ISBN: 978129024764

Published by:
HardPress Publishing
8345 NW 66TH ST #2561
MIAMI FL 33166-2626

Email: info@hardpress.net
Web: http://www.hardpress.net

929.2   M761

Columbia University
in the City of New York

Library

Robert Mortimer Montgomery

THE MONTGOMERY MANUSCRIPTS.

CONTAINING ACCOUNTS OF THE

COLONIZATION OF THE ARDES,

IN THE

COUNTY OF DOWN,

IN THE REIGNS OF ELIZABETH AND JAMES.

MEMOIRS OF THE FIRST, SECOND, AND THIRD VISCOUNTS MONTGOMERY, AND CAPTAIN GEORGE MONTGOMERY:

ALSO,

A DESCRIPTION OF THE BARONY OF ARDS,

WITH VARIOUS LOCAL AND HISTORICAL FACTS CONNECTED WITH THE COLONIZATION OF ULSTER.

ALSO, AN APPENDIX,

CONTAINING

INCIDENTAL REMEMBRANCES OF THE TWO ANCIENT FAMILIES OF THE SAVAGES,

FORMERLY THE LORDS OF THE LITTLE ARDES.

Printed from Original Manuscripts and Transcripts of MSS. composed by William Montgomery, Esq. second son of Sir James Montgomery [between the years 1698 and 1704.]

BELFAST:

PRINTED AT THE NEWS-LETTER OFFICE.

1830.

PREFACE.

A considerable portion of the MONTGOMERY MANUSCRIPTS was printed in the *Belfast News-Letter* so early as 1785 and 1786,* when their publication was suspended in consequence of their extent, which in some degree unfitted them for the columns of a newspaper. Besides, it was suggested that their intrinsic interest and importance to a large proportion of the Nobility and Gentry of the Counties of Down and Antrim, required their publication in a permanent and portable form, and hence the origin of the present undertaking. The influential part which the family of MONTGOMERY acted in the affairs of Ulster after its colonization by the Scots, is matter of historic record, and will be found minutely detailed in the subsequent pages; while, in consequence of the matrimonial and other alliances, that were gradually formed between the several branches of that distinguished family and other families of rank at the time, there are not a few gentlemen in the counties referred to, who will naturally feel an interest in recurring to these simple, but authentic memoirs of their ancestorial dignity. The gratification which the recorded fame of ancestry may fairly minister to the ambition of posterity, is not, however, the only advantage derivable from the publication of these Memoirs. Their importance as historical documents will be readily recognised by those who have studied the transactions of the agitated period to which

---

* They were again re-printed in part in the *News-Letter* in 1822.

they refer, while, as illustrative of manners and customs and habits of thought, that are now comparatively antiquated, their value cannot fail to be estimated even by those who have no hereditary interest in their details. In this view, it is hoped, that though the locality of the scenes that are described, and the individuality of the personages who are chiefly engaged in them, may limit to a portion of the community, the specific interest of the volume; yet it will possess independent merit sufficient to engage the attention of the majority.

In the early parts of the volume, references have been made to an Appendix, which has not been printed, and the omission of which requires explanation. The reasons of its omission were these—after a considerable portion of the Montgomery Manuscript had been printed off, a second Manuscript by the author of the former, was discovered. It contained an interesting history of the family of the Savages, formerly the Lords of the Little Ards, and its publication was found to be necessary, not merely to complete the narrative of the former, but for reasons equally cogent with those which had originally induced the determination of publishing that Manuscript. Hence, the omission of the proposed Appendix became indispensable, as the size of the work had been limited. Besides, no great inconvenience can result from this omission, as there are numerous sources of information accessible to those who may be inquisitive regarding matters of mere antiquarian curiosity; while the full insertion of the Appendix would have required either a separate volume, or would have enlarged this to an inconvenient size, and would, besides, have proportionably increased its price.

The orthography of the original manuscripts, with its ncidental pecularities of contraction, has been strictly preserved. The printer has even followed the occasional defects of his copy, without attempting their correction, which, in many instances, might have been easily done. It now remains that we close this preface with a brief notice of the author of the following memoirs. He was the son of Sir James Montgomery, and was born at Aughaintain, in Tyrone, on the 27th of October, 1633. He represented the borough of Newtownards, in the Irish Parliament, which, shortly after the restoration, passed the celebrated act for the settlement of military adventurers in Ireland. In his habits he appears to have been studious, to have possessed persevering industry, extensive knowledge, and acuteness of observation, notwithstanding the quaint, parenthetical style of his composition—a fault which is attributable, not to him, but to the age in which he lived. He wrote these memoirs in the interval between the years 1698 and 1704. In a historical view, their authority is indubitable—It has been alluded to by Lodge, in his *Irish Peerage*, and as they have never before been printed entire, it is presumed that the present publication will furnish valuable hints to the national annalist, as well as acceptable information to the northern public in general. Copious extracts from the original MSS. of the Lords Mountalexander and of Captain George Montgomery, were first published in the *Belfast News-Letter* of the years 1785 and 1786, with the consent of the late Daniel Delacherois, of Donaghadee, Esq. (in whose family they had been preserved,) when a great portion of the Original MS. became missing, and after repeated searches to recover them, it was found that a copy of them had been taken, which, being traced out, was obligingly communicated. When compared with the parts printed in 1785 and 1786, they were found exactly to correspond, and have been used in completing the present publication.

THE MONTGOMERY MANUSCRIPTS

SOME FEW MEMOIRES OF THE MONTGOMERIES OF IRELAND.

CHAPTER I.

BEING to write of the MONTGOMERIES of Ireland, (now planted therein) recourse must be first had to what I have credibly heard, as truth never doubted of (that my enquiry could find out). And 2dly, to those authentick papers and parchments, which I have carefully perused, and which came to my hands among those left to me by my father, many others of them being lost or embeazled or burnt in Rosemount House: out of the remainder whereof, or from such as I have seen elsewhere, relations shall be made. 3dly, and lastly, I must, in this treatise, make use of my own certain knowledge and memory in those affairs, having had conversation or concern with most of their familys (both the dead and yet surviving of them) to whom I have been a contemporary within the space of above those fifty years now last past, wherein I did more or less make observations as I best could, whilst I grew up in age, and acquaintance with them, and thus furnished, I begin this following narrative (as near as I can) according to the order of time, wherein the several events came to pass, the like not having been attempted that I can any ways learne. Therefore, Imprimis, (as in duty I am bound) with the Montgomeries of the great Ardes, who were the first and chiefest of all that sirname, that came from Scotland, and mostly the procurers of other Montgomery families, and of many of divers sirnames besides them ; to follow and plant in this kingdom, of whom the most conspicuous and powerfull, and the 1st introducer and encourager was Hugh Montgomery, the 6th Laird of Braidstane, whose genealogy is as next followeth, viz.—The said Hugh was the eldest son of Adam (the second of that name) the fifth Laird, who married the daughter of Montgomery, Laird Haislhead, (an ancient family descended of the Earls of Eglintoune). This second Adam (besides breeding his four sons) purchased land from one of the said Earles (I have the deed thereof); which Adam was the eldest son of Adam, (the first Montgomery of that name) and 4th Laird of Braidstane. This Adam married Colquhon's sister, the Laird of Luss, (chief of his ancient sept). This Adam the first, (last mentioned) was son to Robert the 3d Laird of that name, who was the son of Robert, the 2nd Laird of that name, who was the son of Robert, the 1st of that name and 1st Laird of Braidstane, who was the 2d son of Alexander, one of the Earles of Eglingtoune, all of them Montgomeries; which Earles are (in a little book called Indiculum Scotiae, or the present state of Scotland, written by A. M. in Anno 1682) placed the 11th in that degree of nobility, which agrees with the list next spoken of, tho' in King Charles the Martyr's reign, rivaled (as I have heard said) for prudency by the Conninghams, Earles of Glencairne; whom I find by an antient list (of the Scottish Peers) written in King James the 6th his time, left to me by my father (who was expert in the heraldry of both kingdoms, having given me Guillim's book and some notes of his own of that science;) I say I find by the said list, (now by me) that Glencairne was but the 15th Earle, yet at this present time, and many years before it, he might arrive to be 12th, and so next after Eglintoun—the said list runs thus, viz:—

The Sirnames, Earles of	The Titles as followeth.
1, Duglas,	Angus.
2, Campbell	Argyle.
3, Lindsay	Crawford.
4, Hay	Erroll.
5, Keith	Marreshall.
6, Gordon	Southerland.
7, Arreskin	Marr.
8, Lesley	Rothes.
9, Duglas	Mortoun.
10, Graham	Monteith
11, Montgomery	Eglintoun.
Graham	Montrosse.
Kennedy	Cassills.
Sinclair	Caithness.
15, *Conyngham	Glencairne.
Arreskin	Buchan.

&c. to yᵉ Nº. of thirty in all.

* Precedency of Eglintoune.

Since the said King James, his time of living in Scotland, when he went into England he created (by advancement) divers Lords to be Earls, as also did King Charles, the 1st and 2d. There were likewise divers Earles, as Argyle and Montrose, advanced to be Marquises. The old Earldoms of Rothes, Southerland, and Monteith, are also extinct for want of male heires, by which events, it seems to me, that Eglintoun should have the 7th place among the Earls, and Glencairne the 9th, unless by special grants (in the letters patent) others, now at present Earles, had precedency given them, being favourites; but as the precedency of Eglintoun was complained of by Glencairne, the debate might have been occasioned thus, viz. one of the Earles of Eglintoun, I think that Hugh who was insiduously slain at the river of Annock: 2d Adam, Laird of Braidstane, and was purchased from him, A. D. 1586, (as hath been mentioned out of John Johnston's book of Encomiums on the Scottish heroes aforesaid,) and his brother Robert dying A. D. 1596, both without male issue to inherit the honour and title of Earl, the same being extinct (or asleep) for divers years; nevertheless the said Hugh left one only daughter who succeeded him in the estate. This lady was marry'd to Seaton, Earl of Winton the 20th, according to the said list in that degree, and was his 2nd Countess. She bore to him Alexander restored to his honour and degree, which had always been prior to Glencairne.

I well knew this Alexander (he was commonly called Grey Steel for his truth and courage) in King Charles the 2d's time; as also I was intimately acquainted with Hugh, his eldest son, who succeeded him, as I had been in Ireland with Colonel James, the said Alexander's 2d son, whose regiment of foot came over into this kingdom with the Scottish army Ao. 1642, and was quartered in and about Newtown of the Ards. I knew also Major General Robert Montgomery, the said Alexander's 3d son, in Scotland, before Dunbarr fight, and in London also, Ano. 1665; but most of all I am known to Alexander the present Earle of Eglinton, having often many years ago conversed with him, and last of all in Edinborogh, A°. 1689, (I being a voluntary exile during the troubles then in Ireland), in which year his Lordship told me there had been seventeen Earles of his ancestors all Eglinton, of the name Alexander (which in English is a worthy helper of men) and none of them all of any other proper name, but the two Hughes and the said Robert aforesaid (who enjoyed the honor those ten years, in which he revenged and survived his said brother slain at Annock as aforesaid,) yet his ancestors, whilst Lords Montgomeries of Ardrossan, had divers other names.

Now none of the Earles of Eglintoune did forfeit their honor by treason, and so could not lose their degree in the file of Earles, and therefore, and for the reasons aforesaid, as well as for the said 2d list, the rivalship of Glencairn is (in my opinion) injurious and a tort done to the family of Eglintoune, and much more will it be so, if in any Parliament a protestation be entered by Glencairne against the other Earles precedencys. I hope there is not, nor will be any such protestation, because the difference about it (as I have been credibly reported,) was ended and taken away by King Charles 2nd upon his happy restoration. This much I have written as in part belonging to the said 6th Laird's genealogy, and in honor to our Chief in Scotland.

Now this 6th Laird (by which title I will design him till he was knighted) had three brothers, who lived to be men respected for their abilities, viz. George, of whom (because his happy living was in England and Ireland) I will especially remember hereafter. He was (as my father writes) for his worth and learning, by the late Queen Elizabeth, prefer'd to the Parsonage of Chedchec, and Deanery of Norwich; Patrick also who by his prowess and conduct (going from Scotland, a Captain of a regiment of foot, into France) did arrise to great credit, and a Colonel's post under King H. the 4th, and was killed in a fight where he had commanded five hundred horse; he had no wife, neyther had John his youngest brother, who was graduated Doctor in physick in a French University or College; he returning homewards came to London, where having practised his art (with good repute) he died of that sweating imoveable sickness which raged in Queen Elizabeth's reign.

But I return to the history of the said 6th Laird, who leaving Glasgow Colledge and his parents at home, he travelled into France, and after some months stay at Court there, he settled himself in Holland, and became a Captain of foot in a Scottish regiment, under the Prince of Orange, grandfather to our present gracious Sovereign King William.— He was in service some years there, till hearing of his mother's, and (soon afterwards) of his father's death, and that his sisters were disposed of in marriage, and knowing that there were debts on his estate, on that account (his brothers having formerly received their portions,) he then obtained leave to dispose of his command and arrears of pay, and so returned to Braidstane, and appearing at the Court in Edenborough, he was respected as a well accomplished Gentleman, being introduced to kiss King James the 6th hand, by divers Noblemen on whose recommendation he was received into favour (and special notice taken of him) which encreased more and more, by reason of a correspondence he had with his brother George (then Dean of Norwich in the Church of England) whereby he received and gave frequent intelligence to his Majesty of the Nobility and State Ministers in Queen Elizabeth's Court and Council, and of the country Gentlemen as they were well or ill affected to his Majesty's succession.

The said Laird upon his return above said, having paid the said debts and settled his estate, (his friends advising him) he marryed about Ano. 1587, the Laird of Greenock's daughter, with content to the said Earle and all his relations in kindred, and lived in peace and amity with all his neighbours, till grossly injured by —— Maxwell, Laird of New Ark, near Greenock; which abuse his martial soul could not brook. This occasioned divers of the 6th Laird's attempts against the said Maxwell, who declined to give him gentlemanly satisfaction, but the bickering on both sides surceased on a reconciliation (made by their friends) between them.

The said Laird having now acquired or conciliated an interest in the *bonnes graces* of his Prince as above said, it happened he had an affront put upon him by the Earle of Glencairne's eldest son, Mr. Conningham, for reparation whereof he challenged the same Gentleman to a combat, but Mr. Conningham avoided the danger by a visit to London (the Queen being still and for some years thereafter alive tho' old:) yet was soon followed by the said Laird, who came to the city; and his errand for satisfaction was told soon enough to Mr. Conningham, whereupon he went clandestinely into Holland on pretence to improve his parts at the Court in the Hague. The said Laird being thus twice disappointed of his purpose (stayed a few days at the English Court,) and then rode to his brother George, Dean of Norwich, and instructed him how to continue his said intelligence, to be communicated to King James by one of their near kinsmen; which affairs adjusted (undervaluing costs, toyle, and danger) the Laird took ship at Dover, and arrived in Holland, going to the Hague (unheard of and unexpected,) where lodging privately, till he had learned the usual hours when Mr. Conningham and the other gentlemen and officers walked (as merchants do in the inner courts of the palace, called Den Primen Hoff,) the said Laird there found Mr Conningham, called him coward, fugitive, and drew his sword (obliging his adversary to do the like) but the Laird pressing upon him, made a home thrust (which lighted on the broad buckle of his sword belt), and so tilted Mr. Conningham on his back; yet it pleased God that the buckle (like a toorget) saved his life. This was a sudden and inconsiderate rash action of the Laird, who thought he had killed

Mr. Conningham. Putting up his sword quickly and hastening out of the Court, he was seized on by some of the guard, and committed to the Provost Marshall's custody, where he meditated how to escape, and put his design that night in some order (an hopeful occasion forthwith presenting itself); for no sooner was the hurry over, but one Serjeant Robert Montgomery (formerly acquainted with the Laird) came to him; the condolement was but short and private, and the business not to be delayed. Therefore the Laird gave the serjeant a purse of gold, and said, I will call you cousen and treat you respectfully, and you must visit me frequently, and bring me word from the officers (my former comerades) what they can learn is resolved against me, entreating them to visit me. Then he employed him to bespeake some of them that night to come to him the next morning, giving him orders at fittimes to deal liberally with the Marshall (then a widower,) and his turnkeys, letting words fall (as accidentally) that he had such and such lands in Scotland to which he designed (in six months) to return, and also to talk of him as his honourable cousen then in restraint, for no worse deed than was usually done, in Edinborough streets, in revenge of any affront, and especially to magnify himself to make love secretly and briskly to the Marshall's daughter (to whom the keys were often trusted), giving her love tokens and coined gold, as assurances of his intire affection, and at other times to shew her the said purse with the gold in it, telling her a Scotch kinsman had brought it to him, as rent of his lands in Scotland, and sometimes also to shew her handfulls of silver, urging her to take it, (or at least a part of it;) often persweading her to a speedy and private contract in order to a marriage between them. The serjeant thus instantly pursuing his love suit, he ply'd his oar so well that in a few nights he had certain proofs of the bride's cordial love and consent to wed him.

In the mean time while the Laird engaged many of his comerades (and they their friends) to intercede for him, likewise (with great secrecy as to his concern) the sergeant procured a Scottish vessel to be hired, and to be at readiness to obey orders, and weigh anchors when required. And now it remained only to facilitate the escape; wherefore the Laird had divers times treated the Marshall and his daughter in his chamber, both jointly and severally, and one night a good opportunity offering itself of her father being abroad, the Laird (as the design was laid) had the daughter and his sergeant into his room, and there privately contracted or espoused them together by mutual promises of conjugall fidelity to each other, joining their hands, and making them alternately repeat (after him) the matrimonial vow used in Scotland, they exchanging one to the other the halves of a piece of gold which he had broken and given to them to that purpose. So, no doubt, the sergeant kissed his bride and she him, and drank a glass of wine to each other on the bargain. Then the Laird carressed them both, and revealed to them his design of getting out of restraint, to abscond himself till he might get King James' letter to the Prince, that his hand should not be cut off; but that receiving on his knee the Prince's reprimand, and making due submissions, and humbly craving pardon and promising reconciliation and friendship to Mr. Conninghame, he should be absolved from the punishment due for his crime. But this was a pretence to the bride only; all this was contrived, carried on, and done without the knowledge of the Laird's servant, who was only employed to cajole and treat the Marshall and his turnkeys liberally, and to perform menial attendances and offices about the Laird's person when called; so that the intrigues prospered (with admirable conduct) without the least umbrage of suspicion, either to the household or to the comerades aforesaid, lest any of them should be taxed with compliance or connivance to the escape.

In this little history I have been the more exact to give the reader (at least) one single instance of the Laird's bold resolution, and of his sagatious ingenious spirit, as well as of his great prudence (which appeared also in the sequel of this affair;) as likewise to be briefe in my future report of another like escape for Con O'Neil, which the Laird devised and got done (almost in the same manner), as shall in due place be remembered. And now there remained only to appoint the night when the Laird was to leave his lodgings (and the preparatorys for it to be advized on); all which being concerted between the Laird, the sergeant and his bride, a treat of a dinner was made for some of the said officers and for the Marshall, which almost being ended, the sergeant came into the room and reported, that, in consideration of the Laird's valorous services and civil behaviour whilst Captain in the army, and of the officers' intercessions, Mr Conninghame having received no wound, (for divers respects on his own account, and to make amends to the Laird) joining with them, the Prince was pleased to pardon the Laird's rash passionate crime, and to restore him to his liberty; he making submission, and craving remission for his fault, and promising, not only reconciliation, but friendship to Mr. Conninghame as aforesaid, was pretended—all which was to be performed solemnly two days thence. These news were welcomed by all at table with their great joy and applause given of ye Prince, who thereby should endeare the Scottish forces the more to serve his highness: then the healths went round and the glasses set about the trenchers (like cercoletts) till run off, the meat being removed, and sergeant gone to feast with the Laird's servant, who treated him and his sweet bride with the officers' and Marshall's men, where there was no want of wine for sake of the good news. After eating was done, the Laird and officers and Marshall (who no doubt had his full share of drink put upon him) continued at the wine (as their attendants also did below them,) both companies being answered by the bride and her cook-maid, when wine was called for, then the reckoning was paid as daily before then had been done frankly, without demurring at all, or even examining how the particulars amounted to the total sum charged by the bride. In fine the Marshall and his man minded no more the keys or to look after the Laird being secured, by reason of the news and wine, and the trust they reposed in the bride.

And now the play was in its last scene, for the sun being a while set, the Marshall was led (as a gouty man) to his bed, and after him his two men (as manners and good breeding required) led to their garrett; and the officers with their servants being gone to their lodgings, and night come, the sergeant and his bride packed up her necessaries and as much of the money and gold as she could find, the maid being then busy in the kitchen, and at the same time the Laird and his servant put up their linens; which done, the bride sent the maid a great way into the towne on an Aprill or speedless errand, and the sergeant called the Laird and his servant down stairs. So the four went forth, leaving candles burning in the room, and locking the street door, putting the key under it into the floor. They went away incogniti; which transaction amazed the Laird's servant, as not having perceived the least of the whole design till that minute—though he was trusty enough, yet perhaps the Laird did not think his discretion capable to retain such a secret in his drinking with the Marshall and his men, to which he was obliged by the Laird (as the sergeant had been) as is aforesaid. What needs more discourse of the feats, but that the

Laird and his company (though searched for) got a board, and safely landed at Leith, without any maladventure or cross fortune. All which particulars concerning the Laird's quarrell at Mr. Conninghame, and the events following thereupon, and the sergeant's courtship, with the debauches at the treats, and the escape aforesaid, might afford matter for a facetious pleasing novell, if they were descanted on by one of the modern witty composers of such like diversions (as they call them) which I think is not an appellative name expressive enough of their nature, because they are instructives and recreatives also.

CHAPTER II.

Next day or two after arrival, the Laird with his retinue mounted on hired horses and journeyed to Braidstane, where receiving the visits of friends and neighbours congratulating his return (which had prevented the news of his adventures then also unknown to the mariners), he minded his affairs, and getting an account of all the intelligencies his brother George had sent to his friends, (pursuant to their agreement at last parting, when the Laird went to Holland) hesent a footman (for there was no conveyance by post (A) between the kingdoms before King James' accession, to the English crown) with letters of intelligencies and of business and advice, and in requittal he received more and fresher informations (touching the English Court and the Queen from his said brother), who was lucky to be well furnished, and therefore his said brother sent back speedily the messenger, who, coming safe to Braidstane, delivered his packet. In perusal whereof the Laird thought it necessary (and conducing to his designs for lands in Ireland) that he should forthwith go to the Court and impart to the King what his brother had sent; and so the Laird hastening thither he was graciously received, but not without a severe check given him by his Majesty, who nevertheless enjoyned him to beg pardon of the Earle of Glencairne, (then in Edinborough,) and to promise friendship to his Lordship's son and family, which submission being made in his Majesty's presence, that sore was plaistered and afterwards fully cured. As soon as Mr Conningham came back to Scotland, his father caused him to confess to the Laird, that he had wronged him and was sorry for it, desiring his forgiveness, and promising his own friendship to the Laird and

See Note (A) in Appendix.

his family whilst he lived; and thus by his Majesty's care was the revival of the old bloody fewd between the Montgomeries and Conninghams fully prevented; the like reconciliations between all other families having already been made by the industrious prudence of that King, who being in the yearly expectation he had of the Queen's death, would leave all quiet at home when he was to go to receive the English crown.

And now Halcyon days shined throughout all Scotland, all animosities being compressed by his Majesty (who in a few months afterwards) having certain intelligence of Queen Elizabeth's sickness, and extreme bodily weakness, and not long thence of her death, which was on the 24th of March (according to the English computation) A°. D°. 1602, James the 6th being proclaimed King in London and Westminster, by the Lord Mayor, with the Lords of the Privy Councill, and by them solemnly invited to take progress and receive the crown, with the kingdoms of England, &c. into his gracious protection. Accordingly his Majesty (as soon as conveniency would allow) went to Westminster, attended by divers Noblemen and many Gentlemen, being by greater numbers conveyed to the borders, where he was received by English Lords, Esqrs. and Gentry in great splendor. Among the Scottish Lairds (which is a title equivalent to Esqrs.) who attended his Majesty to Westminster, he of Braidstane was not the least considerable, but made a figure, more looked on than some of the Lords' sons, and as valuable in account as the best of his own degree and estate in that journey.

When the said Laird had lodged himself in Westminster, he met at Court with the said George (his then only living brother), who had with longing expectations waited for those happy days. They enjoyed one the others most loving companies, and meditated of bettering and advancing their peculiar stations. Forseeing that Ireland must be the stage to act upon, it being unsettled, and many forfeited lands thereon altogether wasted, they concluded to push for fortunes in that kingdom, as the Laird had formerly done; and so setling a correspondence between them, the said George resided much at Court, and the Laird returned to his Lady and their children in Braidstane, and imploying some friends who traded into the next adjacent coasts of Ulster, he by them (from time to time) was informed of the state of that country, whereof he made his benefit (though with great cost and pains, as hereafter shall be related), giving frequent intimation of occurrences to his said brother, which were repeated to the King. After the King was some months in his palace at Whitehall, even in the first year of his reign, the affairs of Ireland came to be considered, and an office of inquest by jurors was held before some judges, whereby the forfeited temporal lands, and abby lands, and impropriations, and others of that sort, were found to have been vested in the Queen, and to be now lawfully descended to the King; but the rebellion and commotions raised by O'Doherty and his associates in the county of Donegal, retarded (till next year) the further procedures to settlement. (B)

In the mean while, the said Laird in the said first year of the King's reign pitched upon the following way (which he thought most fair and feazable,) to get an estate in lands even with free consent of the forfeiting owner of them, and it was thus, viz:—The said Laird (in a short time after his return from the English Court), had got full information from his said trading friends of Con O'Neil's case (c) and imprisonment in Carrickfergustowne, on account of a quarrell made by his servants with some soldiers in Belfast, done before the Queen died, which happened in manner next following, to witt:—The said servants being sent with runletts to bring

See Note (B) in Appendix. See Note (c) in ditto.

wine from Belfast aforesaid, unto the said Con, their master, and Great Teirne as they called him, then in a grand debauch at Castlereagh, with his brothers, his friends, and followers; they returning (without wine) to him, battered and bled, complained that the soldiers had taken the wine, with the casks, from them by force. Con enquiring (of them) into the matter, they confessed their number twice exceeded the soldiers, who indeed had abused them, they being very drunk. On this report of the said servants, Con was vehemently moved to anger; reproached them bitterly; and, in rage, swore by his father, and by all his noble ancestors' souls, that none of them should ever serve him or his family (for he was married and had issue) if they went not back forthwith and did not revenge the affront done to him and themselves, by those few Boddagh(D)Sasonagh soldiers (as he termed them). The said servants (as yet more than half drunk), avowed to execute that revenge, and hasted away instantly; arming themselves in the best way they could, in that short time, and engaged the same soldiers (from words to blows), assaulting them with their weapons; and in the scuffle (for it was no orderly fight), one of the soldiers happened to receive a wound, of which he died that night, and some other

See Note (D) in Appendix.

slashes were given; but the Teagues were beaten off and chased, some sore wounded and others killed; only the best runners got away Scott free. The pursuit was not far, because the soldiers feared a second assault from the hill of Castlereagh, where the said Con, with his two brothers, friends and followers (for want of more dorgh) stood beholders of the chase. Then in a week next after this fray, an office of enquest was held on Con, and those of his said friends and followers, and also on the servants, and on all that were suspected to be procurers, advisers, or actors therein, and all whom the Provost Marshall could seize (were taken), by which office the said Con, with some of his friends, were found guilty of levying war against the Queen. This mischief happened a few months before her death; and the whole matter being well known to the said Laird, and his brother, and his friends, soon after the King's accession to the English Crown, early application was made to his Majesty for a grant of half the said Con's lands, the rest to Con himself, which was readily promised; but could not, till the second of his reign, by any means be performed, by reason of the obstacles to the settlement of Ireland aforesaid.

But I must a little go retrograde, to make my report of their affairs better understood.

The Laird having met with his brother, and returned from London (as before mentioned), came home, (his second son being then about the third year of his age), and industriously minded the affairs in Ireland; and, by his said brother, gave frequent intimations to the King, or his Secretary for Scotland, of all occurrences he could learne, especially out of Ulster (which had never been fully made subject to England); which services of the Laird, and the King's promise, were by his brother renewed in the King's memory, as occasion served to that purpose. And the effects answered his pains and expectations, which was in this manner, viz.—The Queen being dead, the King filling her (late) throne, O'Doherty soon subdued, and the Chief-Governors in this kingdom of Ireland foreseeing alteration in places, and the King's former connivance of supplies, and his secret favor to the O'Neils and M'Donnells, in counties of Down and Antrim (being now well known) as to make them his friends, and a future party for facilitating his peaceable entry and possession in those northern parts of the country (if needful), it so came to pass that the said Con had liberty to walk at his pleasure (in the day time) in the streets of Carrickfergus, and to entertain his friends and tenants in any victualling house within the towne, having only a single sentinel to keep him in custody, and every night delivered him to the Marshall. And thus Con's confinement (which lasted several months after the Queen's death) was the easier, and supportable enough, in regard that his estate was not seized by the escheators, and that his words (at his grand debauch aforesaid) were reputed very pardonable, seeing greater offences would be remitted by his Majesty's gracious declaration of amnesty, which was from time to time expected, but delayed on the obstacles aforesaid.

In the mean time, the Laird used the same sort of contrivance for Con's escape as he had heretofore done for his own; and thus it was, viz.—The Laird had formerly employed, for intelligence as aforesaid, one Thomas Montgomery, of Blackstown, a fee farmer, (in Scotland, they call such gentlemen feuers), he was a cadet of the family of Braidstane, but of a remote sanguinity to the Laird, whose actions are now related. This Thomas had personally divers times traded with grain and other things to Carrickfergus, and was well trusted therein; and had a small bark, of which he was owner and constant commander; which Thomas being a discreet, sensible gentleman, and having a fair prospect given him of raising his fortune in Ireland, was now employed and furnished with instructions and letters to the said Con, who, on a second speedy application in the affair, consented to the terms proposed by the Laird, and to go to him at Braidstane, provided the said Thomas would bring his escape so about as if constrained, by force and fears of death, to go with him.— These resolutions being, with full secrecy, concerted, Thomas aforesaid (as the Laird had formerly advised) having made love to the Town Marshall's daughter, called Annas Dobbin (whom I have often seen and spoken with, for she lived in Newtown till Anno 1664), and had gained hers and parent's consents to be wedded together. This took umbrages of suspicion away, and so by contrivance with his espoused, an opportunity, one night, was given to the said Thomas and his barque's crew to take on board the said Con, as it were by force, he making no noise for fear of being stabbed, as was reported next day through the town.

The escape being thus made and the bark, before next sun set, arriving safe at the Larggs, in Scotland, on notice thereof, our valorous and well-bred Laird kept his state, staying at home, and sent his brother-in-law, Patrick Montgomery (of whom at large hereafter, for he was also instrumental in the escape) and other friends, with a number of his tenants, and some servants, all well mounted and armed, as was usual in those days, to salute the said Con, to congratulate his happy escape, and to attend him to Braidstane, where he was joyfully and courteously received by the Laird and his Lady with their nearest friends. He was kindly entertained and treated with a due defference to his birth and quality, and observed with great respect by the Laird's children and servants, they being taught so to beheave themselves. In this place the said Con entered into indenture of articles of agreement, the tenor whereof was that the said Laird should entertaine and subsist him, the said Con, in quality of an Esq. and also his followers in their moderate and ordinary expenses; should procure his pardon for all his and their crimes and transgressions against the law (which indeed were not very heinous nor erroneous) and should get the enquest to be vacated, and the one-half of his estate (whereof Castlereagh and circumjacent lands to be a part,) to be granted to himself by letters patent from the King; to obtain for him that he might be admitted to kiss his Majestie's hand, and to have a general reception into favour; all this to be at the proper expenses, cost and charges of the said Laird, who agreed and covenanted to the performance of the premises on his part. In consideration whereof, the said Con did agree, covenant, grant and assign, by the said indenture, the other one-half of all his land estate, to be and enure to the only use and behoof of the said Laird, his heirs and assigns, at which time the said Con, also signing and registering; but no sealing of deeds being usual in Scotland, he promised by an instrument in writing to convey part of his own moiety unto the said Patrick and Thomas, as a requital of their pains for him, which he afterwards performed, the said Laird signing as consenting to the said instrument, the said agreements being fully indorsed and registered (as I was told) in the town council book of the Royal Burgh of Air or Irwine, the original of that indenture to the Laird, I had and shewed to many worshipful persons, but it was burnt with the house of Rosemount, the 16th February, 1695.

Upon the said agreement the said Laird and Con went to Westminster, where the said George had been many months Chaplain and Ordinary to his Majesty, and was provided with a living in London, in Commendum, worth above 200*l.* per annum, and the Laird was there assumed to be an Esq. of the King's body, and soon after this was knighted, and therefore I must call him in the following pages by the name of Sir Hugh Montgomery, who made speedy application to the King (already prepared) on which the said Con was graciously received at Court, and kissed the King's hand, and Sir Hugh's petition, on both their behalfs, was granted, and orders given, under the Privy signet, that his Majesty's pleasure therein should be confirmed by letters patent, under the great seal of Ireland, at such rents as therein expressed, and under condition that the lands should be planted with British Protestants, and that no grant of fee farm should be made to any person of meer Irish extraction; but in regard these letters took no effect, as in next paragraph appears, I shall make no further mention thereof, but will proceed to what afterwards happened to the said Sir Hugh and Con.

CHAPTER III.

Now these affairs, as also Con's escape and journey with Sir Hugh, and their errand, took time and wind at Court, notwithstanding theirs (and the said George's) endeavours to conceal them from the prying courtiers, (the busiest bodies in all the world in other men's matters, which may profit themselves) so that in the interim one Sir James Fullerton, a great favourite, who loved ready money, and to live in Court, more than in waste wildernesses in Ulster, and afterwards had got a patent clandestinely passed for some of Con's lands, made suggestions to the King that the lands granted to Sir Hugh and Con were vast territories, too large for two men of their degree, and might serve for three Lords' estates, and that his Majesty, who was already said to be overhastily liberal, had been over-reached as to the quantity and value of the lands, and therefore begged his Majesty that Mr. James Hamilton who had furnished himself for some years last past with intelligencies from Dublin, very important to his Majesty, might be admitted to a third share of that which was intended to be granted to Sir Hugh and Con. Whereupon a stop was put to the passing the said letters pattent, which overturned all the progress (a work of some months) that Sir Hugh had made to obtain the said orders for himself and Con. But the King sending first for Sir Hugh, told him (respecting the reasons aforesaid) for what loss he might receive in not getting the full half of Con's estate, by that defalcation he would compensate him out of the Abbey lands and impropriations, which in a few months he was to grant in fee, they being already granted in lease for twenty-one years, and that he would also abstract, out of Con's half, the whole great Ardes for his and Mr. James Hamilton's behoof, and throw it into their two shares; that the sea coasts might be possessed by Scottish men, who would be traders as proper for his Majestie's future advantage, the residue to be laid off about Castlereagh, (which Con had desired) being too great a favour for such an Irishman.

All this being privately told by the King, was willingly submitted to by the said Sir Hugh, and soon after this he and Con were called before the King, who declared to them both his pleasure concerning the partitions as aforesaid, to which they submitted. On notice of which procedure, Mr James Hamilton was called over by the said Sir James Fullerton, and came to Westminster, and having kissed the King's hand, was admitted the King's servant (but not in a great while knighted, therefore hereafter I shall make mention of him as Sir James Hamilton, in its due place); all which contrivance brought money to Sir James Fullerton, for whose sake and request it was the readilyer done by the King. Sir Hugh and Mr Hamilton met and adjusted the whole affair between themselves.

Whereupon letters of warrant to the Deputy, dated 16th April, 3d Jacob. 1605, were granted to pass all the premises, by letters patent, under the great seal of Ireland, accordingly, in which the said Sir James Fullerton obtained further of the King, that the letter to the Deputy should require him that the patent should be passed in Mr James Hamilton's name alone, yielding one hundred pounds per annum to the King; and in the said letter was inserted that the said lands were in trust for the said Mr. Hamilton himself, and for Sir Hugh Montgomery, and for Con O'Neill, to the like purport already expressed.

Then the said Con, Sir Hugh Montgomery, and Mr. Hamilton entered into tripartite indentures, dated ulto. of the said April, whereby (inter alia) it was agreed that unto Con and his followers their moderate ordinary expenses from the first of August preceding the date now last mentioned being already paid them, should be continued them, 'till patents were got out for their pardons, and also deeds from Mr. Hamilton for Con's holding the estate, which the King had condescended to grant him. Soon after this, Mr. Hamilton went to Dublin to mind his business and to ply *telis extremis* for the furtherance of it.

All this being done, and Sir Hugh having

no more business (at present) at Whitehall, he resolved with convenient speed to go through Scotland into Ireland, to follow his affairs, which he did so soon as he had renewed his friendship with the English and Scotish Secretarys; and laid down further methods, with his said brother, of entercourse between themselves for their mutual benefit; and the said Con, well minding Sir J. Fullerton's interposition for Mr. Hamilton (whereby he was a great loser), and that the patent for his lands was to be passed in Mr. Hamilton's own name, and only a bare trust expressed for his, Con's use, in the letters of warrant aforesaid, he thought it necessary that Sir Hugh and he should look to their hitts. They therefore took leave at Court; (and being thoro' ready) they went to Edinborough and Braidstane, and after a short necessary stay for recruits of money, they passed into Ireland, taking with them the warrant for Con, his indemnity, pardon and profit.

Mr. Hamilton having gone to Dublin, as aforesaid, then, (viz.) on the 4th July, 1605, (being two months and four days posterior to the said tripartite indenture) a second office was taken, whereby all the towns, lands, manors, abbeys, impropriations, and such hereditaments in upper Claneboys and Ardes, were found to be in the King; it bearing a reference (as to spiritual possessions) for more certainty unto the office taken concerning them, primo Jac. A°. 1603, and also it was shuffled into it that Killough was usually held to lye in the county of Down; this office being returned and inrolled in September then next following, it was (by inspection thereof) found to vary from the jurors' briefs and notes, and from many particulars in the office taken 1st Jac. and the matter of Killulta was amiss.

About this time, the inquisition found against Con and his followers for the feats at Belfast aforesaid, being vacated and taken off the file in the King's Bench Court, and the pardon for himself and all his followers, for all their other crimes and trespasses against law being passed under the great seal, and the deed of the 6th Nov. 1605, from Mr. Hamilton of Con's lands, being made to himself;— Con then returned home in triumph over his enemies (who thought to have had his life and estate,) and was met by his friends, tenants, and followers, the most of them on foot, the better sort had gerrans, some had pannels for saddles, (we call them back bughams) (E) and the greater part of the riders without them; and but very few spurs in the troop, yet instead thereof they might have thorn prickles in

See Note (E) in Appendix.

their brogue heels (as is usual), and perhaps not one of the concourse had a hat; but the gentry (for sure) had on their done wosle barrads, the rest might have sorry scull caps, otherwise (in reverence and of necessity) went cheerfully pacing or trotting bare headed. Con being so come in state (in Dublin equipage) to Castlereagh, where no doubt his vassals (tagg-ragg and bob-tail) gave to their Teirne More, Squire Con, all the honour and homage they could bestow, presenting him with store of beeves, colpaghs, sheep, hens, bonny blabber, rusan butter (such as it was); as for cheese I heard nothing of it, (which to this day is very seldom made by the Irish), and there was some greddan meal strowans, with snush and bolean, as much as they could get to regale him; where I will leave him and them to congratulate each other's interview, till other occasions to write of him offer themselves, and he gave them not many months after this time. But good countrymen (Erinagh or Gelagh), Irish or English, if you believe not this treat as aforesaid, neither do I, because I could not see it, nor was I certainly informed; many histories have stories in them, for writers make King's and Gentlemen's speeches which, perhaps, they never uttered; however, the worst on my part in this is, that it is a joke, and such I hope you will allow it, and also the Pope's own country Italian proverb, used in the holy city, and the mother (church) Rome itself, viz.—*Si non e vero e ben trovato*—if it be not truth, it is well invented for mirth's sake, and so I intended it, for it is not unlikely.

But before I recount the after actions I mean to treat of, I must mention two transactions more between him and Sir Hugh, viz: On 14th March, the same 3d Jac. according to English suputation, Ano. 1605, but by the Scottish account, 1606, (for they have January(f) for the first month of their year, as the almanacks begin the calender), Con specifying very honorable and valuable considerations him thereunto moving, makes and grants a deed of feofment of all his lands unto Sir Hugh Montgomery, (then returned from Braidstane to prepare habitations for his family). John M'Dowel, of Garthland, Esq. and Colonel David Boyd, appointed to take and give livery of seizin to Sir Hugh, which was executed accordingly the 5th September following, within the six months limited by the statutes in such cases made and provided, the other was added from Con conveying by sale unto Sir Hugh Montgomery, the woods growing on four townlands therein named—this sale was dated the 22d August, 4th Jac°. 1606. Patrick Montgo-

See Note (r) in Appendix.

mery and John Cashan being Con's attorneys, took and gave livery of seizin; accordingly this much encouraged the plantation which began in May this year. Likewise the said Mr. Hamilton (as he had done to Con) by deed dated next day after that conveyance to Con, viz. on the 7th November, 1605, grants to Sir Hugh Montgomery divers temporal and spiritual (as they call them) lands in Clanneboys and Great Ardes, thus part of the trust and covenants in the tripartite indenture was performed to him. So Sir Hugh returned from Dublin, and (as hereafter shall be said) taking possession, he went forthwith to Braidstane, and engaged planters to dwell thereon.

Now, on the whole matter of Sir Hugh Montgomery's transactions with and for Con O'Neil, the benefits done to him will appear very considerable, as the bringing them to pass was very costly and difficult, as followeth, viz.—Con (by the said transporting and mediation for him) had escaped the eminent danger of losing both his life and estate; because, by the said inquest against him, his said words (and perhaps his commands too) were proved fully enough; or they might have been entered therein, and also managed (in future) so dexterously by the covetors of benefit arising out of the forfeitures, as to make him guilty of levying war against the Queen, which (by law in Ireland) is treason. Moreover, Con's title was bad, because *imprimis* by act of Parliament, in Ireland, 11th Elizabeth, Shane O'Neil, who had engaged all Ulster in rebellion, being killed by Alex. Oge M'Connell, (so the statute sur-names the M'Donnell) the whole sept of O'Neill were all attainted of treason, and the whole country of Clanneboys, and the hereditaments belonging to them, or any of their kinsmen and adherents, (besides Shane's patrimony in Tireowen) now vested in the Queen's actual possession, and did lawfully descend to King James, and was his right as wearing the Crown. And Con's title being but a claim by tanestry, whereby a man at full years is to be chosen and preferred to the estate (during his life) before a boy, and an uncle before a nephew-heir under age, whose grandfather survived the father; and so many times they preferred persons, and their descendants, intruded by strong hands, and extruded the true lineal heir. And Con's immediate predecessors, Brian Fortagh O'Neill, &c. Con's reputed grandfather, and father, were intruders (as himself also was) into the Queen's right and possession, in those troublesome times especially, whilst Hugh O'Neill, whom the Queen restored to his predecessor's possessions, and to the title of Earl of Tireowen (alias Tireogen in Irish speech,) rebelled and ravaged over all Ulster, and most other parts in Ireland, until the latter end of the year of the Queen's reign, of whose death he had not heard till he had submitted himself prisoner to the Lord Deputy Chichester, (G) in Mellefont. The said Brian Neil and Con so intruding into Clanneboys and the Great Ardes, in those days of general confusion, and (for peace sake) winked at, they continued their profession, and at some times more avowedly (by reason of the fewness and weakness of the English garrisons) did take up rents, cuttings, duties, and cesses; coshering (H) also upon their underlings, being therein assisted by their kindred and followers, whom they kept in pay, as soldiers, to be ready on all occasions (when required) to serve him.

This being the pickle wherein Con was soused, and his best claim but an unquiet possession, usurpation and intrusion against the laws of the kingdom, neither his ancestors nor himself being released from that attainder aforesaid, nor he anywise set *reclus in curia* for joining with Hugh O'Neil, it must needs follow, by all reasonable consequences, that Sir Hugh Montgomery had done many mighty acts for the rescue and welfare of

(G) See Appendix.   (H) See Appendix.

Con himself, his friends and followers, as hath been fully proved were done for him and them ; the very undertaking and prospect of which welfare could not but be very strongly obliging on Con O'Neil, kindly and with hearty thanks to accept of and to agree to the articles signed to Sir Hugh Montgomery at Braidstane, aforesaid.

CHAPTER IV.

WE have in the foregoing narrative a few of the many generous acts of the 6th Laird of Braidstane ; let me trace him on the back scent, as well as I can for want of papers, and of the original articles of Braidstane, between him and Con alone, and of the consequencial proceedings thereupon interrupted by Sir James Fullerton, 2d Jac. till we find the time about which he was knighted, pursuant to which I observe, *imprimis* by the letters patent passed (5th November, 3d Jacobi, Ao. 1605), to Mr. James Hamilton, who therein is named James Hamilton, Esq. and called by the King his servant. Our 6th Laird is stiled Sir Hugh Montgomery, knight, in which patent the letters to the said Deputy Chichester for passing it (dated 16th April foregoing), that Nov^e. is *intermini* recited. Item in a deed, 1st October, that same year 1605, it appears that James Hamilton, Esq. servant to the King, (as aforesaid) pursuant to the first trust, grants unto our said Laird (by the name of Sir Hugh Montgomery, Knight, one of the Esqrs. of his Majesty's body,) the abbey and lands of Movilla, (1) &c. which is a prior date by a month and five days to the patent last named. This was so early done because abbey lands were first passed. James Hamilton, Esq, by patent, dated 20th July the said year, 1605, Sir Hugh Montgomery not being then come to Dublin, but in September ye next month following, the said 20th July, notwithstanding all the expedition he and Con had made through Scotland, that they might look to their hitts aforesaid.

Item, I observe by the tripartite indenture, dated ult^o. April, 1605, aforesaid, that James Hamilton, Esq. was to bear equal share in the expences of Con and his followers from the 1st of August preceding that indenture. This August was A^o. 1604, which was 2d Jacobi, and was many months after Con was brought to Whitehall by our Laird, in all which time, and till the said letters to the Deputy, dated the 16th of April, 1605, our

(1) See Appendix.

said Laird and his brother George, the Dean, had solicited Con's pardon, and the grant for half of his estate, the other moiety to the Laird himself, and obtained the King's letters of warrant to the Lord Deputy to pass letters patent conformably to the said articles at Braidstane. But this affair taking time, and wind, at Court, was interrupted by Sir James Fullerton, as you have already heard; and that thereupon the said Con and Hugh Montgomery, of London, Esq. and James Hamilton, of London, Esq. adjusted affairs between themselves, so that it seems our Laird was knighted in April, 1605, or not long afterwards, but of Knights Bachellor no record is kept, so that for want thereof I must desist my enquiry.

Item, we have heard also how that after the said overthrow given to the Laird and Con by Sir James Fullerton's procurement of a letter of warrant to the Lord Deputy, Arthur Lord Chichester, dated the 16th April, 1605, aforesaid, was granted to pass Con's estate and some abbey lands, by patent, to James Hamilton, Esq. in his sole name, in trust for himself, our Laird and Con, and that ye last day of ye said April, ye tripartite indenture was made between the said three persons.

Now to faciliate the performances thereof,

Mr. Hamilton returned soon to Dublin with an order for an inquisition on the lands of the said Con, and on yᵉ abby lands, which was held the 4th July, 1605, and being returned enrolled in Sept. next following, and wherein was a reference (for more certainty) unto the office taken 1st Jac. Aº 1603, and from which and yᵉ jurors and breefs the last above said inquisition did much vary, as hath been before now related. However, Mr. Hamilton, yₑ 20th of yₑ said July, passed letters patent in his own name, of the premises; and Sir Hugh Montgomery being arrived in Ireland, with Con, they went to Dublin as aforesaid, where, pursuant to the former said agreements, he did, 1st October next following, (as is said) grant the lands of Movilla, Newton, and Gray Abbey, (κ) &c. to Sir H. Montgomery; then on the 5th Nov. 1605, passed a more ample patent of Con's estate, and of all the abby lands therein; and, pursuant to agreement with the said Con, Mr. Hamilton grants him his lands in and about Castlereagh, ye very next day after the date of the said ample patent last above mentioned. So Con's whole affair being done for him, and he releasing Sir Hugh Montgomery and Mr. Hamilton of all contracts and expenses relating thereunto, soon returned to Castlereagh, where I left him treated by his friends

(κ) See Appendix.

and followers as before herein is briefly related. In this dispatch is seen Sir Hugh Montgomery's kindness to Con and himself.

Observe further, as aforesaid, that the said Mr. Hamilton, on the 7th day of the said November, 1605, again grants to Sir Hugh Montgomery, the lands of Newtown, Gray Abbey, &c. This was done the next day after Mr. Hamilton had given the deed to Con. No doubt this dispatch pleased every of the three parties for their respective private reasons: Con being contented to the full for aught I find to the contrary, and Sir Hugh with whatever he got *(de bene esse)* in part for the presents, that they both might more closely follow the plantations they were bound to make, and therefore Sir Hugh, also, after a small stay, returned from Dublin, and on the 15th January of the same year 1605, livery of seizin of Con's lands was taken by Cuthbert Montgomery, and given to Sir Hugh in trust for Con's use, and much about the same time livery of seizin was given to Sir Hugh, pursuant to the said deed, dated the 7th of November abovesaid, Jo. Shaw and Patrick Montgomery, Esqrs. being appointed attornies by Mr. Hamilton to take and deliver the same accordingly.

These few last rehearsals, being the sum of the chief transactions between Mr. Hamilton, trustee aforesaid, and Sir Hugh Montgomery and Con before, A°. 1606, I thought it necessary to be recapitulated before I proceed to other matters done between them after the 22d of August, 1606, on which day the said Con had sold to Sir Hugh Montgomery the woods of four town-lands as aforesaid, and then I will (as well as I can) give the narration of Sir Hugh promoting and advancing his plantation after the last mentioned August. But first I must intimate two things, of which I shall not write hereafter: The first is that Mr. Hamilton and Sir Hugh were obliged in ten years time, from November, 1605, to furnish British inhabitants (English and Scotch Protestants) to plant one-third of Con's lands granted to himself. The second thing was that Mr. Hamilton passed another patent in February, 1605, which is posterior as you now see to that of the 5th of November the same year, according to English account or supputation current in Ireland, by virtue of which patent in November now mentioned, it was that Mr. Hamilton gave the deeds aforesaid of the 6th and 7th of the same month, unto Con and Sir Hugh, as is (herein) before-remembered.

These two remarks being made, I now go on with Sir Hugh Montgomery's plantation, which began about May, 1606, and thus it was, viz :—Sir Hugh, after his return from Ireland to Braidstane, in winter 1605, as he had before his coming into Ireland, spoken of the plantation, so now he conduced his prime friends to join him therein, viz :—John Shaw, of Greenock, Esq. whose sister Elizabeth he had married divers years before that time, and Patrick Montgomery, of Black-House, Esq. who married the said John Shaw's sister, Christian. These two Gentlemen had been in Ireland, and given livery of seizin as aforesaid to Sir Hugh, who also adduced the afore mentioned Colonel David Boyd, who bargained for 1000 acres, in Gray Abby parish, Scottish Cunningham measure, at 18 foot 6 inches to the perch or pole. Sir Hugh also brought with him Patrick Shaw, Laird of Kelseland, (his lady's father's brother) and Hugh Montgomery, a cadet of the family of Braidstane, and Mr. Thomas Nevin, brother to the Laird of Mouck Roddin and Cunningham, gentlemen, his near allys, and also Patrick Moore, of Dugh, Neil and Catherwood, gentlemen, with many others, and gave them lands in fee farm in Donaghadee parish (all which parish, except some of the town parks, is under fee farm or mortgage,) under small chief rents, but did not assertain the tythes to any of them, nor would he put them into the clergy's hands, because he would keep his tenants from under any one's power but his own. Besides his Lordship considered that the contentions (which too frequently happen) concerning tythes, might breed dislike and aversion between the people and Minister; therefore he gave unto the incumbents salaries with glebes and perquisites or book-money (as they are commonly called) for marriages, christenings, burials, and Easter offerings, the clerk and sexton also had their share of dues; and the people in those days resorted to church and submitted to its censures, and paid willingly those small ecclesiastical dues, and so were in no hazard of suits in the Ecclesiastical Court, but of their landlord, if he pleased to chastise their stubborness or other misbehaviour.

There came over also divers wealthy able men, to whom his Lordship gave tenements in freehold, and parks by lease, so they being as it were bound, with their heirs, to the one, they must increase the rent for the other, at the end of the term, or quit both, which makes the park lands about towns give ten shillings per acre rent now, which at the plantations the tenants had for one shilling rent, and these being taken, the tenants had some two, some three and some four acres, for each of which they passed a boll of barley, rent. They built stone houses, and they traded to enable them buy land, to France, Flanders, Norway, &c. as they still do.

Here is to be noted, that Sir Hugh got his estate by townlands, by reason of his agreement with Con O'Neil, whereas other undertakers of plantations in Ulster had several scopes of lands (called *proportions*) admeasured to them, each containing one thousand acres, profitable for plough and good pasture, mountains and bog not reckoned in the number, but thrown in as an appurtenance. In the Queen Elizabeth's reign, ye perch or pole was 24 feet long, Parliament reduced it to 21 feet, ye English perch being but 16 feet 6 inches, but Sir Hugh sett his land by Cunningham measure, as the planters were used to have it at home, which is 18 feet 6 inches a perch.

I desire that this brief account may serve as a sampler of Sir Hugh's 1st essay to his plantation, for it would be tedious (as it would be impossible for me) to enumerate all the substantial persons whom he brought or who came to plant in Gray Abby, Newton, and corner parishes, among whom Sir William Edmeston, 7th Laird of the antient honorable family of Duntreth, was very considerable, both for purse and people, but after some years he sold his interest and settled his family in Broad Island, and there built two slated houses, on ye Dalway's estate, near Carrickfergus.

Therefore let us now pause a while, and we shall wonder how this plantation advanced itself (especially in and about the towns of Donaghadee and Newton), considering that in the spring time, A°. 1606, those parishes were now more wasted than America, (when the Spaniards landed there), but were not at all incumbered with great woods to be felled and grubbed, to the discouragement or hindrance of the inhabitants, for in all those three parishes aforesaid, 30 cabins could not be found, nor any stone walls, but ruined roofless churches, and a few vaults at Gray Abbey, and a stump of an old castle in Newton, in each of which some Gentlemen sheltered themselves at their first coming over.

But Sir Hugh in the said spring brought with him divers artificers, as smiths, masons, carpenters, &c. I knew many of them old men when I was a boy at school, and had little employments for some of them, and heard them tell many things of this plantation which I found true. They soon made cottages and booths for themselves, because sods and saplins of ashes, alders, and birch trees (above 30 years old) with rushes for thatch, and bushes for wattles, were at hand.

And also they made a shelter of the said stump of the castle for Sir Hugh, whose residence was mostlie there, as in the centre of being supplied with necessaries from Belfast (but six miles thence), who therefore came and set up a market in Newtown, for profit for both the towns. As likewise in the fair summer season (twice, sometimes thrice every week) they were supplied from Scotland, as Donaghadee was oftener, because but three hours sail from Portpatrick, where they bespoke provisions and necessaries to lade in, to be brought over by their own or that town's boats whenever wind and weather served them, for there was a constant flux of passengers coming daily over.

I have heard honest old men say that in June, July, and August, 1607, people came from Stanraer, four miles, and left their horses at the port, hired horses at Donaghadee, came with their wares and provisions to Newton, and sold them, dined there, staid two or three hours, and returned to their houses the same day by bed-time, their land journey but 20 miles. Such was their encouragement from a ready market, and their kind desires to see and supply their friends and kindred, which commerce took quite away the evil report of wolves (L) and woodkerns, which envyers of planters industry had raised and brought

(L) See Appendix.

upon our plantations; but, notwithstanding thereof, by the aforesaid Gentlemen's assiduity to people their own farms, which they did, A°. 1607, after Sir Hugh and his Lady's example, they both being active and intent on the work (as birds, after payring, to make nests for their brood,) then you might see streets and tenements regularly set out, and houses rising as it were out of the ground (like Cadmus's colony) on a sudden, so that these dwellings became towns immediately.

Yet among all this care and indefatigable industry for their families, a place of God's honor to dwell in was not forgotten nor neglected, for indeed our forefathers were more pious than ourselves, and so soon as said stump of the old castle was so repaired, (as it was in spring time, 1606,) as might be shelter for that year's summer and harvest, for Sir Hugh and for his servants that winter, his piety made some good store of provisions in those fair seasons, towards roofing and fitting the chancel of that church, for the worship of God; and therein he needed not withdraw his own planters from working for themselves, because there were Irish Gibeonets and Garrons enough in his woods to hew and draw timber for the sanctuary; and the general free contribution of the planters, some with money, others with handycrafts and many with labouring, was so great and willingly given, that the next year after this, viz. A$_o$. 1607, before winter it was made decently serviceable, and Sir Hugh had brought over at first two or three Chaplains with him for these parishes. In summer 1608, some of the priory walls were roofed and fitted for his Lady and children and servants (which were many) to live in.

Now the harvests 1606 and 1607 had stocked the people with grain, for the lands were never naturally so productive since that time, except where no plough had gone, and where sea oar (called wreck) is employed for dung, to that degree that they had to spare and to sell to the succeeding new-coming planters, who came over the more in number and the faster, because they might sell their own grain at a great price in Scotland, and be freed of trouble to bring it with them, and could have it cheaper here. This conference gave occasion to Sir Hugh's Lady to build water mills in all the parishes, to the great advantage of her house, which was numerous in servants, of whom she stood in need, in working about her gardens, carriages, &c. having then no duty days' works from tenants, or very few as exacted, they being sufficiently employed in their proper labour, and the publique. The millers also prevented the necessity of bringing meal from Scotland, and grinding with quairn stones (as the Irish did to make their graddon) both which inconveniencys the people, at their first coming, were forced to undergo.

Her Ladyship had also her farms at Greyabbey and Coiner, as well as at Newtown, both to supply new-comers and her house; and she easily got men for plough and barn, for many came over who had not stocks to plant and take leases of land, but had brought a cow or two and a few sheep, for which she gave them grass and so much grain per annum, and an house and garden-plot to live on, and some land for flax and potatoes, as they agreed on for doing their work, and there be at this day many such poor labourers amongst us; and this was but part of her good management, for she set up and encouraged linen and woollen manufactory, which soon brought down the prices of y_e breakens and narrow cloths of both sorts.

Now every body minded their trades, and the plough and the spade, building, and setting fruit trees, &c. in orchards and gardens, and by ditching in their grounds. The old women spun, and the young girls plyed their nimble fingers at knitting—and every body was innocently busy. Now the Golden peaceable age renewed, no strife, contention, querulous lawyers, or Scottish or Irish feuds, between clanns and families, and sirnames, disturbing the tranquillity of those times; and the towns and temples were erected, with other great works done (even in troublesome years) as shall be in part recited, when I come to tell you of the first Lord Viscount Montgomery's funeral, person, parts, and arts; therefore, reader, I shall be the more concise in the history of the plantation, and of his loyal transactions; not, indeed, with his life, for the memoires (out of which I have collected observations thereof) are few, by reason of the fire, February, 1695, and other accidents, and by my removal into Scotland, since A^o. 1688, whereby such papers were destroyed or lost.

Yet I find by a fragment (of a second information to the Herauld, concerning the Lord Viscount's coat of arms,) written by Sir James Montgomery, that in a few years from the beginning of the plantation, viz. in A^o. 1610, the Viscount brought before the King's muster-master a thousand (M) able fighting men to serve, when out of them a militia should be raised, and the said Sir H. (for the great encouragement of planters and builders) obtained a patent dated the 25th of March,

(M) See Appendix.

11th Jac. which is the 1st day of A$_o$. 1613, *Stilo Anglecano*, and but one day more than ten full years after the Queen's death, y^e 24th March, 1602; being the last day of that year; by which letters patent, Newton aforesaid is erected into a corporation, whereof the said Sir Hugh is nominated the 1st Provost; and the Burgesses are also named. This corporation hath divers priviledges, the most remarkable are that every Parliament they send two Burgeses to serve therein; the other is that it can hold a Court every 2d Friday for debt, trespass, and damage, not exceeding three score six shillings and eight pence, sterling. The town hath in it an excellent piece of freestone work of eight squares, called the cross,(N) with a door behind, within are stairs mounting to the towers, over which is a high stone pillar, and proclamations are made thereon; on the floor whereof at each square is an antique spout which vented claret, King Charles the 2d being proclaimed our King of Great Britain, France, and Ireland, &c. A°. D°. 1649.

(N) See Appendix.

CHAPTER V.

THE foregoing things done, and in progress to their greater perfection, I begin again with Sir H. Montgomery and Con O'Neill's further dealings together. The last I mentioned was Con's conveyance to Sir Hugh, dated 22d August, 4 Jacobi, of the wood growing on the four townlands. I find also that, in pursuance of articles of the 24th December, 3d Jacobi, and of a former treat and covenant, and Sir Hugh's part to be performed, mentioned in Con's deed of feofment, dated the 14th May, 3d Jacobi, (for Con made then such a deed poll, which was accepted, because of mutual confidence between them). I say, pursuant to the premises, Sir Hugh made a deed of feofment, dated 15th May, 1610, purporting a gift in taile to Con and his heirs male of all his own lands, excepting ten towns. And the same day Con releases to Sir Hugh all the articles and covenants he had on Sir Hugh; and releases also thereby, the said excepted ten towns, and this done in consideration of 35*l*. paid in hand, and of 1000*l*. sterling, (formerly given, at several times, to ye said Con) and now remitted by the said Sir Hugh.

And so here I leave off to write of Con, but will relate some troubles which came upon Sir Hugh, but not so grievous as those which were occasioned by that killing dart, when Sir James Fullerton, when he procured the letters to ye Lord Deputy, with that clause, that ye patent for Con's estate should pass in James Hamilton's name alone; but Sir Hugh's courage and conduct (at long run) cured in part that great hurt.

The first succeeding troubles and costly toils which I read of after this last spoken of transaction with Con, which Sir Hugh met with, sprang from the petitions and claims of Sir Thomas Smith, against him and Sir James Hamilton; they began in April, 1610, and the 6th April, 1611, Sir Thomas gets an order of reference to the Commissioners for Irish affairs (of whom Sir James Hamilton was one) to make report of his case (for he claimed by grant from Queen Elizabeth, and the Commissioners judged it fitt to be left to law in Ireland). What he did pursuant to his report I know not, but on the 30th Sep. 1612, inquisition is taken, whereby Sir Thos. his title is found void and null, for breach and non-performance of articles and covenants to the Queen. See Grand Office, folio 10 and 11..

But it seems this was not all the trouble put upon Sir Hugh, for I find (folio 50 of Grand Office) he gave unto the Lord Deputy, Sir John, the King's letter, dated 20th July,

14th Regis, inhibiting any lands to be passed to any person whatsoever away from Sir Hugh Montgomery, to which he had claim by deed from James Hamilton or Con, and this caveat with a list of the lands he entered in the Secretary's office in Dublin.

Between this and the year 1618, divers debates, controversys aud suits, were moved by Sir Hugh against Sir James Hamilton, which were seemingly taken away by an award made by the Right Honourable James Hamilton, Earle of Abercorn, to which both partys stood; in conformity to which award, and the King's letter relating thereunto, at least to the chief parts thereof, Sir James Hamilton conveys several lands to Sir Hugh Montgomery, and both of them in the deed are stiled Privy Counsellor; which deed bears date 23d May, 1618, George Medensis, and William Alexander, &c. subscribing witnesses. I presume this might be done at London, for much about this time Sir Hugh and his Lady lived there, and made up the match between their eldest son and Jean, the eldest daughter of Sir William Alexander, Secretary for Scotland, whom I take to be one of the witnesses in that great concern, by reason, the match aforesaid was about this time or some months afterwards completed.

The produce of this marriage, which lived

to come to age, was two sons and a daughter, which only survived that comely pair. The eldest left behind him two sons, now alive. One of which hath also two males living and life like. And of the 1st Viscount's second and third sons, there are in good health two old Gentlemen, past their grand climacterick; and the eldest of them hath his son married above 11 years ago; of whose loins there are three male children, unsnatched away by death, and he may have more very probably. The other old Gentleman is father to two proper young Gentlemen, one lately married, and the other able to ly at that wedding-lock above four years past.

Yet, for all our expectations, I neither can (nor will) divine how long these three families may last, seeing that neither the said Earle of Abercorn, nor heirs of his body (that I can learn) hath any children, only his brother's (the Lord of Strabane) offspring enjoy the title, either from his said father, or by a new creation of one of the two late Kings, the Stewards; and seeing, likewise, the 1st Viscount Clanneboy left but one son, who left two, who are both dead, without leaving any issue behind them, the more is the pity, for many reasons too well known, as by the records in Dublin doth appear. This consideration, on the duration of families, is to prevent overmuch care to raise posterity to grandeur.

The said Sir Hugh had (no doubt) further troubles between the said year 1618 and 1623, because, at his chief instance and request, and for his greater security, the King granted a commission and order, directed unto Henry Lord Viscount Faulkland, Lord Deputy of Ireland, for holding an inquisition concerning the lands, spiritual and temporal, therein mentioned, which began to be held before Sir John Blennerhassett, Lord Chief Baron, at Downpatrick the 13th October, 1623. This inquest is often cited, and is commonly called the Grand Office. Again, Sir Hugh (that he might be the more complete by sufferings) is assaulted by Sir William Smith, who strove to hinder the passing of the King's patent to him; on notice whereof, Sir Hugh writes a large well penned letter (which I have) with instructions to his son James how to manage that affair. This is dated 23d February, 1623, about four months after the Grand Office was found. I have the original every word written by himself. I should greatly admire at the exactness thereof, both in point of fact and law, but that so ingenious a person and so long bred (by costly experience) to the law (as for 20 years before this Sir Hugh was used) could not want knowledge to direct his son to pass that ford which himself had wridden through.

But to continue the troublesomeness of Sir Thomas Smith. King James died Ao. 1624, and on the 11th April, 1625, the Duke of Buckingham writes to the Judges to make report to him, in William Smith's and Sir James Hamilton's case, that he might inform the King thereof, which they did in the same manner as the Commissioners for Irish affairs before had done (in Ao. 1611,) viz:—That Smith should be left to the law in Ireland, and herein the said James Montgomery was agent, for I have a letter dated from Bangor, 4th November, 1625, to him, signed J. Clanneboy (who was then possessed of Killileagh) advising him to consult Sir James Fullerton, &c. in the business against Smith, for James Montgomery was then going to Court about it, his father, some months or days before that time, being created Lord Viscount, for his patent was prior to the said Clanneboys, and so henceforth I must stile him the first Lord Viscount Montgomery.

The 30th April, 1626, Sir William Smith, in a new petition, complains against the Viscount Montgomery, and prays orders to stop the letters patent to him for any lands; and obtained warrants of Council, dated May and

F

June next following, requiring the said Lord Viscount to appear before some English Lords authorised to report their cases, that both his Lordship and Smith might be heard; which orders were served on James Montgomery, as agent to his father; but the said agent being then Gentleman Usher of the Privy Chamber in ordinary to King Charles, Hamilton petitioned his Majesty, setting forth that Sir Thomas and Sir William Smith's cases (both in the late King's time and in the beginning of his Majesty's reign) were adjudged to be left to the law in Ireland; and that no stop was put to the passing the respective patents, in behalf of the Lord Chichester, the Lord Claneboys, or Foulk. Conway, thereupon, A. D. 1626, 2 Car. said Lord Montgomery's patent for his lands, conform to Abercorn's award, was ordered by the King to be passed, under the broad seal of Ireland, which bears date ———

Moreover, to the Lord Montgomery further trouble arose. For I find there was a decree in Chancery the 12th December, 1626, touching underwoods and timber; whereby the Lord Montgomery was to have those growing in Slutevils and Castlereagh, as should be awarded or recovered from Francis Hill, Esq. So the reader may oberve, that from the date of the tripartite indenture, ulto. April, 3d Jac. Ao. 1605, till December, 1633, there arose many difficulties between Sir James Hamilton and Sir Hugh Montgomery, (Viscount 1623), occasioned by that ominous and fatal interposition of Sir James Fullerton aforesaid, and chiefly by the clause he procured to be inserted in the letter of warrant, dated April, 3d Jac. Ano. 1605, whereby Mr. Hamilton was nominated as the only person in whose name alone the letters patent for Con's estate and the abbey lands in upper Claneboy, and the great Ardes were to be remembered.

Yet in all my reach of papers and enquiry of knowing more, I cannot find or hear what became of Sir James Fullerton, or of his posterity, or whether he died childless, there being none of that sirname (that I can learn) in Scotland, above the degree of a gentleman, only I read in Bishop Ussher's life, that he lies in St. Erasmus Chapel, where that Primate was buried.

There arose also difficulties (after December, 1633,) between the first and second Viscount Montgomerys, plaintiffs, and the Lord Claneboys, defendant, concerning the articles of agreement made 17th December, 1633, not being fully performed to the Lord Montgomery, *(ut dicitur)*, which ended not till the rebellion in Ireland began 1641, verifying

the Latin adage, *Inter Arma Silent Leges.*—
So I find that many are the troubles of the
righteous, but the Lord delivereth them out
of them all.

All which differences sirceasing that last
named year, and so were sedated, or buried, or forgotten, that they were never
stirred up again, I shall therefore leave no
memory of the Montgomerys' losses therein
by mentioning them either by word or writing, because of the love and kind deference
now among us, all Montgomerys and the
Hamiltons of that family; but now I will readdress myself to the narrative of the said Lord
Montgomery, only, (as in parenthesis) I here
insert that Con, the 1st January, 1616, made
a deed purporting a lease unto Ellis Nyneil,
his wife, and unto Hugh Buy O'Neil, his son,
of the townlands of Ballycargbreman, Bressag,
&c. delivered the deed to his said wife,
for the use of his said son, being a child
of five years old, and there present in
the house; also that the said Con had two
brothers (whether uterin or by marriage
I know not) viz :—Tool O'Neil, and Hugh
Mergagh O'Neil, to each of whom he gave
lands, and they sold their interest therein. As for Con's other actions and dealings (because most of them were failures to
the first Lord Montgomery) I bury them in

silence and oblivion, having occasion, hereafter, to write of his only surviving issue, Daniel O'Neil, Esq. who, Ao. 1641, attempted (as the Smiths aforesaid had done) to reverse or greatly impair the two Viscounts' titles; but he died a Protestant, as is thought, without issue, after King Charles the Second's restoration, being married to the old Countess of Chesterfield. Thus, many time innocent children are punished for their parent's faults; yet not without procuring the same business of their own.

CHAPTER VI.

I HAVE long retarded the history of the said Montgomery's progress in his plantation, and other affairs, by these foregoing interjections, concerning the Smiths and Con—with other difficultys and troubles. It may be remembered, that I told you, reader, that some of the priory walls were roofed and fitted for Sir Hugh and his family to dwell in; but the rest of these walls, and other large additions of a gate, house and office-houses, which made three sides of a quadrangle, (the south side of the church being contiguous, made the 4th side) with coins and window frames, and chimney-pieces, and funnels of freestone, all covered; and the floors beamed with main oak timber, and clad with boards; the roof with oak plank from his Lordship's own woods, and slated with slates out of Scotland; and the floors laid with fir deals out of Norway, the windows were fitly glazed and the edifice thoroly furnished within. This was a work of some time and years, but the same was fully finished by that excellent Lady, (and fit helper mostly in Sir Hugh's absence), because he was by business much and often kept from home, after the year 1608 expired; yet the whole work was done many months before Sir Hugh and she went to London, Ao. 1618, as the dates of coats of arms doth shew in the buildings, and as old men, who wrought thereat, told me.

And so I shall here surcease from any further relation of the plantation and buildings, because of my promise to relate more of this matter when I come to speak of Sir Hugh Montgomery, his funeral, person, parts and acts; and I will now enter upon his actions about and from the year 1623, repeating as little as I can of what hath been said, because I intend not to mention any of his law troubles, so unpleasing to my memory.

Imprimis, in or about Anno 1623, the marriage between Sir Hugh Montgomery's eldest son, Hugh, (he was called from his travels being then in Italy) and Jean, eldest daughter of Sir William Alexander, the King's Secretary for Scotland, was solemnized. The new wedded couple were comely and well bred personages, who went that summer with Sir Hugh (now Viscount) Montgomery and his Lady, to their new built and furnished house aforesaid in Newtown. Some years before this time, Sir Hugh had married his eldest daughter to Sir Robert M'Clellan, Baron of Kirkcoby, who (with her) had four great townlands near Lisnegarvey, whereof she was possessed in December, 1622. Sir Hugh and his Lady, also, had likewise given him a considerable sum of money as an augmentation to the marriage portion; but the said Sir Robert spent the money and sold the lands after her Ladyship's death, and himself died not long after her, both without issue.

Item, in or about the same year, 1623, the Viscount married his other daughter, Jean, to Pat. Savage, of Portaferry, Esq. (o) whose predecessors (by charter from the Queen Elizabeth, and formerly as I am credibly informed,) were stiled, and in their deeds of lands they named themselves Lords of the little Ardes. This family is reputed to be

(o) See Appendix.

above 400 years standing in Ireland, and those Lords were men of great esteem, and had far larger estates in the county of Antrim, than they have now in the Ardes. One of the Earles of Antrim married Shelly, a daughter of Portaferry, and the late Marq. and Earle thereof, called those of this family Easens; and the Lord Deputy Chichester would have had the Patrick's immediate predecessor and brother to have married his niece, but it is reported that Russell, of Rathmullen, made him drunk, and so married him to his own daughter, who was mother to one O'Hara, in the county of Antrim. This Patrick was reputed to be the 17th son, and succeeded to the manor of Portaferry, by virtue of ancient deeds of feofment in tail, for want of heirs males by his eldest brother. He was the 1st Protestant of his family, through the said Viscount's care to instruct him. As to portions, the said Viscount gave 600*l.* (a great sum in those days); he was Captain of a troop Ao. 1641, in the regiment of horse, under the command of the second Lord Viscount Montgomery. And the said Jean died Ao. 1643; he himself also departed this life in the beginning Anno 1644, leaving orphan children only two daughters and Hugh (his 9th son) to the care of Sir James Montgomery (their mother's brother), who performed that trust with full fidelity, and to their great advantage, compounding many debts, paying them out of the rents, which then were high (for he waved the benefit of the wardship he had of the said Hugh's estate and person). He bred them at Rosemount, his own house, according to their quality, till harvest time Ao. 1649, that Oliver Cromwell's army (triumphing over us all) obliged himself and his son to go into Scotland, and leave them at Portaferry aforesaid.

The said Hugh Savage lived till about Ao. 1666, and died without issue. He was educated at Rosemount and Newtown with me as two brothers; and he boarded himself many years with me, never having had a wife; but his encumbered estate came (by virtue of the said Hugh and father's feoffments) to his nearest kinsman, Patrick Savage, Esq. who now enjoys it, he having, by his prudent management, recovered it out of some great encumbrances thereon, and brought it to great improvements of rents.

And now I have ended the bad success of the said last recited two matches by our first Lord Viscount, let us now, as order requires, relate what his Lordship did for his other offspring and first of his son James Montgomery (often before named). Him his Lordship called home from his travels, after he had been in France, Germany, Italy, and Holland, (divers months in each of these countrys); and finding him fit for business, sent him to Court in England, Ao. 1623, to obviate the mischief feared from Sir Thomas Smith's complaints (as hath already been said) ; and there the said James continued to study the laws at the Inns of Court, and attending all his father's business which came before King James or King Charles, till Ao. 2d Car. that patents were passed to his father for his estate; and then being called home (for now the clouds of danger, from the two Smiths aforesaid, were blown over), he was, some months after that time, employed as his father's agent, both in the country and in Dublin, so that he became an expert solicitor, courtier, and statesman, as before his travel he had been a pregnant scholar, and taken his degrees as of Master in the liberall arts in the University of St. Andrews. The certificate, under the seal, I have shown to many persons who had esteem of learning.

Now before I leave this brief acccount of him, I take the liberty to relate one instance of favour to him from the Royal Martyr, viz. His Majesty went to shoot at the Butts; (p) necessaries were brought, the King desires Mr. Montgomery to try one of the bows, and

(p) See Appendix.

he shot three or four ends with his Majesty so very well that he said, " Mr. Montgomery that bow fitts your hand, take them and a quiver of arrows and keep them for your use." I was told this by my father, who carefully preserved them, and divers times (in my sight) used them at Rosemount, charging me to do so likewise; they were left to his nephew Savage's care, Ao. 1649, who restored them to me at my return; the bow was too strong for me, and he using it, it broke in his hands; one half of it was desired and made a staff for the old Countess of Strevling, when she was entertained here by her daughter, the 2d Viscountess Montgomery, at Mount Alexander house.

His Lordship, to compensate the said James's constant, dutiful, well performed services, and to give him a 2d son's portion, settled on him about ten townlands, five of them about Gray Abbey aforesaid, the rest in the barony of Castlereagh, and one summer, Ao. 1631, matched him to Katherine, eldest daughter of Sir William Stewart, Knight and Baronet, a Privy Councellor.

Then about this time his Lordship called home his third son, George Montgomery, Esq. from his travels in Holland, through London, where he stayed some months at Court. Thence to Scotland, where he had visited (as he had been ordered) the family of Garthland, and there stayed some time to be acquainted with the Gentlewoman designed to be his wife, which, in Ao. 1633, came to pass, his Lordship having first settled on him the lands, value about 300*l.* per annum, which Hugh (the said George his son) now enjoys. These M'Dowells, Lairds of Garthland, near Portpatrick, have now stood in that place above 1000 years; and were, in the first century, stiled Princes of Galway, by allowance of the then Kings in Scotland.

Now having spoken of the said Lord Montgomery's offspring, as to what his Lordship did for them, I think it a due gratitude in this place to remember his Lordship's said brother George, the best and closest friend he had, they two being, like Castor and Pollux, to supply one another's absence. You have heard in what station he lived before Ao. 1603, and what preferment King James gave him, in the first year of his reign. Soon after this, his Majesty, finding the Dean of Norwich, his chaplain, Geo. Montgomery (q) aforesaid, his abilitys for state affairs and his great skill in ecclesiastical matters, and the Church of Ireland being under very bad circumstances, and being careful that abuses should be redressed, (I say) his Majesty thereupon sent over the said George, Ao. 1605, 3d Jac. in

(q) See Appendix.

quality of a Privy Councellor, to be informed and to acquaint him in what condition the Church and State stood in that kingdom, and to be one of the Commissioners for settling clergy affairs: this proved much for their and that Church's benefit, and his carriage therein so well pleased the Primate, Archbishops, and Bishops, that he was their darling and chief advocate, but his employment ran counter to some English Lords and others of the laity, who had grasped over hardly too much of the tithes due to the Priest's office.

After a few years toilsome pains to understand the business of his errand and of the commission for settling the affairs aforesaid, the Chaplain George aforesaid was employed Ao. 1606, 4th Jac. by the Primate and the Bishops in Ireland, to represent to his Majestie the grievances of the clergy, to the great thwarting and hinderance of the laity aforesaid, in their will and designs, on which (as I have heard from his daughter, the old Lady of Howth,) they had a great grudge against him; but he, having the best cause in hand and his native Prince's favourable hearing in God's and his servant's concern, did prosper in that message, and at the Council

Board (where he sat) had the King's orders confirmed and by others obeyed.

Now Chaplain Montgomery became more and more esteemed of the superior and inferior clergy, and was recommended by the Bishops that he should have the diocess of Derry, and with it Clogher and Raphoe in commendam, which were then very low in tithes and revenues, by reason of O'Doherty's rebellion, in which Derry was sacked and burned, and the lands being as it were a waste wilderness without English plantations and garrisons; and laying further Church business on him, as their agent at Court, he went the second time into England. I was credibly informed, that divers Lords (some of them Privy Counsellors) gave him the compliment of seeing him to the ship, telling him, at parting, that he should fail in that enterprize which he then undertook, and that his answer was—My Lords, I am going to the King, and you know it is the business of God's oppressed church, which his Majesty and the laws protect, and if the divine permission suffer my errand to miscarry, through yours and other men's profanement, I shall lament the misfortune in England, and our sins which may draw on us that punishment, and be contented with my livings in England, for I am not pursuing preferment for myself, but the service of the Church in Ireland; and I will cast my cap at this kingdom, and never return to it. But, be assured, whether I come back or not, the sinful politick measures taken against God's Church will not prosper.

Then the said Chaplain doubled his diligence at Court, the more for the opposition he met with; and he obtained for the Church and himself what was committed to his agency. Then he returned with strict orders that the petitioned for desires of the Primate and other Episcopalians should be granted, and himself to be preferred to the dioceses aforesaid. All which affairs were accomplished as soon as might be done by the Government; for his consecration stuck not at all for want of the Bishops' ordaining hands; and this was very lucky for those northern parts, because his residence therein and watchful unwearied industry mightily advanced the British Protestant plantations, and the Bishop's revenues to treble the value he found them at, as will appear in the sequel of this discourse concerning that Lord Bishop.

And here I must make a large stop for want of councilable books, and the first Lord Viscount Montgomery's and the Bishop's own papers, out of which (if by me) I could have plentiful memoires of this good Bishop's memorable services for his God, King and country. I must therefore have leave to spare fruitless pains, being troubled with the gout. I take him where I find him, signing George Medensis to a deed from Sir James Hamilton to Sir Hugh Montgomery, made in parcel, pursuant to Abercorn's award, dated 23d May, in the year of God, 1618, as aforesaid; and after this, for want of the said books and papers, I can say little of his transactions for the publick, but much of his usefulness in the plantation, of the marriage in bestowing his daughter, and his promoting Dr Ussher to succeed him, and of some other things of lesser moment relating to him. I premise, to this future narrative of this Right Reverend Father, that it is most probable he was no lazy Bishop nor idle patriot, in the posts he held, but very prudently and sincerely, as well as piously, active in business, fearing God and hating covetousness, to which last quality he had no temptation, as being a widower long before his death, and having but one child, a daughter, to prefer; yet he lived with great hospitality, gathering little or nothing but what he employed to religious uses, and building for his successor Bishops, and in charity to the poor; and I must be excused for my prolixity in writing (if it be such) of this very eminent Prelate, who left behind him no male or other issue capable to transmit to after ages a due memory of his pious actions, and the precious endowments of his Heaven-born generous soul.

Now, as to his Lordship's usefulness in advancing the British plantation in those three northern dioceses, the footsteps of his so doing are yet visible; so that I need but tell the reader that he was very watchfull, and settled intelligences to be given him from all the sea ports in Donegal and Fermanagh, himself mostly residing in Derry but when he went to view and lease the Bishop's lands, or settle preachers in parishes (of which he was very careful.) The ports resorted from Scotland were Derry, Donegal, and Killybegs; to which places the most that came were from Glasgow, Air, Irwin, Greenock and Larggs, and places within a few miles of Braidstane; and he ordered so that the masters of vessels should, before disloading their cargo, (which was for the most part meal and oats), come to his Lordship with a list of their seamen and passengers. The vessels stayed not for a market. He was their merchant and encourager to traffick in those parts, and wrote to that effect (as also to the said towns wherein he was much acquainted and esteemed), and had proclamations made in them all, at how easy rents he would set his church lands, which drew thither many families; among whom one Hugh Montgomery, his kinsman, a master of a vessel, and also owner, was one who brought his wife, children, and effects, and were settled in Derrybrosh, near Enniskillen, where his son, Mr Nich. (my long and frequent acquaintance) aged above 85 years, now lives in sound memory, and is a rational man, whose help I now want, to recount particulars of that Bishop's proceedings in that country, whilst his Lordship stayed there; which was, at least, till near Ao. 1618 aforesaid, that he was Bishop of Meath.

One other Montgomery, named Alexander, (a minister), his Lordship settled near Derry. He was prebend of ditto, and he lived till about 1658; of whose, and the aforesaid Nich. their sons, I shall have occasion to speak, before this be done. Thus, by the Bishop George's industry, in a few years, the plantation was forwarded, and Church revenues encreased greatly. I was credibly told, that for the encouragement of planters on Church lands, he obtained the King's orders to the Governors, and an act of council thereon, that all the leases he made (which were for 31 years) should not be taken from the planters or their posterity, at the expiration of their term, but renewed to them as they held the same, they paying their Bishop one year's rent for a renewal of their lease, to the other 31 years, which was a very encouraging certainty for planters; but the Parliament since that time have taken other measures more for Bishops' than tenants' profits.

In or about this first (or rather second) visitation of the said diocess, his Lordship married the Lord Brabason's daughter, by whom he had divers children, none surviving him except Nicholas Lord Baron of Howth, his Lady, with whom he gave in marriage portion three thousand pounds sterling, a round sum in those days.

You have heard that 23d May, 1618, his Lordship signs Medensis as witness to a deed of lands made to his brother, Sir Hugh Montgomery. About this time (or how soon after his translation from Derry to Meath I know not) he erected a Bishop's house at Ardbrackin, near Navan, and repaired the Church near it, which was without a roof Ao. 1667, and therein built a vault for a burial place of his wife and children who died some years before himself. I have seen the monument and took the figure off it with a black lead pen; it had (under an open arch) on it, divers stone figures carved out from the table stones, where the inscriptions were engraven representing his Lordship's wife and the children kneeling one behind the other, with the palms of their hands joined and erected before their chins, which, with the rest of the monument, were much defaced, and my draft thereof is (to my grief) lost.

CHAPTER VII.

Now let us recur to Ao. 1618, and soon after it we find his Lordship in Westminster, where he departed this life Ao. 1621, or beginning 1622. I touched the grudge some lay lords and others had against him, and it seems their animosity arose from his hindering them to be confirmed in their sacriledgious acquests, not suffering the Church to be despoiled of her rights, nor the King's goodness to be overreached and abused by their misinformations. For thus it was, viz.—Dr. Ussher, for his printed books against the Popish religion, and other divinity tracts, and for his printed disputations against MaCoon, (R) the learned Jesuit, was had in great esteem by the University at Dublin; they having, for those actions and his wonderful learning, given him a degree for a Doctor of Divinity, when he had but newly passed the years of age which

(R) See Appendix.

the canons require should be elapsed, before a man can be regularly admitted to full orders of Priesthood ; but they took not ordinary rules with him whom they found God had highly honoured with such extraordinary gifts and graces as he had by the divine bounty bestowed on him, for the future particular welfare of the Church in Ireland, and the universal good of all true Christians.

This said University, this dear alma mater as he was its *humilis alumnus*, did moreover get some Lords of the Council and other Officers of State to write letters of recommenda- to their correspondents at Court, in favour of Dr. Ussher (unsolicited by him, who was contented enough with the livings he then had, being unmarried), that he might be parson of Trim. Every step in this business and of the Doctor's speedy coming over, and of the house he was to lodge in, was soon known to the Bishop of Meath, who, from the time of his being settled in England, long before the Queen died, never would want exact intelligences (the best rudder and wind by which Statesmen steer their courses, according to the old verified axiom—*Vigilantibus et non dormientibus sauciunt Leges*); for the Doctor was not an hour or a little more alighted from his horse at his inn (where he intended to stay incognito all next day, to rest himself, after his wearysome journey, and till he had got new habits, according to the English clergy made); but fresh news thereof came to the Bishop, who sent his Gentleman to the Doctor with positive request that he should come forthwith to his Lordship in his company, for the Bishop stayed in his lodgings to receive him, and this present visit the Doctor must not omit, unless he desired to return *re infecta*. Upon this strict message, the Doctor caused his clothes to be brushed, and went (like Nicodemus) when it was night with the Gentleman to the Bishop, when after caresings, salutation and a glass of wine, they sat down together, to do which the Bishop found some difficulty from the Doctor's native humility, and from the great deference he had for the Bishop. This being overcome, the Bishop began thus as followeth, viz.—Doctor I very well know your errand, and how unexpectedly and unwillingly too you were engaged in it, because you had not first obtained my leave to move in ye suit, and that you are not recommended by any letter to me; and here the Bishop mentioned all the persons from whom and to whom the recommendatory epistles (as St. Paul calls such like letters) were written, and the time he received them, and the time he hastened away with them, when he landed, at what inn he was advised to alight from his horses, (which he was to have at his arrival in England) and how his Lordship had laid watch to send him immediate notice when he should come to the inn, he was advised to, and here his Lordship held his tongue. This harangue would have amazed any young man, but the Doctor, who knew there was no familiar demon or other spirit that ministered that intelligence, but only the Bishop's watchfulness for his care of his diocess, had procured his Lordship that wonderful information, in so many points, which were carried on with all the secrecy that might.— And now the Doctor being mute awhile, admiring the Bishop's conduct, he rose from his chair and began to apologize for consenting to meddle in that business, before he applied himself therein to his Lordship, and had his allowance thereunto; and so going on in his excuses, the Bishop interrupted him, and rising, said, I will be brief with you, who may not know the meanness of the revenues of that diocess for a Bishop thereof, whose station ties him to almost continual attendance at the Council Board, and to be in readiness at all times to go thither, when called; and, therefore, you shall not be Parson of Trim, the King having already granted to me that the parsonage shall be annexed to the Bishoprick, for the reasons aforesaid. But trouble not yourself, Doctor, (said the Bishop), at this repulse; I know you deserve a much better living than Trim, and I will be solicitor to the King that you may be better provided for. I will discourse his Majesty to-morrow morning, and prepare the King to receive you (as I am assured he will do) gratiously; only, Doctor, deliver not your letters but as I shall advize you, and so take your designed rest after the journey, and give me notice when your new habits are on, that I may apprise you a time when you shall next come to me, and may bring you to kiss the King's hand, when he is best at leizure to talk with you, of whose abilities he hath, from myself, abundantly heard, besides what the public fame has reported to his Majesty. The Doctor, thereupon, gave his humble and hearty thanks, promising to obey all his Lordship's commands. And so the Bishop dismissed the Doctor with his episcopal benediction, and sent his said servants to conduct him back to his inn.

Next morning, the Bishop went to the King, and had his further order to confirm the parsonage of Trim to his successors, Bishops of Meath, and acquainted his Majesty of the Doctor's coming to Westminster, and of his errand and recommendations, and prayed his Majesty's leave and orders to speake to the Archbishop of Canterbury and Bishop of London to provide the first good living that fell for the Doctor, and to accept him for his Chaplain in Ordinary (as his Majesty had done for himself), and to let him know when he should bring the Doctor to kiss his Majesty's hand, and to have the honor of discoursing with him, to all which the King agreed.

Then the Bishop sent that evening for the Doctor, telling him what had passed between the King and him, concerning promises and the time appointed for his reception; so the Bishop brought the Doctor the day following to see the Court, where every body was curious to see him of whom so much had been spoken, especially the clergy regarded him, observing the countenance and deference which the favourite Bishop (for the King commonly called him his black Ireland Bishop) gave publicly to the Doctor; yet none of them could draw from him his errand. The time being come for the Doctor's private appearance before the King, who said, I long grieved to see you, of whom I have heard a great deal of praise, and then told the Doctor he thanked the Lords and others

H

who had recommended so worthy a man as he to his favours, and calling for the letters, and reading the subscribers' names, saying he should love them the better all his life, for their love to him, but added he need not read them because this Bishop there had fully enough interceded for him, giving the Bishop order to see that the Doctor should be admitted at present his Chaplain in Ordinary, till further provision (by his careful enquiry) might be made for him. Then after the Doctor had made his submissions and thanks on his knee, the King bade him rise and discoursed him on divers abstruse points of religion, and received learned pertinent answers, the King saying again Doctor I find you are sufficiently able, and therefore you must soon preach before me, as my Chaplain, for I can advance you. And the King would not allow of his excuses as to his youth and the envy it might bring on him; no matter for all that, said the King, seeing I shall be careful of you, and my Bishop here is your solicitor; but I will order you the text and time for preaching. And so that interview passed over.

But I must not here break off my discourse of what was further done for the Doctor, it being a part of the history of Bishop George, of whom I am writing. The Doctor (a while after this) being admitted the King's Chaplain, was called before his Majesty, who told him he must preach, within a week, in his presence, and, opening a Bible, recited an historical verse in the book of Chronicles (which was very hard bones to pick); yet, the Doctor handled them so warmly, that he extracted abundance of good oyle from them, to the admiration of all that heard him.— Upon this charge, the Doctor, falling on his knees, vowed his dutiful obedience to all his Majesty's commands: but begged that at least the time might be granted him for preparation allowed to his other more learned Chaplains, lest he should be called an arrogant novice, on whom his Majesty had now looked (as he hoped) with gracious and favourable eyes. No more words, Doctor, said the King, you shall pass this and future tryals before myself, for I will not refer you to the report of others. So the King rising from his chair, and the Doctor from his knees, the assembly (as I may call it, because there were many spectators) was dissolved, the Doctor still attending the Bishop, and both of them saluted by the lay and clergy courtiers.

Now, as to the Doctor, I need say no more, but he performed his task beyond expectation, by preaching in the King's audience, and also at the intreaty of the Archbishop and Bishop aforesaid, to whose care he was recommended. The Doctor was provided for; nevertheless the Bishop, George, had reserved the best good turn for him of any; and thus it was, the Doctor being provided for of a good fat benefice (as they call those of the greatest profit) and in his turn paying his attendance and preaching as Chaplain to the King, the Bishop finding him well liked of all and very deserving, obtained of the King that the Doctor should be his successor in the diocess of Meath, and got his boon confirmed when he fell ill in his last sickness. This pleased very well courtier divines expectants for English livings, there being as yet no great temptation to covet those in Ireland, and they feared a new favourite at Court (for the King was much addicted to over love them); and the Bishop having procured the necessary licenses from the King in behalf of the Doctor, he sent for him from his living (much better than the parsonage of Trim), and informed him of what was done, giving him the letters with his advice and charge not to neglect his business, because his Lordship said he trusted in God that the Doctor should be a great instrument for the welfare of the Church in Ireland, and his Lordship wrote letters to his friends to assist the Doctor.

This being the last public actions (I hear of) done by the Bishop, he died soon after in Westminster, which was the latter end of Ao. 1621, or beginning of Ao. 1622, for I find by the Doctor's letter to Dr. Teatly, the Archbishop of Canterbury's Chaplain, dated the 16th of September, 1622, that he subscribed Jac. Midensis, (see his fragment remains collected by Dr. Burnett, printed 1657) leaving a petitionary letter (which I have by me) to King James, in behalf of the family of Howth, in which he had settled his daughter as aforesaid; and so piously dying, he was embalmed, coffined in lead, and transported to Howth, then, pursuant to testament, thence taken to Aberbrecken, to rest with his wife and children.

I cannot sufficiently say or express his due eulogium, but this may be added to the premises, that for his honor and in memory of his contributions to the reparations in Christ's Church, Dublin, I saw his coat of arms over the door which lets into the quire of said Church, in which place only divine service and sermons are now used. The said coat was the same with the uppermost of those three which is over the gate house entry at

Newton, except that instead of helmet, tors and crest, it was surmounted by an episcopal mitre, and bore a distinction of a second brother, the arms being the bearing of the Lairds of Braidstane, before the first Viscount Montgomery was nobilitated; but this coat, with the rest of the contributer's arms, are now totally expunged.

I saw likewise, Ao. 1696, his Lordship's picture and his wife's, at Howth house, but little regarded since the late Lady, his grand-child, died; those of them which were carefully preserved in Newtown-house, till the late Earle of Mount Alexander died, were, about Ao. 1664, burned there with the several pieces, could cost no less than twenty pounds each, being done sitting in chairs and to ye feet. To conclude with his Lordship, he was a faithful servant to God and his Church, and King, and an excellent friend, especially more than a brother to his brother (the sixth Laird of Braidstane), where he was born A. D. 1562, and at his death 61 years of age.

Having brought this Rev. Prelate to his tomb, I can do no less (being under greater duty) than to convey his eldest brother to his grave in peace to Newtown Church, which he had re-edifyed, and shall rehearse some of his peaceful actions (for I will not mention any more of his law troubles), but proceed in my intended narrative.

CHAPTER VIII.

IT hath been said very briefly what his Lordship did as to providing wives for and settling his two younger sons. Now before these last two marriages his Lordship was a widower many months, and being at leisure, as well for diverting melancholy as to look after his affairs at Braidstane, he went into Scotland, and visited his chief and superior, the Earl of Eglington, paying him all the gratefull returns of former kindnesses and countenances in his affairs from first to last. For this Earle, besides his assistances in his business in Scotland and England, before his Lordship was Viscount, had not only given him a certificate (which in Scotland is called a bore brief,) of the said genealogy and extraction from his family of Eglington, but also afterwards (the more to make his descent appear *lucidus in futuro*, and to shew his present respects), he consents that the Viscount's coat armorial should agree with his own in all things, except that the Viscount's hath not the same crest nor motto, and but one of the Earle's supporters, with this other difference (for a distinction as a cadet) that in the nombril of his Lordship's shield he should bear an escutchion charged with the same sword and lance, sattire wise, as he had over all his coat when he was Laird of Braidstane; and he, with his Lordship's 2d son, Sir James Montgomery, managed that affair, as appears by copys of his letters to the said Earl and the Herauld yet extant. Let me have the favour, reader, to insert (as a parenthesis) a very probable conjecture, viz. that the said 1st Viscount was god-son unto Hugh, Earl of Eglington, who was insidiously slain at the river of Annock, the 18th day of April, A.D. 1586, for the reasons formerly mentioned, there being in those days no scruple for a man to be a god-father, and to answer at the font for a friend's child.

This lately said visit of our Viscount, to the said Earle, and his friends and kindred, was received with great love and respects by them all, which they continued till and after his funeral; and after it, to the two succeeding Viscounts, whilst they lived, as their heirs have a kind deference and regard to our present second Earle of Mount-Alexander.

At this time, it was during his Lordship's stay in Scotland, he married the Viscountess of Wigton, and brought her to Newtown, to fill up the empty side of his bed, not minding profit from her jointure lands, which he left to her Ladyship's own disposal and ordering; but she not liking to live in Ireland, though great improvements were made, both as to his large store-houses in Newtown, sufficient for two succeeding Viscounts to dwell in, and also at Dunsky Castle which his Lordship had bought in his first Lady's time, with the lands belonging to it, and Portpatrick town, also from Sir Robert Adair, of Kinhilt, and had put many convenient and handsome additions to it; she, notwithstanding, after some months stay, returned to Scotland, and did remain therein, which obliged his Lordship to make yearly summer visits to her, and to send divers messages (by his son George) to persweade her Ladyship to return and cohabit with him, whose attendance at Council Board, and business in law, at Dublin, and private affairs at home, would not allow his Lordship dwelling with her in Scotland.

His Lordship brought over a page to his Lady, Edward Betty, the prettiest little man I ever beheld. He was of a blooming damask rose complexion; his hair was of a shining gold colour, with natural ring-like curls hanging down, and dangling to his breast, and so exact in the symmetry of his body and limbs to his stature, that no better shape could be desired in a well carved statue.— His wit was answerable to what his comely face might promise; and his cunning no less, for many times, when gentlewomen, that did not frequent Newtown-house since the first Viscount's death till the second Lord brought his lady to live therein, came to pay visits to her Ladyship, this beautiful man‧ nick was often mistaken for one or the other of his Lordship's sons, and taken up by the gentlewomen on their laps, and they kissed him to make him prattle, which he could very well do as a child. He kept them in their ignorance so long as to have occasion enough to make his Lady sport, nay sometimes he would protract his convers till his Lady came from her chamber to see the female visitant, his unmannerlyness being reproved by his Lady, so to impose on the gentlewomen, as to sit on their knee and promote the error. You may believe the mistaken ladies blushed and were extremely ashamed, and this happened when he had passed twenty years of age. I did copy (after Vandyke's original) the picture of the Royal Martyr's dwarf, Jeffrey, holding a silken cord, a monkey on his shoulder, as a fancy to set him off, who, although he was very comely, well proportioned and so diminutive as that the

King's long porter's boot, (as I was told Ao. 1664, by old courtiers), covered his brow when he was put in it, yet he was not to be compared, for shape aud beauty and far less for wit, with our homuncio Edward, whose bones lie at the foot of the three Viscounts, whom he successively served, but did not survive the last of them, whose imprisonment at Cloghwooter Castle broke our little man's great heart, that he died for grief thereof and despair of his Lordship's release, who was detained about two years in the restraint aforesaid.

As to his Lordship's said Lady, the Countess of Wigton, she continuing in her refractory humours, went to Edinboro to reside there, being 60 years old, and falling sick, his Lordship her husband personally attended her till she died in that emporium; his Lordship buried her where she had desired, giving her all the observation and obsequies due to her peerage: but returning from her interment, his coach overturned, and he received bruises, the pains whereof reverted every spring and harvest till his own fall. And now his Lordship might have bid his last adieu to his native country and Braidstane, because he never again crossed the sea after he returned to Ireland, which he did soon after his compliments were paid to his most honoured Earl, and to the beloved Montgomery Lairds, with his kindred and loving neighbours.

We have his Lordship now in Newtown and in the neighbourhood, composing some differences (as to his lands) which had not been perfected to him, pursuant to articles made the 17th Dec. 1633; other whiles his Lordship attended the Council Board. Thus and in the service of God, his King, and country, as formerly, he spent the residue of his life, which ended May 1636, in a good old age of 76 years.

Now reader, I have given some general notice of the affairs of the noble first Viscount Montgomery. I will only add to them a character of his person and internal parts, or endowments of his soul, and an account of his acts (as brief as I can), not to mutilate them, and the order of his funeral, with some other remarks. As to his birth, it was about Ao. 1560, when Hugh Earl of Eglinton, by his parchment deed, signed and sealed (yet extant), not only confirmed all the lands of Braidstane aforesaid, but also sold all the lands of Montgomery, *minnock als vocat* Blackstown mynnock and Amiln unto Adam Montgomery, of Braidstane, (he was our first Viscount's father), and his heirs and his assigns, &c. by deed aforesaid, dated 25th Nov. 1652. This Earle (some small time before or after this deed) is supposed (very probably) to have been god-father to our Viscount, the said Earl slain, as aforesaid, being the first Hugh of his family, as our Viscount was the first of that name in his own.

Imprimis, then his Lordship was of a middle stature (I had his picture as large as the life), he was of ruddy complexion, and had a manly, sprightlie and chearful countenance; and, I believe, his temperament was sanguine, for his body and nerves were agile and strong, beyond any of his sons or their children, according to all the stations of youth, manhood and old age, no wise troubled by cholicks, gravel or gout, or pains, but what were occasioned by the bruises aforesaid, being of a sound vigorous constitution of health, and habit of body, seldom having sickness, because he was greatly sober and temperate in meat and drink, and chaste also, and used moderate exercises, both coursing badgers and hares with grey hounds on foot, (before he was nobilitated) and afterwards frequently with hounds, hunting (on horses) the deer and the fox in his woodlands yearly at the fittest seasons, and wolves (s) when occasion offered. His Lordship kept a blood

(s) See Appendix.

(in Scotland called a sleuth) hound to trace out thieves and woodkerns (so were torys then termed) which was a great terror to them, and made them to forbear to haunt in his bounds; he also had an huntsman for those games, and a falconer to manage his hawks, netts and spaniels; but he delighted little in soft easy recreations, (fit only, as he said, for Ladies and boys) from his youth taking most pleasure in the active sports which the tennis court, the foyles, the horse, the lance, the dogs, or fowling-piece gave him; for he could endure fatigue, yet was always complaisant in bearing company to ladies, or his guests, at any house game, but would not play for sums of money.

Secondly, as to his mind, his Lordship enjoyed a continual presence of it, ready on all emergent difficulties, which did extricate him out of them. He was not passionate nor precipitate in word or deed, though he had ardour and martial inclinations enough. He retained his Latin, Logicks, and Ethicks, which he had acquired in Glasgow, and very promptly and aptly he applied verses of Roman poets, or sentences out of Tully and other authors, and the adages of his own country to the discourse in hand, without ostentation. He spoke and wrote with gravity, either as to law or gospel. I have by me his letters of learned and full instructions to his son, J. Montgomery, for obtaining the Smiths' pretences, and his skill in law is evidently seen in removing thereby his other troubles. I have also his pious letters (like a learned divine's), condoling and consolating his said second son upon the death of his lady, dated February, Ao. 1634; but in this point, his actions, in their place to be related, will describe him more fully.

His Lordship was very obliging by his condescending humility and affability; his usual compilation was kind (often in his ultry grand climaterick years), calling inferior men, my heart, my heart, and naming them; his worst word in reproaching them was baggage, and his most angry expression was beastly baggage, and commonly followed by the lifting up the staff at the trespasser, or a committal to constable or stocks; this was his latter days intercomuning with his misdoing servants and yeomen tenants; but towards gentlemen or the nobility, his behaviour and discourse was no otherwise than as befitted him. His Lordship was a good justicier, dispensing to men their rights, inflicting the punishments of the law with the tender pity of a parent. Item, over and above all these and other commendable qualifications, as courage, liberality, constancy in friendship, which he placed discerningly, and other his excellent virtues, (whereof I have heard a great deal) his Lordship as a truly pious soul, which on very good grounds I verily believe (as generally others did, and all the old people yet do) is now in the Heavenly Paradise, blessed with the fruition (in part) of his Lord and Master's joy, reserved for all his elected servants till the consummation of their happiness be given them at the great day of general judgment, which in order leads me to the relation at least of a few of his generous, noble and pious acts.

In the third place, then, as to or for his acts beyond seas, or in Scotland, no more remarkable are come to my knowledge than what I have already expressed, and as for those good ones done in Ireland, what is herein before said shall not be repeated, and for the residue of them they are so numerous and so many of them escaped my memory (besides those which were never in it) that therefore and to avoid being tedious, or to seem affectedly and partially bent to over-magnify my ancestor, I have rather chosen to mention only a few of them as followeth, viz :—First of all he sent over to Donaghadee (т) (by the understanding Irish then called Doun da ghee, *i.e.* the mount or burial place of the two Worthies or Heroes) before him some hewn freestone, timber and iron, &c. of which he caused to

(т) See Appendix.

be built a low stone walled house for his reception and lodging, when he came from or went to Scotland. Mariners, tradesmen, and others, had made shelter for themselves before this time, but the Viscount's was the first stone dwelling house in all the parish. Then he repaired the old stump of the Castle in Newtown, as aforesaid. After a while's residence at Newtown, he assiduously plyed his care and pains to repair the chancel (a word derived from the upper part of the church, separated by a screen of nett or lattin work from the body thereof, like the sanctum sanctorum of Solomon's Temple), for the communion table, which place the ancient clergy (in and after Constantine the Great's days) called cancelle of the church. It is now a chappel, and all that part thereof wherein sermons and divine service are used, itself alone being above — feet in length, and 24 in breadth. In process of time the rest of that church was repaired, roofed, and replenished with pews (before his death), mostly by his Lady's care and oversight, himself being much abroad by his troubles aforesaid. His Lordship, in his testament, left a legacy sufficient to build the additional church, contiguous to the body of the old one, and the steeple, which are now in good repair, which was performed by the second Lord Viscount, soon after his father's death, for he then came to dwell in his father's house in Newtown. Next, after this church, the said first Viscount repaired two-thirds of that which belonged to the abbey of Comerer, the Lord Claneboy finishing the other third part thereof, for he had the third part of the lands and tithes in that parish, as also the advowson to present (every third turn) a clerk of priestly order as Vicar, to officiate therein.

The said first Viscount Montgomery also wholly repaired the church of Grayabbey, (in Irish, it is called Monastre Lea—in the patent, called also Abathium de jugo Dei and Hoar abbey) placing his Chaplain, Mr David M'Gill, (who married his Lady's niece), as Curate therein. Then his Lordship built the great church and bell-tower in Donaghadee, near the mount and town, and Portpatrick church also; both of them large edifices, each having four gable ends (for the figures of them are crosses) raised on new grounds and slated, now in good repair, as the rest are, and apparent to the view of all men.

Lastly, his Lordship being tenant to the Bishop of Down (as he was also to the Lord Primate,) he repaired a church on the episcopal lands in Kilmore parish, furnishing all those six houses of God with large Bibles, of the new translation, and printed Ao. 1603, with common Prayer Books, then likewise set forth, both sorts being in folio, and fair Dutch print (except the contents of chapters, and explanatory interjections, marginal notes, &c. and such like). One of those Bibles, now covered, my father and I preserved by transporting them to Scotland, with our best things, when he fled thither Ao. 1649 and I Ao. 1689, it being bestowed to be used in Grayabbey Church, where it is now read, his Lordship being always a firm professed friend to episcopacy and our liturgy, as all his race have continued to be and are at this day. There is one of the said common Prayer Books (much mangled because ill kept and not used, because of the new ones established by law,) which hath his Lordship's coat of arms, as Laird of Braidstane) stamped on the cover with leaf gold, as all the other said service books and Bibles had.

His Lordship likewise furnished the said six churches with large bells, one to each of them, having in like manner the said coat-armorial on them. They are all extant (except those of Comerer(v) and Kilmore, which were taken away in the rebellion, begun Ao. 1641, and since then), which makes me and others take it for granted that, considering his Lordship's piety and liberality, the said books and bells were his free gift to the said churches,

(v) See Appendix.

and an humble offering to God, who had preserved and exalted him—for these words, *Soli Deo Gloriæ,* are in great letters embossed round this bell in Grayabbey, and, I believe, is so on the other three; and I cannot imagine any reason why the bells should differ, or that they and the books were not his Lordship's gift and offering as aforesaid, because I have enquired heretofore at the oldest sensible men who dwelt in those towns, and of some yet alive, who averred for truth my assertion; and, for my part, I have searched all the papers I could come at, for making the whole narrative, and cannot find one iota or tittle to contradict my belief, nor to gainsay the testimony of the old, honest, unbiassed men aforesaid.

His Lordship also built the quay or harbour at Donaghadee, a great and profitable work, both for public and private benefit; and built a great school at Newtown, endowing it, as I am credibly told, with twenty pounds yearly salary, for a Master of Arts, to teach Latin, Greek and Logycks, allowing the scholars a green for recreation at goff, football, and archery, declaring, that if he lived some few years longer, he would convert his priory houses into a College for Philosophy; and further paid small stipends to a master to teach orthography and arithmetic, and to a music-master, who should be also precentor to the church, (which is a curacy) so that both sexes might learn all those three arts; the several masters of all those three schools having, over and beside what I have mentioned, wages from every scholar under their charge; and, indeed, I have heard, in that church, such harmony from the old scholars, who learned musick in that Lord's time, that no better, without a full quire and organs, could be made. For the precentor's method was this—three trebles, three tenors, three counter-tenors, and 3 bass voices, equally divided on each side of them (besides the Gentlewomen scholars which sat scattered in their pews), which sang their several parts as he had appointed them, which overruled any of the heedless vulgar, who learned thereby (at least) to forbear disturbing the congregation with their clamorous tones.— The scholars of the great school also came in order, following the master, and seated themselves in the next form in the loft or gallery, behind the Provost, who had his Burgesses on each hand of them.

But, alas! this beautiful order, appointed and settled by his Lordship, lasted no longer than till the Scottish army came over and put their Chaplains in our Churches; who, having power, regarded not law, equity or right to back or countenance them; they turned out all the legal loyal Clergy, who would not desert Episcopacy and the service book, and take the Covenant, a very bitter pill, indeed, to honest men; but they found few to comply with them therein; and so they had the more pulpits and schools to dispose of to other dominies, for whom they sent letters into Scotland.

All those mighty and (as I may justly term them) pious works were performed by his Lordship before his second marriage. In the patent for his lands, which, by the trouble aforesaid, he could not get passed till 2d Car. Ao. 1626, which was then positively ordered by his Majesty, at the earnest solicitation of James Montgomery, Gentleman Usher in his Privy Chamber aforesaid. His Lordship had grants therein of fairs and weekly markets in Donaghadee, Grayabby and Comerer, towns aforesaid, with a free port to each of them; from whence all goods *(except linen yarn)* might be exported, and the ordinary customs, both inward and outward, were granted to himself and his heirs, which he took at very low rates, the more to encourage importers, and such as would come to plant on his lands; which usage did wonderfully further and advance his towns & plantation with trade, which was begun and to a great degree encreased in the first seven years after it began, which was Ao. 1606, as aforesaid; and thus it continued growing better and better till his Lordship's death, and afterwards, also, even until the Lord Strafford's administration, when patents were renewed, and the grants of ports, customs and officers were retrenched by Parliament, and vested in the crown again. His Lordship also (before he was nobilitated) had his coat armorial, according to the bearing of his ancestors, gilded on his closet books, as the Bible and Prayer Books were.

His Lordship had also granted to him many franchises, immunitys and privileges in his lands and courts, and to his senischall, which, whether they stand on the old bottom, or be fallen, because of taking out the new patent, 13 Car. upon the Commission, for remedy of defective titles, I will not say *pro* or *con*, but leave it to those who shall be concerned, and so surcease mention of his other acts; and shall tell of him things which his Lordship never did nor knew, viz.—the last memories, I mean his funeral, which I here write of him, who was, by the Irish, to the highest degree, beloved whilst alive and lamented when dead.

CHAPTER IX.

LASTLY as to his late Lordship's funeral, it was managed by the said Sir James, joint-executor, with his eldest brother to the defunct's will, as the alteration of his coat armorial had been. I here transcribe from his pen the order of it as concerted between him and Ulster King at Arms, and Albone Leveret, Athlone (whose acquittances for fees I have) being his pursuivant. The solemnity was performed with all the pomp that the rules of heraldry would admit and decency did require. For the preparations thereunto no time was wanting, his late Lordship (as hath been said) dying in May, 1636, and his corpse being embalmed and rolled in wax searcloths was close coffined, (no more now Lord or Montgomery) was locked up in a turrett till a week before its interment, at which time (being in September the said last mentioned year), it was carried privately by night a mile out of town, and in a large tent laid in state, and attended with the formalities of wax candles, friends and servants, till the day of the procession on foot from the said tent to the Church. The persons who made up the procession were all clothed in blacks (called in Scotland dueil weeds from this word dueil, borrowed from the French, signifying mourning) and were seen in the following order, which the reader may please to peruse, if he doe not already know well enough the manner of burying Viscounts, which is, viz.—Imprimis, 2 conductors (with black truncheons) named Thomas Kenedy and John Lockart, both of Comerer—2dly, poor men (the oldest could be had) called salys (i. e. almsmen) in gowns, to the number of 76, the year current of his late Lordship's age, walking two and two, with their black staves—3dly, the servants of Gentlemen, Esquires, Knights, Barons, Viscounts, and Earles hereafter named, viz. by two's as they went.

Hy. Savage, of Arkeen (v)	1
Hu. Kennedy, of Greengraves	1
Rt. Barclay, Dean of Clogher	2
Robt. Adair, of Ballymenagh	1
Archd. Edminston, of Duntreth	2
Sir Jos. Cunningham, Kt	1
Sir Wm. Murray, Kt. and Bart	1
Mr Jo. Alexander	1
Sir Edw. Trever	2
Jo. Shaw, of Greenock, Esq	1
Geo. Montgomery, Esq	2
Sir Anthy. Alexander, Kt	1
The Lord Alexander	2
The Lord Viscount Claneboy	3
Sir Wm. Semple, Kt	2
Charles Alexander	1

(v) See Appendix.

N. Montgomery, Esq. of Langhshaw 1
Pat. Savage, of Portaferry, Esq 5
Sir Jas. Montgomery, Kt 6
Sir Wm. Stewart, Kt. and Bart...................... 5
The Lord Montgomery, the Earle's son.............. 2
The Earle of Eglinton 5
Besides the attendants on their two Lordship's bodies.

4th, Then marched the standard borne by Lt. Robert Montgomery.

5th, After it followed the servants to the 2d Viscount, the chief mourner, viz.

John Boyd.	James Fairbairn,
William Catherwood,	Hugh Montgomery, of Grange, jun.
Mr Samuel Row,	
Henry Purfrey,	Edw. Johnston, of Greengraves,
Hugh Montgomery, of Newtown,	

6th, Next came the servants to the defunct,

Jo. Loudon, his clerk,	Jo. Jerden,
Jo. Montgomery, of Newtown,	Jo. Gillmore of the same.
	Archibald Millen,
Thos. Aitkin,	Jo. Millen of Grayabby,
Matthew Haslepp,	Wm. Burgess.

7th, In the 7th space came two trumpeters fitly equipped, sounding the death march.

8th, Walked the horse of mourning, led by the chief groom, Jo. Kennedy, and one footman.

9th, In the next place went the Divines neither Doctors nor Dignitaries.

Mr James Mirk,	Mr James Montgomery,
Mr Hugh Nevin,	Mr William Forbes.
Mr Js. Blair, Portpatrick	

10th, Then came the Gentlemen and Esquires, who were mourners, viz.

Jo. Cunningham, of Newtown,
James Lenox,
James Coningham, of Gortrie,
Water Hows Crymble, of Donaghadee,
Hugh Montgomery, of Derrybrosk,
Richard Savage,
William Melville.
Tho. Kenedy, of Pingwherry,
James Edminston,
Jo. Gordon, of Pingwherry, sen.
Mr Jo. Echlin, of Ardquin,
Mr William Cunningham, of the Rash,
Malcom Dormont,
Thomas Nevin, of Monkroddin, jun.
James Melvill, Esq.
John Crawford,
Andrew Cunningham, of Drumfad,
Pat. Muir, of Aughneil,
Hu. Kenedy, Drumawhay
William Montgomery, of Ballyheft,
Hugh Echlin,
Lieut. Thomas Mellvill,
Mr William Adair,
Jo. Gordon, of Aghlain, jun.
William Burley, Gent.
Thomas Boyd, of Whitehouse,
Hugh Hamill, of Roughwood,
Henry Savage, of Arkeen Esq.
Thomas Nevin, of do. sen.
William Montgomery, of Briggend,
Mr Marcus Trevor,
Mr William Stewart,
Robert Adair, of Ballymenagh,
Arch. Edminston, of Duntreth, Esq.
Mr John Trevor,
Alex. Lecky, of Lecky,
Hugh Kenedy, of Girvan Mains,

11th, In this space went together the late Lord's Phisitians, viz. Hugh M'Mullin, practitioner, and Patrick Maxwell, Dr. in physick, and next after them came,

12th, Alexander Colvill, Dr. in Divinity, Robert Barclay, Dean of Clogher.

13th, Then there walked Knights and Noblemen's sons, mourners, viz.

Sir Jas. Conningham, Kt.
Sir William Semple, Kt.
the Lord Semple's son,
Mr Charles Alexander,
Sir James Erskin, Kt. and Privy Counsellor,
Sir Wm. Murray, Kt. and Bart.
Mr John Alexander,
Sir Ed. Trevor, Kt. and Privy Counsellor.

14th, Went Mr. Robert Montgomery, Clerk, the Curate in Newtown, alone.

15th, Dr. Henry Leslie, Lord Bishop of Down and Connor, who preached the funeral sermon.

16th, Then followed the great banner, advanced by William Montgomery, of Ballyskeogh.

17th, Neile Montgomery, of Langshaw, Esq. bore the cushion with a Viscount's coronet on it, and a circolet about it.

18th, Athlone, Pursuviant at Arms, appeared marching by himself, and presenting to view the spurs, gauntlet, helm, and crest.

19th, Then the defunct's Gentleman Usher, named Jo. Hamil, walked bare-headed next before the King at Arms.

20th, Ulster King at Arms carried the sword, target or shield armorial.

21st, Then was drawn (by six led horses, cloathed in black) the hearse, environed with a circolet mounted on the carriage of a coach, supported with posts or pillars, under which was laid the coffin, inclosing the remains of that late worthy Viscount, covered with a velvet pall, and on it pinned taffeta escutchions of his Lordship's own, and his matches coat's armorial, and elegys of the best sort also affixed thereto. The hearse on each side being accompanied by six men, with single banner rolls without; and even in rank with them went six footmen belonging to his late Lordship and his three sons, each having a black battoun in his right hand.

22d, Next immediately after the hearse followed now the Right Hon. Hugh, 2d Lord Viscount Montgomery, of the great Ardes, the chiefest mourner; after him, walked Sir Jas. Montgomery, George Montgomery and Pat. Savage aforesaid, as next chiefest mourners, (I dare say it), both in hearts and habits.

23d, Then walked the Viscount Claneboy and the Earl of Eglinton together; the Lord Alexander and the Lord Montgomery together; John M'Dowal, of Garthland and the Baron of Howth's son; — St. Lawrence, Esq. and Sir William Stewart. Knight Bart. and Privy Counsellor, in one rank. All these, as chief mourners, who were attended by some of their own servants, appointed to wait on them and be near their persons; six men, also covered with long black cloaks, marching by two and two, in the servants' rear, a great mixed multitude following and going about the herse at decent distance; only all the women in black, and those who had taffeta scarfs and hoods of that colour, went next the six men in cloaks. The great bell then in the west end of the Church tolling all the while that the procession was coming from the tent.

24th, And now all being orderly entered and seated, and the coffin placed before the pulpit, and the service ended, the Lord Bishop preached a learned, pious and elegant sermon (which I have seen in print long ago, from whence I might have borrowed some memories if I had it now). This done, and the corpse moved to the upper end of the chancel, was (after the office for the dead performed) there inhumed. The Church pulpit and chancel being circoled with black baze, and stuck with scutchions and pencils of the defunct and his matches, at due distances; the whole edifice thoroughly illuminated by wax candles and torches. The full obsequys were thus ended.

Divers elegant elegys and epitaphs were made by Newtown school (as was their grateful duty) and others on his Lordship's death, as encomiums of his life (whose love to the learned was eminent) but these being too long and bulky to have room here, I will only in a few lines write my remarks on worldly grandeur and prophesy as a poet of the defunct.—Take them ; thus they are :

As shaddows of dark clouds doe fleet away
On sudden sunshines of an April day,
So all the glorys of our Birth, Acts, State,
Swiftly (like powder fir'd) evaporate.
Not th' less his Justice, Piety and Name,
Shall be preserv'd (in memory) by Fame :
For written Monuments more lasting are
Than those of Stone, or Metall, rear'd by farr.
And Sun, Moon, Starrs (tho each a centinell)
Doe by their beams, dangers and safetys tell :
Yet virtue (to give life) wants parallel.

In confirmation hereof *vivit post funera virtus,* says Ovid,

And only the actions of the just,
Smell sweet and blossom in the dust.

This funerall was extraordinary great, and costly ; all the noblemen and noblemens sons, and the gentry which came from Scotland, and the knights, gentry, and heralds, with their retinue, and the rest which came from Farmanagh, Tirowen, Donnegall, Armagh, and Antrim (which was no smal number) with the attendants of all these mourners, and their horses, besides the phisitians, divines, and bishop ; and their servants, etc. were all entertained to the full, in meat, drink, lodging and other accommodations. The better sort of them in the Viscounts house, and the residue in the town, where wine (because there was no excise or new impost) was plenty at his Lordships expence; the atcheivments (alone) costing above 65*l.* at the lowest rate that they could be bought by Sir James Montgomery, who was one of the executors to the late Lord his fathers last will and testament.

His late Lordship was generally well reported of, and even by those with whom he contended at law to gain possession of his own right, and they could not do otherwise (except clandestinely) because his Lordship took all the civil and fair wayes imaginable to obtain his lawful purposes. And he was universally revered, loved and obeyed by the Irish, and much esteemed of by Con O'Neil and his followers, but especially of his tenents of that nation, who loudly lamented for their loss of him, now he was dead: because he had been in general carefull to protect them all (within his reach) from injurys, and familiarly conversing with them his own tenents, when he used his summer recreations of hunting and fishing in his woodlands, rivers and loughs, by which means his British planters seldom lost any goods (by stealth or robbery) that were not retrieved.

But for all the said costly pomp and

what was expended at the 2d and 3d Lords burialls, there is not as yett, An. 1698, any monument (but this) erected to the memory of any of them. Such hath been (as it is easy to be demonstrated) the troublesomness of the times elapsed since the said funeral.

I shall only say, it hath been a frequent fate of great and good personages, to have no tombs; and the luck of sordid capricious rich men, to have them, but then this latter sort do often build them, (as Abraham bought a field and a cave for a burrial place for him and his, and Jacob erected a pillar over Rachel) in their own life time, otherwise their heires, notwithstanding all the lands or money is left to them, are seldom so respectful or grateful as to doe it, tho it were prudence to gett a good name and repute thereby both alive and dead.

But lett us see the poets ill advised angry distich, and let who will discant on it, viz.

Marmoreo tumulo Licinus jacet, at Cato parvo ;
Pompeius nullo : Quis putet esse Deos.

Which I English thus :

Glutton Licinus, in gilt marble sleeps,
In a smal urn Utica Cato keeps:
Pompey the Great no lodging hath ; yet wee
Miscall them Gods, were lesser men than Hee.

I will now make a few generall remarks of the Mongomerys, and first of their ages ; the first Viscount's forefathers lived long by reason of temperance, abstaining from excess, as wine, women, and variety of food, and useing corporeall exercises, abandoning idleness and a lazy life and soft pleasures, which hath corrupted the healths of the last century.

His Lordship was past the middle of his 76th year, his son George lived to 68; of the others shortness of life you shall hear in the sequel of this narrative : But to proceed on this head, imprimis, I know An. 1646 (when at Newtoun school) many artificers, and yeomen (whom his Lordship conduced to plant) that lived to great ages. Among which one Adam Montgomery (who told me many things of Braidstane, when I was young, which I studied not to remember) he lived to about 105 years as I am told, and as himself said he was a little before his death. Also John Peacock of Tullycavan, my fee farmer, lived above 100 years a healthy man, and had travelled much with the first Viscount.— There was John Montgomery of Ballyrolly, who lived so long in sound health (but not memory) that he would play at hide and seek, and such like childish games, with his wife and his great grand children. Also the Goodwife of Busby, after the 85th year of her age, walked to a communion in Comerer : and many more instances of longevity might be given, but I forbear them.

As to the sirname of Montgomery, the Scotish rithmers designe them by calling them Poet Montgomerys,(w) many of them haveing been excellent in that art. This was their character in time of peace, which I read to be ascribed to some Roman Emperors, and to some Christian Kings, as a commendable quality or indowment, and a mark of the elevation of their spirits to high notions, fitting them for oratory, and lofty fluent speech, takeing them off from grovelling on vulgar appetites as worldlings doe; by this sirname in time of commotions and warrs were stiled the martiall Montgomerys, as their due epithet; and that they deserve it, I can give many instances, but too much of one thing is good for nothing.

To these two characters his late Lordship and his brother Patrick gave proof (as their progenitors did) to the first of them in France and Holland, and his Lordship, and his brother George (falling into peaceable times) shewed themselves suitable thereunto. I must here mention and discover a little of his Lordships temper (which I guess was fitt both for peace and warr) and it is from his devise which he assumed when he went to travell; it was this, viz. a lute with two hands out of clouds, the one stopping, the other moving the strings, and this motto (the French and

(w) See Appendix.

Scotch call it aditon) viz. " Such Touch, Such Sound," but this is not certain.

To the like purpose Sir Ja. Montgomery had for his devise (as may be seen within the porch of Rosemount house, and on his monument in Grayabby church aforesaid,) viz. a sword and a lance (still part of our familys arms) saltirewise, surmounted on an open book, on the leaves whereof is written the words *Arte, Marte,* surrounded by a laurel and a bay branch, bearing fruit, interwoven within each other: and under all for a motto appears those words, viz. *In utrumque Paratus.*— Thus it may be said of him, *Proles sequitur suum patrem,* in these brave qualitys and accomplishments.

Another generall observation (and so I shall omitt the rest) is, that it cannot be said (with any seeming truth) either that his late Lordships progenitors or himself, or his descendants, ever imployd any coin to buy imployments, or preferrment, but by their services, and at expence or hazard of their blood and lives they obtained the like favors, which they had of their respective princes: so they may say as they have found, *tandem bona causa triumphat.* Furthermore they were always loyal to the crowne and never tainted or stained in their blood, and for maintenance of this honour, I here lay aside my pen and throw down my gantlet to answer all opposers of this my averment.

And now I proceed to his late Lordships heire and successor : and though my recitall is short of his merits, yet I shall be much briefer in what I shall write of his Lordships descendants, not repeating but touching (as shall be requisite) the mentions I have interwoven before : because I have seen but few records of their Lordships actions, except what my own knowledge can afford, or is come by the credible reporte, which must needs be litle, for I was in my grandfather Stewarts house, till I was sent for to the Ards, a heedless boy of ten years and six months age an. 1644; kept at school till harvest 1649; that Oliver Cromwell's army chaced me into Scotland, and then out of it into Holland, when I came an. 1652 into England, and so returned into Ireland an. 1653. I was kept soliciting for my birth right, till King Charles the 2d's happy restoration May 1660, and for eight years after it, imployd in my proper affaires ; mostly abroad not at all resolving (but rather discouraged for want of papers) till anno 1697, that I should make these collections, concerning the Montgomerys in general, or of the family of Ardes, and others of that sirname in Ireland, or to write of them particularly.

L

—But the gout (I thank God for it, and for my health, and ability which had furnished me with some preparations) hath since that year given me occasion and leizure to scribble these and divers other sheets.

CHAPTER X.

SOME MEMOIRES OF SIR JAMES MONTGOMERY, KNT.

HAVING already given a summary account of the two first Viscts. (x) and the next two Earles (Montgomerys) I cannot (for I ought not) neglect to remember ye other posterity of ye Laird of Braidstane, the founder of this family, of and in the great Ardes.

In doing whereof, memoires now (at least) fall due (if not sooner) unto ye second sonn of ye first Viscount, viz. to ye Hon. Sir James Montgomery, Knt. which title was no advancement of his preheminence in heraldry, but a particular mark of the King's favour to him his meniall servant (as his being Gentleman Usher of ye Privy Chamber in ordinary, was also). And as to his being Collector, it might signify much dureing his commission (especially in the field) to give him a higher place, than as he was a Lord's second sonn.

(x) See Appendix.

But let that case bee as it will, it is left to be determined in ye court of honour.

He was (as you see) personally dignified, by these designations to be eminent in peace and warr.

Wherefore, with Virgil and Lucan, *Arma virumque cano, et bella plusquam civilia :* because his life was divided (partly per palo) between those states of legall and military governments, wherein he was exercised almost in a continual warrfare ever since he could manage the pen, or wield the sword ; and had also his death in hostility upon another element than that wherein he was born and bred, as will appear in the pursuits of this history, and his actions were so much concerned for three first Viscounts, his father, brother, and nephew, that they are necessarily interwoven herein before, so that there is little left to say of him hereafter, but some past passages must be transiently touched to make the relation now regular of one piece.

This Sir James Montgomery's birth was at Braidstane, anno 1600 : the said Hugh, the 6th Laird, and Dame Elizabeth Shaw aforesaid, were his parents : Sir James Montgomery's sister Jean being married (as hath been already said) unto Patrick Savage, of Portaferry, Esq. anno 1623. The said Patrick's estate was much in debt, and not one stone walled house in that town, till that match (as was often credibly told me) only some fishermen's cabins and an old Irish castle out of repair near it, nor any mills, and very little grain to employ one (that country being much wasted) till our Viscount's plantation, which was not suffered to spread into that little Ardes till their own greater was furnished with inhabitants : and no trade by sea (nor encouragement for it) before the said year 1623.

The most effectual way he took was to get the wastes filled with Brittish planters in the lands, and builders of stone houses in the town and mills on the loughs, which soon brought traffick and merchandize wares to Portaferry, and afterwards so perfected the prosperity of that town and estate, by passing two several patents to remedy Mr. Savage's defective titles, the first of them dated ——, the other is tested by ——

The other thing memorable of Sir James Montgomery (before the grand Irish rebellion) is his concerting with our two Viscounts, how only such as they thought best, should be elected Knights of the Shire, to serve in the Parliament anno 1640.

Their Lordships, both in affection and prudence, pitched on their brother, the said Sir James and John Hamilton, Esq.

Those gentlemen were (as is required by the writt) Idonii, fit persons, and fully qualified to sit in Parliament, each of them had been for 23 years conversant and employed in business of the county (of which they had exact tallys and keys) and of the respective familys therein, and those two Lords plantations did now surmount all wastes, so that these gentlemen's good conduct could not fail to have the farr major number of votes in the election, although the *Trevors, Hills, M'Gennisses, O'Neills, Bagnall's,* * and other interests were combined against them: diverss sham freeholders being made to encrease their number of choosers, which the dexterity and diligence of those gentlemen discovered before ye face of the county, to the utter shame of the servants and agents who had practised the cheat, to sett up other pretenders who stood to be Knights for the Shire.

It was contended much in the fields, and there you might have seen the county divided into four parties, each having him mounted on men's shoulders whom they would have their representative, and neither of them would yield ye plurality to ye other; and the sheriff would not determine ye con-

* Ancestor of the Nedham's, of Newry, and of the Uxbridge family.—Editor.

troversy on view, but like a skilfull gardner, brought all the swarms into one, and so the poll (carefully attended, & ye truth of each man's freehold searched into) ended the difficulty by the reckoning made of them : which gave it by a great many votes to Montgomery and Hamilton, many of the Lord Cromwell's tenents appearing to their sides, the rest of them being newters, or absent. (y)

I was told (as I remember) by persons acting at that election, that Sir James Montgomery had many more voices for him than Mr. Hamilton, for not a few joyned him, out of the other partys, which were all generally for him, to be as one chosen : so that his business lay most to strengthen the Hamiltons, who brought a third part more voters of their own people than Sir James could conduce of his brother Montgomerys; but all the Savages, with their interest, the Fitzsymonds, the Echlins; also Mr. Wards, and most of Kildare's and Cromwell's tenents, were for him and his colleague partys.

Our two Viscounts (who though present) behaved as spectators only. This election was evident proof, what their Lordships could atchieve by their own Scottish interest ; and so their regard was the greater with the Governors and Parliament.

(y) See Appendix.

Now omitting (as much as I can) rehersall, I come to the 23d of October, 1641.

Sir James, as you heard, the summer of this year, had defeated *Daniel O'Neill's* mischief threatening designe, and was now a widower at home, assisting in his brother George Montgomery's and Patrick Savage their affairs, and minding his own, when the said rebellion broke forth; and having opportunity of Mr Galbraith, he wrote to the King, then in Edinburgh, and by the same hand received the (yet extant) Commission for his regiment and troops, (which he raised by his own money and credit). He armed and otherwise fitted them for service, and went into the barrony of Lacahill about the beginning of December, 1641, and subsisted his men by the grain which the enemy had deserted on his first appearance (which was wonderfull soon); and by help of the grain of substantial Brittish inhabitants living next the Ardes, and by preys of cattle taken from the Irish beyond Dundrum. Thus he protected Lacahill for diverse months against all the great body of the Irish dwelling on *Mr Bagnal's* and the *M'Genisses* estates, and those in Kinalerty and Iveagh Barronys,* who were assisted by their neighbours in the

* Hy. Veach, or Iveagh, is now the two baronies of Upper and Lower Iveagh, the country of The Magennis, or MacEnos.

Fews and other places of the county of Ardmagh, Sir James being desired to return thither, as he did on the 20th of April, 1642.

This Dundrum is an old castle, five miles from Downpatrick, and belongs to the Blondells, a family of knightly degree†. Sir James had placed a strong garrison there, and from thence had sent divers parties, which drove preys from the Irish, beyond this place, which galled them to the heart, and they watched all opportunitys for revenge, (which he knew well enough they would do); but was not thereby deterred from laying seige to Newcastle, where the Irish had a garrison, it being a pass to secure the sea coasts towards Carlingford, which was fully in their possession; also it was an inlet for all the Irish in that tract to come into Lacahill, and to settle themselves in the castles of *the Russels,* and of others, whom Sir James had expelled out of that barrony.

As Sir James lay before Newcastle aforesaid, with a brass field piece and some falconets of his own, the like whereof the enemy had not, he so warmly plyed it, that the besieged conditioned to give it up if not re-

† It had been built by John de Courcey, for Knights Templars, till their overthrow in 1313; was then granted to the Prior of Down, till the dissolution of Abbies; when it was granted to Lord Cromwell, Viscount Lecale, and by him disposed of to the Blundells.—Editor.

lieved by their friends in three days, for which time a cessation of arms was agreed on, but no permission granted to revictual that place. Then Sir James, leaving a sufficient blockade, withdrew thence (not two miles) to his head-quarters at Dundrum Castle, which stands on a high hill, and hath plain prospect of Newcastle and the country round about it.

On the third day, his scouts on all hands brought him certain word of the enemy's approach from all quarters, in great numbers. He rode out with his troope to stop passes, and to view their several partys with his perspective glass, and finding that any one of them was his over-match ; he, therefore, raised the seige, and brought the men to join the rest at Dundrum, himself and the horse and some firelocks (whom he placed in the ditches), staying on the roads to retard the enemy's march ; and so they disputed the highway, killing many of the Irish, beating them back very often, till Sir James (his ammunition being near spent, his foot firemen weary, and his troop almost jaded,) seeing another great party of the enemy marching towards the Castle, and like to intercept his late besiegers and himself, he, therefore, in time sent to Dundrum his commands for fresh men and ammunition ; and with them he staid and made good his retreat to the bridge, called Blackstaff, at the head of the Strand, with all his small party (being not half of his regiment) deserting the garrison, as untenable against such a force. He halted at the said bridge and reinforced his men, which lay at the pass next Newcastle. The tide coming in, made the Irish draw up on Dundrum shore.

Sir James (on his first full discovery of the powers of the Irish) had sent for the rest of his regiment, and the militia countrymen, who, with baggages, boyes, horses and provisions, repaired to him with all expedition; whilst he was refreshing with meat, and encouraging his wearied men by his words, as he had done that day by his conduct, and the example of his actions. He was now well posted at the bridge, on the entry of the barrony, where it is a sort of peninsula.

The timely and martial retreat which Sir James had made, gave them all great confidence in him, and his approved courage animated them greatly; which was confirmed when they saw their comrades and countrymen come to them. Sir James told them he must beat those rebels forthwith, to regain what they had left and could not keep for want of the reinforcement. They joyfully assented; and so Sir James went and ordered them in a battalion, to march in that order straight against the enemy as soon as the tide would permit.

Here I must not omit to mention the keenness and spight with which his men had fought, (I may say without fear or witt,) especially the troopers, for they were men that escaped on horse-back with sword in hand, and had seen (as most of the foot also had escaped and beheld) their houses burned; their wives and children murdered. So they were like robbed bears and tygers, and could not be sattisfied with all the revenges they took, for they spared not the enemy nor themselves. It was a Commander's labour to restraine their chargeing till the due time; and then their enraged and implacable fury was unresistable, for they whetted one another's malice when they went to fight, saying, " let us take amends for the murders and mischiefs those cowardly dogs and their friends have done to us and ours."

The Irish army, of above 3000, were drawn up (as aforesaid) on the shoar and the fields above it; and the tide was going fast out, and they seeing all Sir James's foot, being about eight hundred, (yet with ten colours,) and his small brass guns before them, flanked with the troops and militia men (about 300) in the reare, with baggage men and boys on horse behind them. All those (except the reserves) drawn up at three men deep, and making a long front, the enemy guessed aright that it was Sir James's design to march over the Strand, and to charge them in that order. So they took the wisest and safest course to march off, before the sea was third part ebbed ; and when they were at the back of the next hills, they dispersed in companies to their several passes and quarters.

Sir James had no designe but to fight them on fair ground ; where his troop and brass pieces gave him the advantage against their numbers, and where he was in no danger of ambusses. However, when he saw the Irish intended to draw off their main body, he detached his troop, with a firelok behind each of them, and two soldiers (with their muskets) on every baggage horse, and came up with the rest, and his artillery (as fast as they could march) to sustain his troop and dragoons, who were very eager to regain the honor they thought they lost by their retreat. And being full of revenge, they attacqued the Irish rear, most partys killing many, and giving no quarter, unless to a prime officer, (of such were their best gentlemen,) by whom a ransom, or exchange of friends (detained prisoners by the Irish) was expected.

The troops and dragoons pursued them

two miles, where there was no danger of ambushcade ; and night drawing on, Sir James retired to his men (by this time drawn up,) and they encamped under Dundrum, which was deserted ; Sir James sending, in his view, a party of dragoons, with his brass gunns, to Newcastle, which the Irish had also evacuated of men and arms. He put (and furnished with victuals) a good garrison therein, to be a frontier to the pass (near it) aforesaid, and to be an inlett to scoure in the woods of Ballaghenery and the lands about Tullaghmore.

He strengthened, also, Dundrum Castle with provisions, though the soldiers had no houses, but cabbins, within the old walls to garrison in, who were to clear the fields about Cloghmaghrecatt (Mr Annesly's house within a mile of it), and other lands about itself.

Sir James (upon the Irish drawing off and disappearing) had sent his militia to their posts ; but he kept the baggage horses and boyes in his camp, for the Coyle bridge was broken down, and only a ferry used on that side ; so that Anacloy river guarded that quarter of the barony, and the sea secured the rest. There was no inlett to it, but by the Strand, or the said bridge of Blackstaff, which had a fort and a garrison that had communication with Dundrum Castle, and but the other pass, near Newcastle, which was secured as aforesaid, and the troop quartered near it.

Yet for all Sir James his circumspection, the Irish (by boggs above the fort and bridge aforesaid, between it and the said river,) came by night into Lecaile, and surprised a small garrison, which lay too secure, being surrounded by a lough, all but one togher before the drawbridge. Our men had lain in hutts among the burned walls of the dwelling-house (called Ballydugan), belonging to Mr West, a gentleman of estate thereabouts; but Sir James, gathering some forces and reinforcing the frontiers aforesaid, skirmished with the enemy, who had come out to prey on the country, whom he routed and pursued to the said togher, investing the house with a close siege, and drawing his gunns against it, preparing boats from Portaferry, Strangford, Killeleagh and elsewhere, which might come to him in two or three tides after orders given; and, in the meantime, bestowed some great, and many small shott on the enemy. Some of them were killed with stones that fell from the battered walls, under which they skulked; others were wounded or killed (as they peeped out) by our fowlers, and by our musketeers, who were by experience become good marksmen.

The besieged Irish had some good officers, but they durst not sally, for fear of our men, and of the falconettes planted before the togher. Their soldiers were picked out as the most resolute, and had the provision layd in for our garrison, and good store they brought on their own and the partys backs which conveyed them; and daily expected more thereof, with arms and ammunition. So they were provided, hoping Sir James's departure out of Lecaile, by reason of the descent which they understood that *Con Oge O'Neile* was to make into the Ardes, and were well resolved to abide the uttermost.— But, being told of a storm by water, as well as at the togher (which they knew very feazable), and fully designed by the incensed Sir James, and wanting (as I said before) British hearts in them, and despairing of relief, by the siege being raised, they parlyed; yet no condition was granted, but a convoy for the safety of their lives, and that they should not be stript of their cloths. On which conditions they surrendered.

CHAPTER XI.

I now come to some other passages relating to him, in the beginning of the said rebellion. And first, I find Sir James Montgomery addressed to, by a letter of the Gentlemen of the Ardes and Claneboys, for his protection, dated ultimo January, 1641.* This was whilst he was defending Lecaile against Irish incursions.

I find, by certificate of above 30 Gentlemen of the Ardes, dated the 15th March, 1641,† that Sir James did levy a regiment of foot and troop of horse; and therewith (at his own charges) did maintain Downpatrick against the M'Genneses and M'Cartans, repelling them when they entered Lecaile, and banishing the inbred Romanists of that barrony thereout, taking their castles and putting garrisons therein, till, by advertisement, that *Con Oge O'Neile*, with great forces from Ardmagh and Tyrone, was coming to join the Magonneses; and he was, thereupon, recalled by his brother, the *Lord Montgomery*, to save the sea-ports, by which relief from Scotland and England must come, as expected; and himself to quarter in that barrony.

I have two letters of advice, dated in Feb.

* This must have been 1641-2.
† See preceding note on this year.

ruary, 1641, directed to Sir James, from the Lord his brother, of the danger which the Ardes, with Hollywood parish, and all the sea coasts stood in, from the said Con's descent; which made him march his regiment and troope through the enemy's country of Dufferin and Castlereagh; and to quarter in and about the said parish, to be at hand to join with his said brother, for preserving it, with Newtown, Bangor and Comerer towns and parishes, and chiefly to stopp Con's coming into the Ardes, and sea coasts. For which purpose they made forts (by the vulgar called trenches) at Dundonald, and other passes.

I have a letter from the state of Scotland, to Sir James, desiring him to obey their Major-General, *Robert Munro*, as being the will and pleasure of the Committee for both kingdoms. This was soon after the landing of the Scotts army, or after Sir James's return from Westminster. The letter is dateless.

I have a letter from both Houses of Parliament, under a cover to Sir James, dated Sept. 1643, (soon after his said return), signed by the two Speakers, advising and hopeing that he would oppose the cessation of arms with the Irish, and promising supplys, &c.

I have a copy of letter from the officers of Sir James's regiment, dated the 5th November, 1643, (the powder plott day,) unto Sir Mungo Campbell, offering to incorporate themselves and soldiers into the Scotch army, and his answer the 18th of December following, giving general assurances of kind terms, (such as the officers proposed,) but no certainty, only desiring them (as he was sent from Scotland to solicit other regiments), to opposethe cessation aforeaid.

This mutinous combination was carried on without asking Sir James's advice or privity; but the officer's letter was (on suspicion) intercepted, copied, sealed and delivered to the messenger, who perceived nothing of the discovery, as he knew as little of the contents thereof.

Such was the factious humours of those men, and the country gentlemen blown up by their teachers, who had so hooked them to their line, that they could pull the people on shore with a single hair.

In all the fermentation raised by the *Covenant-teachers* (which were imposed on parishes, and the legal incumbents ejected, by the Scottish army's violence), against the peaceable Irish Papists in the Lower Ardes, yet Sir James procured the Lord Conway's order, dated December, 1642, that only bonds should be taken of Henry Savage, of Ardkeen, Esq. for delivery of his arms in his house, at any time when called for; and the rest of the Papists to be disarmed.

Which privilege Sir James got confirmed and enlarged on another occasion, and there was need and reason for granting that safeguard, because of the unruly Scottish mobb, and common soldiers, who would make the pretence of searching for arms and ammunition an opportunity to quarrel and plunder.

This Gentleman was loyal and moderate in his Romish religion, and read the Holy Scriptures; and, on his death-bed, (whereon he lay long) assured me, that he trusted for his salvation only to the merits and mediation of Jesus Christ. He kept no images in his house, and if he had any picture (or such like) he said he would meditate on it, but not worship it. He used to say, that invocation of Saints was needless, although it were supposed they did hear us, or know our wants; because he was sure his Saviour was God all-sufficient, and our intercessor as a man and priest. He was, by marriage, next cousin to Sir James, and by that way related to some of the officers in his regiment, to whom he was kind, and he was hospitable to the rest; yet, all this did not release the fear he had from the vulgar people and inferior officers.

By the way I must remember, that Sir

Charles Coote brought from the Parliament a Commission to be President of Connaught; and he came with his Lady and her mother, the Lady Hannah, and his eldest son, with one or two younger children, to Rosemount. He left him in the house, but himself (after a day's rest) with Sir Jas. (to whom he was recommended by the Committee of Parliament), as no doubt to many other Colonels, went to the *Lord of Ardes*,* at Newtown.— Sir Charles his great want was men, arms, ammunition, provisions and money. How he was supplied of the last of those I cannot tell; but, as for the other four necessarys, Sir James proposed the way to his Lordship, and they joined to perswade the *Lord Clannboy*,† and he was willing to assist; and then he went with Sir Charles to Belfast and Lisnagarvey. Sir James dispatched also expresses to Sir William Stewart aad Sir William Cole (his fathers-in-law), and to Sir Robert Stewart and Colonel Audley Mervin, with account of what was agreed upon by the two Viscounts, and at Belfast, and by the Commanders of the regiments thereabouts. And the contrivance was thus, viz:—

That every of their regiments should allow fifty men to go with a month's provision of

* Hugh Montgomery, Vicount of Ardes.
† James Hamilton, Viscount Claneboye.

meale (which came according to allowance in the little Ardes) to four pecks and an half for each private man—the peck containing 20 Winchester quarts; and that the officers, serjeants, corporals and drummers should have the like quantity of meale, and the rest of the subsistence raised for them in money, *prout* the establishment, consented to by the country from the beginning of the rebellion, the meal price (which was then half the crown per peck) to be deducted out of the money pay.

By this means, Sir Charles Coote would be enabled to maintain his province, with the help of the Lagan forces (when called for) and our regiments needed not march up thither every summer, where they were always put to great hazard and loss of men, to retake the castles we had ruined the last expedition; into which the enemy crept when we returned and left them, they also building new forts to be wonn from them the next campaigne, which trouble would be now prevented, and Sir Charles hereby enabled to fortify and place strong garrisons in Sligo and the seaport towns, to which provisions, arms and ammunitions would be brought by sea, without danger of the Irish.

Sir James could easily demonstrate those particulars, who run divers bodily risks at the taking of Sligo, and in two several smart fights against the enemy (who were double his numbers), and they now by usage being grown expert in stratagems and feats of war; and were on their own known dunghills with friends at hand.

The advantage, however, was on our side; our men had bold Brittish souls in them, that the Irish wanted, and our officers were better than theirs.

But, after all, what gained we? Nothing but honor and a few cows, which the wearied soldiers (yet dancing with courage and mirth) drove home to their quarters, to be winter kitchen (as they called it) to their bannocks; they got also some garrons, which they sold.

The second act of Sir James his intended kindness, was to get those men fixed to Sir Charles as his proper regiment.

Sir James's third act of friendship was in buying meal, &c. to send to Sir Charles Coote, which he did plentifully, Mr. Jo. Davis, of Carrickfergus, giving bond to Sir James, dated 18th March, 1646 (which I have yet uncancelled) for £778 sterling, for the same, as papers between them doth shew. Other respects done to Sir Charles by Sir James I think not needfull for my narrative of him.

There are (by me) letters from divers persons to Sir James Montgomery, shewing in what high esteem he was had, and how able and ready to serve his country; but I cannot wade in an ocean, and therefore will content myself to have writt the foregoing instances, and will draw this relation of him to a conclusion, by an account of his suffering in Scotland for his loyalty here, and of his exile to Holland, etc. and his death, as followeth.

CHAPTER XII.

You have heard how part of Oliver Cromwell's army coming into this county of Down made Sir James Montgomery flee into Scotland, his native country. He was no sooner known to be there but was cited to compeir (that is their word for appear) before the committee of estates; who accused him to have been most active in contriving and carrying on the late design and engagement with the Viscount of Ardes and Sir George Monro, against the well affected Brittish in the province of Ulster, to the betraying of the cause of God and the covenant in those parts, and to the irreparable loss and prejudice of the well affected people therein. This was a heavy charge, and no lighter burden than was expected. Yet one might have thought they should have pittyed and carressed Sir James for helping to out Colonel Monk, who had surprised their Major General and sent him prisoner to London, and broke their whole army in Ireland. But that disgrace and loss was not resented. They appeared only disgusted that their Kirk party was hindred to sway all in Ulster, without owning the King's Commission.

Sir James pleaded that as a subject of Ireland (where his estate was) he had acted according to law, and by Commission from King Charles ye first and second and against the Irish and *Sectarians*, (as the estates then called the Rumps and Cromwell's party) their and our common enemy; which he thought no crime, and themselves were articling to reward the King as he and the Viscount's party had been endeavouring to hold up his Majesty's right in Ireland.

That he could not hinder, nor did he promote or advise, Sir George Monro's expedition, which their Major General himself could not obstruct. That he had not contributed any to the Duke Hamilton's engagement, (for relief of their late imprisoned and murdered King) though their own Parliament had authorized the said Duke, how well or ill became not him to determine.

That he was fled for his life from those, who were enemys to their and his King, and to get bread and shelter among them till those calamitous times were over which he hoped would soon come to pass, by the treaty on foot and by his Majesty coming for protection to them: as himself now did, and offered to give security for his good carriage during his residence.

But his conjunction with the Lord of Ardes, and slighting the Ministers, and using authority over the godly and well affected to the pretended cause afforesaid and to the Covenanters, was proved against Sir James, who was advised (by his relations) not to stir up nests of wasps, nor depend too much upon his justification, nor to decline their jurisdiction, lest he should be imprisoned.

Sir James had good friends, viz. the Earl of Eglinton, the Laird of Greenock, the Laird of Langshaw (who was his cautioner, as they call a man who is security for his friend in a bond) and divers others, besides his brother-in-law, Sir Alexander Stewart, Bart. who interceeded for him.

The committee of estates reply to Sir James his defence, that he was a native of the kingdom, and that they might cognosce upon his actions, which trenche on their welfare, though he lived not in it; and told him he had been an enemy to God, and to his covenant and cause, and to the adherers thereunto.— Yet in hopes of his amendment and upon the request of his friends, they would only order him to remove out of the kingdom, betwixt and the first of January, without longer delay; and that he should not return without licence and permission, asked and gotten from the Parliament or committee of estates, or secret council for the samin. And that he shall not doe, speak, nor act any thing to ye prejudice of the said cause or covenant, or well affected Covenanters either in Scotland or Ireland, under pain of 20,000l. Scotts money to be paid to the commissary general of Scotland for the use of the public, those presents to be registrat in the buiks of Parliament, etc.— There was no disputeing fitt; so he submitted to their will.

Sir James landed in Scotland in and about the latter end of October 1649, gave bond ye 8th of December, and left the kingdom before next month, which begins their new year 1650.

He being banished (as aforesaid) went to Holland and left more than 100 pieces of gold (with Mr Alexander Petry, minister to the Scottish congregation at Delft) for maintainance of his son William aforesaid, at the university in Leyden, under the care of Doctor Adam Stewart Primarius Professor of Philosophy there.

His Majesty was then come out of Germany from solliciting the Emperor and Princes (as he had done to France and Spaine) and was come to Breda (his brother Orange's town) to meet and treat with commissioners from Scotland; in which affair, hardly any three weeks passed but that the Scottish commissioners were instructed (as I was informed) to urge further and more strict concessions from his Majesty.

Sir James came over in one of the ships which wafted the King and his train from Holland, and he contracted an intimate friendship with Sir Alexander Sutherland whom the King afterwards created Lord Duffus (an excellent man he was) whose truth and worth, the said Sir James his son (the said William) found by receiving, what money, papers, or cloaths were left with him at his house in the far north of Scotland for safety; for he delivered them to the said Captain Hugh M'Gill. Then Sir James came to the west country and was obliged to abscond, and I rode with him, his cloaths-bag behind me for secrecy, till he might gett up his bond, which was cancelled as aforesaid; and I had (that winter) remained at the Colledge in Glasgow, and till the summer following. Then students had the vacance (so they called it) i. e. leave to go home till harvest (which begins the first of August) was past.

In the meanwhile, no malignants (so were the late suffering loyalists termed) were ad-admitted into the army, nor to any office in the King's household, and it was but privately that Sir James might repaire to Court or near the King's psrson, yet sometimes he had secret speech with his Majesty.

The English army, commanded by O. C. was drawn up within five miles of Edinburgh, and the Scotts between Leith and Pictland (comonly called Pentland) hills.

In which, a Committee of ye Kirk had a place, neare Generall Lesly, and were privy to all resolutions made in councils of warr, having an overawing and controlling votes therein ; and it was generally believed that O. C. had secret correspondence with them and their party, among ye officers, and ye event confirmed the report. For ye ministers and some leading officers, after the loss of Dunbarr fight, now called Remonstrators (from a paper called a Remonstrance against ye assembly of the Estates, and of the Ministers at Striveling), for this assembly declared that it was lawfull for the King to imploy any of his subjects, to expell ye Sectarian English out of the country; but those other ministers and officers, having gott together about 6000 men, and more dayly of their peevish gang, refractory to ye laws, comeing in to pursue their remonstrance, would admit of no conjunction with ye King, nor with his sober estates and clergy at Striveling, but being headed by y said Straughan and Colonel Gilbert (comonly called Gibby) Carr, would fight ye Lord's battles by themselves; because he was able to doe his own work with few, as well as with many, and would own his cause and covenant, (which they only expressed) against the sectarians, and, therefore, they rejected the help of 1000 men, which ye King and estates sent, by Major General Montgomery, (Eglinton's 3d son), and threatened to fall upon him and his party, if he presumed to joyne with them, tho' he offered to be under their command; only permitting their leaders to march and fight as volunteers, with ye men they had brought to their party. Now, lett any man judge whether Carr and Straughan were more for the King and country or for Cromwell; but Lambert easily routed them at Hamilton, within six miles of Glasgow.

Sir James Montgomery, about six days before yᵉ said fight at Dunbarr, attending with myself, when yᵉ King viewed yᵉ army, (to their great joy, whereof the Kirk party were jealous,) seeing the King debarred from staying with his army, and advised peremtorily (which he must interpett as a command, being under sadd circumstnnces with the Committees), to retire, and stay in Striveling Castle; and his Majesty did so.

The history of the passages in the west parts of Scotland; how the remonstrators were routed and dispersed; how Oliver Cromwell sent over a party in Fife, thinking to enclose the King, at Strivling; how his Majesty marched to Worcester, and was defeated, and escaped to France—is sufficiently recorded, and belongs not to me.

Then Sir James seeing the King's affairs ruined in all his kingdoms (chooseing the most convenient time) he went incognito as a merchant to Edinburgh, to a stanch friend, and by his means got a pass to travel to London under the name of James Huson, and for his trusty man, (who went as his nephew) under the name of William Thomson, as merchants with bills of exchange and letters of credit for wares to be brought back. And indeed the master was son of a Hugh, and the servant son of a Thomas; so their adopted sirnames (to gain current permission of travelling,) were all truths. James Huson thus travelling by the way of Newcastle upon Tyne found ye roads pestered with marching horse and foot, which were very often inquisitive. Yet none of them did discover him, though he knew some English officers that he mett, and therefore he resolved to run no further risque by land.

James Huson sold his horses and took to sea in a coal's barque for London (that great wood for concealments), and here was Sir W. Cole his father-in-law, that owed him 500$l.$; with acquittall whereof, and other sums which he intended to bestow by his hands, he hoped to get a pardon, and to be admitted to compound for his estate.

Yet it may be observed all the world over, that man may propose, but that God only can, and doth dispose of events. For now our pretended shopkeepers being aboard, and all danger of Oliver Cromwell and his army past, I may name them by their former names.

Sir James had not sailed 8 hours, till night and a storm separated the coal-fleet, which had set out together. On the next morning, being the 12th of March 165$\frac{1}{2}$, the storm being abated, a picaroon (or privateer) of Dunkerk, carrying six small guns and near 60 men, having letters of marque or reprizal, gave chase to our vessel near Flamborrow head.

Sir James viewed the picaroon with the

master's perspective, and thinking their enemy of less force than they were, and the coal barque having three iron guns, 6-pounders and 12 muskets aboard, the sailors and passengers making 14 men besides himself and servant, and being hopefull to stand fight till they might reach ye harbour,—he encouraged the crew and passengers to set all things to rights for defence.

Sir James understood gunnery well, he tackled the two guns on the deck, and whilst in action there, the privateer made a low shott, for they had formerly shott high to make our vessel strike and come under lee, but she bore up to the wind landwards, which shott broke off some of the cabin's topp, the splinters hurt Sir James his arm and face, but did not dangerously wound him; yet for all this he heartened his companions at sea, and assured them, he would either sink or disable the enemy if he offered to board them, and if he made only to give broadsides, there was no hazard of our sinking by their small guns, and that he was going into the cabin to fix a gun which (under God and by their courage) would be means to gaine the port they all aimed at and desired. So leaving the men at their posts and on the hatches, Sir James and William Coninghame his trusty servant (whom he had educated from a boy and preferred to be an Ensign both in Ireland and Scotland) went down and charged the gunn, and heaved up the porthole leafe, but did not thrust out the gun lest the enemy should perceive their intent.

Sir James being out of breath with the toile of this action, sat down on the master's bed, and his servant stood on the other side of ye floore to look out and to be ready. In the mean time the privateer made another low shot (of 4 lb. weight) which entered in at the port-hole, and cut off William Coningham's foot at the ancle, and the ball bounding from the floor shot Sir James in his shoulder in the upper part thereof and towards his neck; which was a gapp incureable; wherefore he bid Coningham call from the cabin door to the master to strick sail and yeeld, for that he had received his death's wound. Alas dear master said Coningham ………. is it so? I have lost a foot, but it is nothing worth to your life; doe as you are bid said Sir James, else neither you nor the rest will get quarters.

In fine, the ship lowered her mainsail, the crew retiring under hatches; the vessel was boarded by the Lieutenant and many men, one of them threw an hand granado into the cabin, which took off two toes from Coningham's other foot; he calling for quarters, and telling the Lieutenant there was a Knight of Ireland who lost his estate for serving the

King whose commission he had, and that he had received his death's wound from their last shot, which cut off his own foot, and that himself was also wounded by the shell of the granado.

On this relation of disasters the Lieutenant commanded all his men to forbear hurting any person, and so comeing into ye cabin, soon understood the mischief that had befallen to Sir James, who was a friend to all the relations he had in Lecaile, and the Ardes; for the Lieut. was one of the *Smiths*, followers of Mr. Savadge of Portaferry. Then the Lieut. weeping for grief prayed his commands, which he promised should be obeyed. Sir James entreated the Lieutenant to be carefull of his servant's cure, and that he might have all papers and other things preserved to him. That as for himself he knew the sea should give up its dead, and therefore desired his corps should be put in his great leather mayle and sunk with sufficient weight, and so reaching his hand to the Lieutenant (which was kissed by him) Sir James prayed that he might be left undisturbed that he might supplicate God to have mercy on his soule.

The Lieutenant set a centry at the cabbin door, and Sir James was layn down in his blood on the bed, at his prayers; none being with him but Coningham, till he expired his last breath, which was in three quarters of an hour after that woeful shot.

After this Sir James his corpse had the marine funeral solemnitys, and all the marriners and passengers were removed into the privateer's pink, and the coal vessel sent for Dunkirk, which was judged a prize.

It had been well for the pyrats they had steered the same course, for the day following they were taken by the Tygre frigatt, which was cruiseing on those eastern coasts.

The frigatt set our men ashore at Harwich. This compliment the pink would have done at her best conveniency, but was thus prevented: for she thinking to snap up some other booty was herself catched.

They had courted the master, Charles Fairweather, and William Coningham, restoring what they had plundered from their bodys, giving their own best portables to them, to purchase their good word that they were civilly treated; but all would not prevail to save Smith the Lieutenant, who (with 17 more Irishmen) was hanged. The rest being English, Scotts, French, Dutch, and Fleemings, were bestowed in prisons.

This account I had from William Coningham's mouth in Harwich, and most of it by certificate of the said master, in Jully following Sir James's death, which I was to prove, before I could be admitted to any part of his estate.

Now, I must conclude my short history of Sir James Montgomery, and give a brief character of him (his actions being often spoken of heretofore), and it must suffice for a burial oration, for I believe the Privateers had no Chaplain to bestow one. I now shall write of my own knowledge, and by certain tradition of discerning, unbiased Gentlemen, who knew him, viz.

Sir James Montgomery was endowed with a large capacity for learning; and he acquired it, with less study than many greater scholars, at St. Andrew's, &c.

He had humane prudence which might stock an able Statesman, and managed it with the moderations and caution of a pious Doctor in Divinity.

He was a polite courtier, in three Kings' Courts, among men; and his qualifications of that sort made his conversation universally pleasant, and also very desirable among ladies. He was not a Proteus or borrower of shapes therein; but did, (without any hesitation,) accommodate his discourse and behaviour to oblige all companies that were fitt for him.

He was talle above the middle size, and not fat; his meene and gate were more suitable to his extraction and station, on all occasions, than is often seen in others.

He was temperate in meate, drink, exercises and sleep, equal to physical rules.

He practised a requisite condescency, even to inferiors, which made him acceptable every where, for he had the epithet of the Courteous Knight (which is more commendable than courtly), from the British; and the Irish gave him the same appellation in their speech, with the addition of Noble (for he was honourable by inclination), they designed him by the title of Ruddery Honoragh Mover, without expressing his baptismal name, or his natural sirname.

He was most adhered to, and obeyed, by his kindred and servants, who were made fitt for preferment, by being about him, those, in the first place, who needed most, for whom, tho' he was carefull to provide, he bestowed no lands, yet payd for some apprentiship for, and for others he did effectually recommend, or himself did, advance them to beneficial posts; because he knew and had read them throly, and had found them true to their trust, as well as able to discharge it. A few instances may serve to prove this, viz—Hugh M'Gill (his female cosen german's son), he made first Cornett, then Lieutenant, to his troop. The same was Controller to the Ordinance aforesaid. He hath left no issue.—Item. the said Hugh's brother, James M'Gil aforesaid, first he made Ensign, and then raised him to be Captain in his regiment.—Those two brothers' grandmother being eldest sister of Sir James his mother.

Hugh Montgomery, of Gransheoch, he made Captain in his regiment, and then procured him to be Major, under Sir Charles Coote, as aforesaid. He made Mr. Nicholas Montgomery, of Derrybrosk, in Farmanagh, and another Mr. Hugh Montgomery, both Lieutenants; also Math. Hamil, whose son, Hugh built B. Attwood house, with David Ramsey his servants, to be Lieuts. under his comand, Jo. Hamill, the first and second Viscounts' Gentleman, he made Quarter-Master.

As for Gentlemen of better sort, who had lands or estates in the Ardes, he gave them commissions, chargeing them to raise a quota of their tenants to serve in their companys; and he proceeded accordingly with the subalterns, whom he choosed out of fee farmers, or other substantiall men, and was very ready to make provision for, and to receive all those who had fled from their burn'd habitations; thus (as it were in an instant) he raised his regiment and troops, placing some officers (who had served beyond seas) among them.

Such was Lieutenant-Colonel Cochran, Major Keith, and some like Lieuts: and serjants.

Sir James Montgomery had seen service and fortifications abroade, and had studdyed the military art and the mathematicks, and left me books and his manuscripts of the same; and particularly he was skilfull in castrametation and gunnery.

It would be tedious to describe him as a Justice in peace and a Commander in warr; which is signified by his device that he put over the entrance door, within the porch of Rosemount house, viz. a sword and lance saltire wise, and surmounted on an open book, connected with a wreath of bays and laurel; on the one leaf is written *Arte,* on the other *Marte,* (this being to the same purpose as *Tam Marte quam mercurio*); underneath is this motto *in utrumq. paratus.*

And at the breaking out of the said grand rebellion, he had on both sides the standard of his troops painted, a dwelling-house on fire, flameing out at doors and windows, with this motto *Opes non Animum,* importing that the Irish burning houses and goods, could not destroy our courages.

CHAPTER XIII.

Hugh, 2d Earl of Mount-Alexander, and 4th Viscount Montgomery, of the Great Ardes, was born 24th of February, 1650, in Newtown house, and was (by reason of his father's troubles) removed, with his sister, the Lady Jeane (elder than hee), unto Mellifont, where his brother Henry (now living, Ao. 1698) was born.

The Lady Mother not parting with these little models of her deare Lord and self, (in all whom was her chief worldly comfort), till she died in Dublin.

But his Lordship (lacking five months of 13 years old at his father's death) left school, and came to the funeral, with his brother and sister; and they stayed some months (being cold weather) with their grandmother and kind Major-General Monro, her Ladyship's husband, sometimes visiting their father's sorrowfull sister and mee, her husband, at Rosemount.

After a while, I conveyed them to Dublin, and they being settled, by common consent of their uncles, Drogheda and Charlemount, and (by them) I being entreated to sollicit this orphant Earle's affaires in London, in order to obtain a reprizal for St. Wolstans aforesaid, their Lordships promising to write to the Duke of Ormond to befriend the cause. The Lord Rannelaugh also promised to write to his sonn, and the desolate good Countess of Mount Alexander promising to write to her mother (the Lady Rannelaugh) to engage her son to advise and assist me therein.

The said Countess likewise entreating me to undertake that jorney, and to prosecute that business; and I having compassion on the orphants' distressed estate and condition, I consented to the Lords and the Countess their requests in that behalf; and promised to go, and doe the best I could for the young Earle, as being my dear wife's nephew; all which I performed, as by the sequel of this narrative will appeare.

I returned to my house at Rosemount, and from thence (in the latter end of February, 1663) I went to Scotland, and rode to Yorkshire, and was in Westminster by the latter end of March, travelling in cold and rainy weather.

And on intimation given to the good Countess of my arrival at Court, her Ladyship acquainted the said three Lords, and wrote her mother, (most affectionately and pressingly), to advise and assist mee in my solicitation, by herself, and by speaking to the Ladys, whose Lords were of that Committee, to which the bill of explanation was given, to be consulted on and drawn up, and that her Ladyship wonld give and gain me respect.

These three Lords also sent the promised letter to the said Duke of Ormond, signed by them, in nature of a petition, for the minor orphant Earle, that his Grace would take him into his protection, signifying that I was gone thither to wayte on his Grace in that behalf.

The Duke received the letter and myself graciously, (for he was feofee in trust, also, to the settlement the late Earle had made, as he had been to his father's as afforesaid;) and presented mee to kiss the King's hand, acquainting his Majesty of my errand in generall; and at this time the King expressed himself sorry for the late Earle's death, promising to be a friend to the orphant. The King also told me he was acquainted with my father in Holland and Scotland, and regretted both his death and the manner of it, saying, he had heard therof; adding, that he had hard measure of his countrymen, for his loyal services.

Indeed, the D. was a true loving friend to the defunct Earle, and often by his Dutches (who had a Montgomery to her chief Gentlewoman her Remembrancer) was he put in mind of the orphant. But great bodys move slowly. The bill was long upon the wheel, before it could be framed to give content to those pretenders to favor, which were included in it.

Whilst I attended every sitting day of the Committee, ordained to draw it up, (where there was no dispatch for the throng of suitors) watching the motions thereof; and making applications to ye Lords, whose acquaintances I had gained, by seeing them at Court, or by means of the Lady Rannelaugh, or her son, or by the D. of Albemarle; whilst thus occupied, our own three Lords in Dublin thought fitt to send to mee an instrument, signed and sealed by ye orphant Earle, whereby his Lordship did nominate me his guardian (for he was then 14 years of age.

I knew intimately Sir Robert Southwall (brother-in-law to Sir H. Percival, my kinsman.) He was one of the four Clerks of the Council, and brought on the cause in his quarter's time of attendance, which was then begunn. And (to make the story short) a full Councel mett on the day appointed, for that and other causes; at which the K. and

Chancellor Hide, the Lords Berkley and Ormond, were present, and those whom his Grace had made friends to our orphant Earle.

Winter, 1664, now came on, and the bill for the Explanatory Act yet under debate. I stayd till it was concluded, and the clause incerted for a reprize in behalf of the orphant Earle, for which there was an order obtained from the King.

After a few yeares the Agents were changed, but in the mean time annuitys or interest of money for debt were suffered to run on, to the great enhancement thereof: and thus matters continued till his Lordship arrived at full age, and he came to live in the Gatehouse of Newtown, the great buildings (some months after his father's death) being burned down by negligence of servants.

His Lordship then finding all his affairs (as the common saying is) at sixes and sevens, he appointed Commissioners to settle his estate and debts, and they acted therein, adjusting matters with tenants and creditors for above two yeares; in which time his Lordship abode most in London and Dublin, and in anno 1672, marryed   daughter of Carey Dillon, and had no portion with her (that I could learn) except goodness, comlyness and breeding. I was not acquainted with her Ladyship, and she dyed in winter, 1673, to his Lordship's and all the Commissioners griefs.

In this time, the Commissioners had begun a suite in Chancery, to discover and redress what they thought amiss in the former agents and receavers, and to bring them to an account of their stewardships, and to refound or compound (if they could make them doe soe); but they were discharged the 14th of November, 1674, from further acting, and required to answer for their proceedings. The which Captain Hugh Montgomery, William Shaw, and Hugh Campbell (who were the main actors) did, in name of the rest, who could not inspect (so narrowly as they) into the managery of every particular, and minute affairs (especially the drudgery part therof,) not living in Dublin, Newtown or Donaghadee. And so the said suite fell to the ground, and his Lordship became £2000 indebted (more than he was), by giving a bond for it, by the advice or arbitration (as was reported and believed) of the said Colonel Dillon; for payment whereof, and other debts, his Lordship was necessitated to sell the whole parish of Newtown.

His Lordship's grandmother dyed in harvest, 1670, and the first Countess (who had a jointure on Donaghadee 12 years) dyed, his father's widdow, Ao. 1675; yett, for all these three disburdenments, and that he was a widdower, without a childe, yet his Lordship had too many heavy burdens to beare, and two other sisters to portion, besides the weight of the £2000 aforesaid.

Amongst his creditors, Alexander Collville, Dr. in Divinity, (a true Church and King's man), had lent to the late Earle, to help to pay his composition mony, in the usurping times, the sum of £1000 ; and Captain Hu. Montgomery and William Shaw aforesaid, were joyned in the bond, with his Lordshipp, for secureing payment therof. So it was their business to be free of that debt, and the long incurred interest mony therof, and also to gett divers hundreds of pounds, due to themselves, and to be released from other suretyshipp incurred with the late Earle. It was their drift and designe (as well as concern) to advise his present Lordship to sell Newtown parish unto the Doctor's only issue son, heire, and executor, Captain Robert Collvill, (a person of a great estate before this time), which was done ; and yett, by reason of the undefrayd minority interest mony, and other debts, his Lordship was not alleviated of all his burdens, but a great many, both old and new incumbrances, stuck to him.

In which plight, his Lordship went to England, and married Elenor Berkley, (daughter to the Lord Fitzharden), who brought his Lordship very little mony, yet run him into further debt. So that, by hers and her accomplices' advices and instigations, (none of his Lordship's kindred, or former Commissioners being consulted,) and by his Lordship's own sense of conscience, honor and justice, (most inclining him,) the mannor of Mount Alexander (the house and demeasnes excepted) was sold to Sir Robert Collvill, to pay the residue of his Lordship's debts.

His Lordship had visited the Duke of York (when he was Commissioner for Scotland) and was graciously receaved, and had gott a foot company; and, in the Earle of Essex Government in Ireland, his Lordship gott his deceased unkle Drogheda's troope. So that, as we commonly say, fortune began to smile upon him.

And his Lordship being at Westminster, at King James' accession to the Crown,) he continued in favour as formerly; and then it was that his Lordship gott the patent for the Corporation of horse breeders in Ulster, and Commission to be Governor of Charlemount, and a Commission for my son (who accompanyd his Lordship thro' Scotland, to the Court at Whitehall,) to be Register to the Admirall Courts, in the countys of Down and Antrim.

Now, his Lordship was Privy Councellor in both the brother's reignes, and frequented their Courts, and was often in Dublin ; and when the Duke of York was Commissioner in Scotland, his Lordship was observing the Parliament and ye judicial proceedings of ye Law Courts (called the Sessions) in that kingdom ; by all which means his Lordship arrived at a great knowledge in state matters. And for country affairs, his Lordship was improved by reading (wherein he still delighted), and by frequenting Assizes and Sessions, for he was made Custos Rotulorum pacis in the county of Downe, after the death of Marcus Trevor Lord Dungannon, who had outed me of that office, by reason I was more than a yeare absent from Ireland as aforesaid ; but his Lordship (as his father had done) appointed me to be his Deputy, Ao. 1683.

Thus affaires stood with his Lordship, till Ao. 1688, about the time that the Lord Iveagh (the Chief of the Magnoises, commonly called M'Gennises) his mobb were gathering together.

Our Earle had then a sealed letter conveyed to his hand, (in the same manner almost as ye Lord Mount Eagle was warned to absent himself from ye Parliament, Ao. 1605, when y$_e$ powder plott was in a readyness), adviseing his Lordship to look to his house and person, and so he had need to doo, for he was one of those ten who were proscribed afterwards, and excepted from pardon by Tireconnel's proclamation.

His Lo^p, therefore confederated with y^e Protestants of Ulster, to stand upon their guard for their safety ag^t such a massacre as was in Ao. 1641, and was by them elected their Genll Comander; and at this time, ye Presbiterians required no renewall of their Covenant, but were joyned with the Established Clergy ag^t ye Papist, ye comon enemy to them and us. Then they scrupled not (nor wee) to hear one anothers way of worship and sermons.

Our Noble Peer having endeavored ye surprize of Carrickfergus (of wch he missed by neglect of some he imployed,) brought the guarison and Major Marcus Talbot (Tireconnel's bastard) to conditions of peace towards ye contry, wherin Archibald Edminston, Laird of Duntreth, being a Col. was valiantly active. But before the rupture came to this pass, Col. Sr Tho. Newcomen, a true Protestant (Tireconnel's bro. in law) then in comand under K. Ja. was obliged (without bloodshed, wher-

---

☞ From this page, throughout the remainder of the work, the original orthography is generally followed by the printer without variation.

of he was wary, for conscience sake) by Sr Arthur Rauden's forming a regim^t of dragoons, to desert Lisnegarvy, and march to Dublin with his 500 new trained Irishmen.

About this time, the Prince of Orange (to whom a convention of all the three estates in England had devolved ye administration of all affaires) sent over the Commissions for wch ye Confederat Protestants had prayd.

Our Earle, therefore, acting the best that might be, and assisted by ye Lord Massareen, Sr Arthur Rauden, Sr Robt Colvill, the towns of Lisburn al^s Lisnegarvy, and all the Protestants elswhere, he drew together part of his troopes, foot, hors and dragoons, (which at best were like ill armed militia men, y^e shores of Carrickfergus being in Irish hands,) and with these forces he marched to stopp the descent of Maj^r Gen^ll Hamilton and his army, wch came by Newry (then a guarison of Irish) to break our forces in this eastmost part of Ulster, and to beleaguer Londonderry (w^c_h had deny'd entrance to y^e Earle of Antrim's Irish regim^t) but our best hors and other forces from Antrim Lisburn and Belfast, not coming up in time, the contry people with Sr Arthur Rauden, and those with his Lo^P, (whom hee comanded personally) was easy routed on y^e 14th of March, 1688, by ye enemy's trained hors dragoons and field peices (whereof wee had none,) and so Hamilton (without peirceing into ye barony of Ardes and Lecale) marched thro Belfast, Lisburn, Antrim, &c. dissipating our forces (wch retired towards Derry) whether hee went to beseige it. What was done thereat, and the rescous it had, will be known whilst the history of K. Ja. (who was there ag^t it), his acts and disappointm^{ts} are read, so I forbeare them, as not belonging to my narrative; yet, I may remarque the providence of God towards the Protestants, in moving K. J. heart to send Scottish Gen^{lls} only to comand over the Irish in this and in the other expedition, for thereby the best sort of y^e British escaped to Scotl^d, England, or the Isle of Man.

But before y^e s^d route, wch was in few miles of Hillsbrough (the place of our magazine,) Col. James Hamilton, of Bangor, being scarce of arms and ammunition, had dispatched my son (then Cap$_t$ of foot) to y^e Isle of Man; the errand being for military stores, required haste, he therefore went in a skiff to a friggot there (which stood for K. W^m· who was now crowned,) and he came back in it to Belfast Roads, and had the news of the said route (called by y^e contry people the breach,) and y^e friggot helped many merch^{ts} and others to escape from y$_e$ Irish.

The next day I saw his Lo͏ᴾ at B.magown, attended by the owner thereof and Cornet Hodges, and his Lo͏ᴾ missing of a vessel at Donnoghadee (to which place he sent my son's groome to look for one,) he rode towards Porteferry, and from thence sailed next day with Sʳ Robᵗ Colvill (in a great storm) to yᵉ Isle of Man, where he stayed awhile, and thence went to England, his Lo͏ᴾ having his young son with him.

His Lo͏ᴾ, after a considerable stay at London, in solitudes and sufferings (not getting any relief or imployment,) he returned and came to Mount Alexʳ Aȯ 1691, living decently and unconcerned in bussynes, for he came not over till K. Wᵐ· left Ireland.

After yᵉ hurry of warr was past, his Lo͏ᴾ not being in condition (or otherwise hindred) to goe into England, he employed friends there to sollicit in his behalf, but no fruits followed his labours. His Lo͏ᴾˢ pretences at Court not succeeding, either thro yᵉ Kˢ frequent goeing beyond our seas, or thro his agents, or his pretended courtier friends, their insincerity (as to seasonable watchings and applications for him,) or for want of money to grease their palmes, for that regina pecunia ruled much at Court, and deficiente pecu deficit omne nia, and this of what was said of Octavius Augustus' Court, viz.

Dat census honores, census amicitias; pauper ubique.

And also remembers me of another saying,

Silicet haud facile emergunt quorum virtutibus obstat, res angusta domi.

Which I English thus—

Not easily scapes hee drowning, whose home straits
His person (in his swimming) obviates.

And his Lo^{p's} case was such at this time, having expended his stock for ye publiq, and there was no faith nor consideration in the Israel of mony mongers for his Lo^p, notwithstanding his many former proofes given of honor and honesty.

King W^m had been divers campaignes abroade and his thoughts greatly taken up by the warrs in Flanders; also England was a while governed by his loving Queen and Council, and after her death, by a Comittee of ye Nobility (called ye Lords Justices of England,) and our solitary suffering Earle was not minded (as to his preferm^t) by them, tho applyd to, and so his Lo^p continued unregarded (as one dead) till it came to pass that his merits and zealous abilitys shined forth, thro that dark cloud of forgetfulness or willing obscurity.

The time and opportunity of his Lo^{ps} appearance (which shewed what capacity he had) was in ye Parliam^ts under Sydneys and Capels governm^ts, then the learned Clergy and whole number of laick Lords and those of the long robe, who sate in ye upper House of Parliam^t with his Lo^p soon found (as those of ye Comons House, ye martiallists, k^nts gentry, and burgesses, had heard proofes of his Lo^ps abilitys to save his K. and contry,) giving wonderfull speedy deferences to his person, and due approbations to his speeches; their esteem was seen in their printed resolves; and their value of him was not misplaced, for he was no bon nor frequenter of taverns or coffy houses, but more retired and grave.

But Sidney was resolved, and had no kindness for any that would not consent to his opinion about the sole right of raising mony off the subjects without their leave, and Capel (his Lo^ps professed friend) died; so he had new acquaintances to make with the succeeding Governors, who at last came to take full notice of his Lo^ps merits and sufferings.

The peace with France being concluded, and ye K. returned to England, his Lo^p was called to sitt at Council board, and com^n was sent for his being Governor of the county of Down, wherein he lived. And Wolseley many months dead, his place, as M^r of ye Ordinance, was reserved, and his L0^p (without his own importunate industry) was so effectually made appeare to K. W^m, that his Ma^{ty} found (now) ye oppertunity (wch he had wayted and wished for) to shew (at first step of his bounty) the esteem and favour he had kept for his Lo^p, the hon^{ble} place and great trust of ye Mastership of all ye Ordinance and Military Stores in Ireland; wherein I leave his Lo^p for a while, designing to write breifly and no further of him, nor of any other Montgomery of this kingdom, than till 1699, save of one or two familys, whereof ye notices are but lately come to my hand; only I may here incert, that before the transcription hereof and of what follows, I am told that his Lo^p is made a Brigadier in the army, and that thereby he is intituled (and also promised) to have a regim^t of foot, when any falls to want a comander, by ye death or other removeall of a Col. These being the beginnings of good aspects towards all our surname, shineing on them, in the person of his Lo^p (the cheif of that nation or tribe in Irel^d.)

CHAPTER XIV.

And now, also, before I conclude with his Lo^p, I will make another interjection, by writing a few lines of his brother, the Honble Henery Montgomery, of Rogerstown, near Dublin.

This Henery was born at Mellifont, in A° 1656, and so named from his godfather unkle, ye Earle of Drogheda. He is of a sweet temper and disposition, affable, curteous and complacent. He hath to wife, Mary Saint Lawrence, eldest daughter of W^m late Ld Baron of Howth, A° 1672, and a great portion (3000 Lib) was due, w_{ch} he rec^d by gales in ten yeares, taking but ye interest for ye principall. It seems he was as little covetous or carefull, and almost as much affectionat to his wives family (wch needed not) as my self was compassionate to ye 2^d Earles deplorable circumstances, in the like case of portion; onely his wisdom exceeded mine, in that he had his whole sum payd as afors^d, wheras I took but ye half due to me (and from our marriage in 1660 to 1674, was not fully paid that mony) without interest required for want therof.

He built a faire house and made improvements at Rogerstown, his brother Houth's lands, within a mile of Lusk (wch the contry people call ye yolk of Fingale) and laid out therein 1500Lib.

He hath lived hitherto without publiq imploym_{ts} saving his being a Justice of ye Peace in the county of Downe, when he dwelt therein.

The Earle (his brother) gave him lands for his portion, near Newtown in the great Ardes, which he sold to Mr. Ro^t Maxwell, and he to Sir Robt Colvil for 3000Lib (double the portion left to him); then he removed, to be near his mother in law (ye Lady Dowager of Howth) and her other daughter, and other allyances thereabouts.

He hath issue now living Elizabeth, a marriagable accomplished lady, fitt to govern a family, and also

Hugh, his eldest sonn, a comely propper man, heir-presumptive (after his father's death) to our Earle of Mount Alexander, and hath Thomas, a pritty nimble witty boy, so called from his mother's brother, ye present L^d of Howth. All whose characters, when they are departed and shall be seen no more on earth, must be had from another pen than mine, for I begg of (and hope in) God, I may never see that day to do it, or to have need to write more of this kind, for I desire not to bee the Visc^t by the death of any of these 4 males, much less of them all, or that the line or title of ye late Noble Earle should faile, (as our neighbour Viscounts, Ardglass, Conway, and Clanbrazils are, sonnless; and ye estates of ye two last named gone out of their posteritys hands,) but that it may encrease and thrive, and see many joyfull years, as they have felt hard times ; and that this dutyfull history may be preserved and continued by our future generations, whilst the sun and moon endure (if God will allow it), and then there will be no need of such records.

I wish also that this Henry and Mary may be remembred and well spoken of, for the care and love they have of entertaining in their house (and their present endeavors to recover what is due to) Jean Montgomery, ye only living offspring of their unkle, ye Hono^{ble} James Montgomery, hereafter to be mentioned in this narrative.

In the interim, I must here again interpose a few lines of our present Earles and this Henry's full sister, the Lady Jean, of whose death and buriall in Chester you have heard.

She was born in Newtoun house in 7^{br} A^o 1649. She had her name from her grandmother by ye father, and yet ye Presbyterian ministers refused to baptize her (so they call ye administration of that sacrament, (as I now think,) improperly; for neither ours nor theirs in these cold climates use immersion of infants, but sprinkling) for they had a pique at her father, for acting by the K^s com^n and not by their directions and authority ; and so he must have stood in ye stoole of repentance (as they call it) before ye congregation, and, in it, must have accused his obedience to ye K{s} com{n} as a sinn comitted by him, ere they would christen his sd daughter; and must hold her up too, and promise for her and himself what they wold please to impose, but his Lo{p} disdained their usurped jurisdiction and would not comply.

His Lo{p} was not displeased that they denyd his mother's request in that behalf, as they had formerly renounced their duty to ye K. when they deserted himself. So a legall minister, named Mr ——— Mathews (whom they had turned out of his office and benefice agt law, as they did all the other other legall clergy) christnd her according to ye Service Book, as all his Lo{pps} other offspring were.

You have likewise heard of this young lady's comlyness, and removalls in those troublesome times.

After her mother's death, she was put in good hands, especially her sd grandmothers, and when her father remaryed, she was under the sd good Countesses view and care, and had the best education Dublin could afford.

You have heard how she was provided for in a portion and she playd on ye guitarr, and sang rarely well and with great art, and her voice was very harmonious, agreeable and charming, as her outward behaviour and humor of mind also was, for she was pious and devout in her closet and ye church, so that there must needs be admirers and servants to those perfections which adorn'd her; by which means she was left out of (and was untouched by) all lampoons, which vexed most of ye maryed and unmaryed ladys of that town. Her friends may happen to see (if they desire it) the elegy I have made on her death. It may partly serve to shew what other young ladys of our family (to whom and to ye males thereof, these my writeings are devoted) should bee, and how to dress themselves by her as at a mirroir.

And now I return to conclude this view of our 2d Earle, with as imperfect a character as it is short, and I would not (if I could) do it more fully to his comendation than as is hereafter, because all his due praise (now he is living) would seem flattery, and but a return for his love to my sonn, on whom I leave that task of gratitude for his Lo^{ps} kindness and respects to him (he being much ye younger of the two.)

And I pray God to give them both many happy years, that his Lo^p (as is very likely) may furnish more and more noble matter for such a theam, and that so my son may gaine the better experience and the more credit in performing this enjoyned duty

The remarks I have made in ye 2d Earle of Mount Alexander, in wch he resembles his most worthy patern and parent, the late Earle, I observe to bee these.

Imprimis. His upright justice, in paying his fathers and his own creditors. So the late Lord sold all his lands in Scotl^d to defray his fathers and grandfathers debts, with use upon use (called the annualls, and the custom in Scotland so to charge debtors) and the principall debt, and the charges of sending out men to the warrs according to his lands. In all which, his late Lo^p was imposed upon neatly by his receavers and agents (they are called factors and doers in Scotland) both here and there, when ye accounts of many yeares came to be taken of the estate for and during ye warrs of Ireland. So this present Earle acted good and suffered loss on ye like account as his father did for justice sake.

2dly. His frugality, and yet he kept a gentile table in his adversitys.

3dly. His Christian fortitude, in bearing crosses, vulgarly called misfortunes.

4thly. His liberality in his former prosperitys.

5thly. His being a beneficiall true friend seasonably, and in the best manner.

6thly. His penning letters gentilely, as to ye reason and succinctly as to the words of them.

7thly. His doeing devotion and alms, without a trumpett or any ostentation.

8thly. His constant adherence to ye lawfull Church wherin he was christened and bredd.

9thly. His right martiall way commanding and governing the royall fort at Charlemont; his s^d company and troops, towards which he was carefull and kind; wth his faithfulness in his present imploym^t over the artillery to save charges to the King, as well as his former prudent and assidous endeavors and struglings ag^t ye Irish.

10. His goodness to servants, in preferring them to places, or enabling them otherwise to live comfortably and creditably.

11. His complacency and winning behavior in conversation, aud generous hospitality.

12. His great ingenuity in poesy, which will appeare, when his modesty will permitt him to shew to others the peices of his composure; some of which I have read with an approveing admiration.

13. His ability for Council and speech at ye Board and on the Earles Bench, wch doth also appear in his next qualification, to wit:

14. His judgem^t in positive and polemic learning, and his apposite ready expressions of

his sentim^{ts} therin, and on all subjects, as well occasional as premeditated, is beyond most of those who have studyed or dared to be teachers in pulpits.

In all these premises (at least) with skill in riding, fenceing danceing, musick, ye French tongue and mathematics (which are endowments gained by God's blessing, on his endeavour to acquire and make them habitual vertues or accomplishments;) I say, in all these, and, as I believe, in more things, his Lo^p doth truely patrizare, according to the old proverb, viz. patrem sequitur sua proles, which is the same with our common saying, As the old cock crows the young cock learns.

Besides and over the aforesaid lovely resemblances, our present Earle hath an excellent hand in faire writing and true orthography for spelling words, and ingraving coats of armes, cyphers and flourishes on copper, brass, silver, or gold.

And as his Lo^p is a skillfull artist in minature, with pen, pencil and crayoon; his Lo^p is likewise a (scarce matchable) artist at violin, flute, recorder, cornet, hautboys, and the huntsman's musical instrum^t, playing on them all, not by help of his nice well tuned eare onely, but by ye diversity of their propper sett noats also, with wonderful skill and dexterity, to ye extraordinary satisfaction of discerning hearers.

All which utensills for ye ey and eare are laid aside or hung up and slighted (like as the Jewish harps were at Babilon) or are with his neglected recreations with ye muses, thrown into unseen places, ever since council board, parliament, assizes, and session business, were his avocations, from those painting and musical divertisements of his melancholy.

Furthermore, at his own or a friend's house, and before a select company (in the time of his retired condition,) he did condescend (sometimes) to shew some rare fates of legerdumain, and did act the mimick, both which he did to admiration, but in the latter of these he personated a drunken man, and lively counterfeited one, that a person of quality who knew his temperance (coming unexpected) wondered extreamely and believed him really fudled to the last degree; wee humored ye mistake till his Lo^p reeled to ye window and rubbing his face of a sudden returned to ye table as sober as ho was at his rare showes, which were hushed up at ye news of the incomers being come to visit his Lo^p.

His Lo^p's recreations abroad are now (mostly) doeing the K. and contry service, and tending ye affaires of his grand mastership, and so they are at home; but at leizure times, in the neighurhood and in and about doores, he entertains himself with requisite visits, or in angling, or in useing the setters for partridge, &c. or by walking to take fresh aire, or in viewing his orchards and plantations and stables, or discoursing with visitants, or peruseing books, or trying experiments and problems in the mathematicks, or doeing private bussynes for himself or friends.

As for meate, drink, and sleep (in which his Lop is temperate to a miracle) and a few of ye last named actions, they are the refreshm^{ts} and recruiters of his natural, vital, and animal spirits, when exhausted by his sedulity in the affairse of his station.

To conclude these remarks, this our present Earle hath gained all his posts to his foot company, to his troope, to his government of Charles Mount, and to his Mastership of ye Ordinance, and title of Brigadier to his chaire in Council Chamber, to the Government of our county and Custosship of its Rolls, all as aforesd without procurement of his father's, or mother's, or lady's friends, or their help, and without mony bribes, but by his own merits; and like the spider (out of his own bowels) hath wrought these webbs, ordinary care, foresight and applications (always herein onely excepted.)

And now I have done with this part of my bold undertaking, tho' I have waved and forgott much, and but meanly expressed my rehearsed notions of his Lop; yet I doe averr and believe my foregoeing assertions of him to be demonstrable truths.

Lastly, as for his Lop' age or era of birth, lett ye next relators speak more fully, when his Lop's life is fulfilled, yet in gen^l and on the whole matter, I repeat what Solon said to Cracesus, in all his riches and glorious grandeur, viz.

<small>Ante obitum nemo supremaq, funera debet dici beatus.
Wee no man fully blest or happy call, before his pious death and funerall.</small>

It may also be observed, from the first to the last part of my narrative of ye Montgomerys of Ards, that ye first of them who chose our motto, *Honneur sans Repose,* and the descendants from him, who have arrived to any name or esteem in these kingdoms, have had great troubles and toyles and losses before, together with, and after attainement of any honours they gott; so the motto (or ditton) hath been a prophesy, or rather a caveat for us in all future adventures, that wee should not, cedere malis sed contra audentior Ire ; ye Scottish proverb is Sett a stout heart to a stay brae.

Be the motto the one or the other, much good may ye affectors of honorable titles have with the uneasyness it brings. I never courted any advancem^t of that sort, els I might have been a Kn^t. and a Barr^t. too, before many my inferioures, both by birth and by my father's merits, and my own sufferings for the King, who is the fountain of honor.

I now remember a reflection I had on ye sd motto, viz.

> Restless, resistless, are the keen atacks
> (In towring minds) which Roman honor makes;
> They, loves, cares, envy, loss, pains, value not;
> Bodys, souls, nor God, so that fame be gott:
> Fals, fickle, fleeting fame (ambition's goale)
> Vain, vulgar voice! betrays poor mortal fools.

Or, in short, thus:

> To all of high rank, birth, or place,
> Honour is still a restless race.

The Lord Visc^t. Claneboy choose for ye motto of his arms (nothing quadrating with ye coat) these words, viz. *Invitum sequitur honos.* But to speak freely of both Braidstane and Mr. Ja. Hamilton, I believe neither of them had been Lords if they had not sought to be so. And now I must subjoin to this Lord's life (wch is but partly described) an appendix, wch relates to his Lo^pp and to his ancestors and sister and the first Countess, laying aside what his Lop hath done since he first was Lord Justice of Ireland; he being now, Ao. 1704, in his 3d Consulship of that office. I hope his Excellency will furnish memoires from his own penn, and give them to my sonn (on whom I lay the task) that he may finish what I cannot doe herein.

CHAPTER XV.

THIRD VISCOUNT MONTGOMERY.

I now return to write of the 3d Visct. as I promised, affectionately and without flattery. Mr. Montgomery (for so he was then called) on the 1st notice of that horrid Irish rebellion, being recalled from his travels beyond our narrow seas, came thro' England and kissed K. Ch. his hand at Oxford, who had the curiosity to look at the palpitat^n of his heart, w^h was plainly discernable at the incision which was made in his side; Sir, said the K. I wish I could perceive the thoughts of some of my nobilities hearts as I have seen your heart; to which this Mr. Montgomery readily replied, I assure your Majesty, before God here present and this company, it shall never entertain any thought against your concerns; but be always full of dutiful affection and steadfast resolution to serve your Majesty. He stayd a few days at Court, and the King had him in particular favour, and here (I believe) was laid that unshaken foundation of loyalty whereon all his succeeding actions were built. He had leave to return to his father, who had wrote to hasten him home, because he feared his drowsy distemper woud grow too fast upon him, w^h perhaps was told to the King. Now, whether it was at this time, that the King gave our Master Montgomery his promise he shoud succeed in his father's commands I know not, but it is likely it was so ; because Dr. Maxwell (who had made the orifice in his side when a boy at school, and prescribed the lotion for it) was then and there attending the K. as his phisician, and might inform his Majesty of the s^d L$^{d's}$ constitution and habit of body, likely to remove him, for this Dr. had been divers years a pensionary phisician to that and the first Lord, and I have named him, joined with another in that quality, at the funeral hereinbefore described ; he was glad to meet with Mr. Montgomery, of the Ardes, his quondam patient (as is lately said) now in good plight of strength and health. The same Mr. Montgomery came home before Ao. 1642 (as I think,) and, no doubt, was welcomed by all, and soon afterw^{ds} was more endeared to this country by the signal proofs of his valor (in the quality of a volunteer against the rebels(to his parents' great joy and fear of his person. This Mr. Montgomery came accomplished in the French tongue, dancing, fencing, touching the lute, riding the great horse, and other academy improvements; yet he laid aside all courtly recreations, and betook himself to fortification and other martial arts, w^h (with other parts of the mathematicks) he had learned abroad; he now using no musick (except in the church and in house devotions) but only the drum and trumpet and bagpipe among the soldiers, in which he delighted, for he was conformist to the adage, *Dulce bellum inexpertis.* It cou'd not be long after his father's death, that his L^{oP} assumed the command of the regm^{ts} and troop, (those dangerous times not admitting any interim from action); but whether the same was resigned to him and confirmation gotten f^m his Majesty (as I think is most probable) or whether the Ld Leicester (I think his name was so) whom both K. and Parliament appointed to be General of the British army, renewed the commission to his L^{oP}, I cannot tell, but I may avow that it was his L$^{oP's}$ due to have the command, because his father raised and many months maintained his own troop of horse and regm^t of foot in Newtown and Donaghadee parishes, and in and about Comer town, by laying out his own money and engaging his credit, and by help of his tenants, whom he gave allowance in rent for it, and by the preys of cows w^h he took from the enemy. I presume his late Lo^p had a certificate (fm' the Ld Chichester and J. Conway, &c. to whom the L^{ds} Justices referred the examination and report of his Lo^{p's} petition, concerning his expenses for the publick, that for the levying, arming, and subsisting his regm^t. and troop the first year, it cost his Lo^p above £1000 (for Sir J. Montgomery had the like certificate for himself,) and that those sums were due unto them from the K. and kingdom, the preservation of this part of the country depending on such supplies and actions; and likewise his Lo^p deserved that honor and command because he had run many hazards of his life, to be an example and encouragement to his followers and others of the nobility in Ulster; but, however that was, his young Lo^p the 3d Visct. became thereby to be youngest, and his uncle, Sr. Jas. M. to be the eldest Colonel, who was now entitled (as I was confidently told) to have the chair as president in all councils of war, before the Ld. Claneboy, Chichester, Conway, and Lo^p, Sr. Jo. Clotworthys, and Sr. Robert Stewart, Audley Mervine, and all other Colonels in Ulster, except Col. Monk, who afterwards (by ordin^{ce} of Parliament) was made governor of this province (there being no governors of countys during the rebellion and usurping times.) What benefit (senority or eldership) in commission brings, is seen in the late reductions of affairs, wh[n] the young[st] Captains are thrown out (who perhaps were the stoutest, because never in danger) and the weary, old beaten commanders continued in pay.

I now presume to give the reader an account of the occurrences concerning our British forces (before I rehearse our worthy 3d Visct.'s actions;) in prosecution hereof, I will, for brevitie's sake, only name papers as followeth, viz. Imprimis, a copy of commissions granted under the signet at Edinburgh, the 16th of Nov. 17 Car. A.D. 1641 silecet.

	Foot	
To the Ld. Visct. of Ardes,	1000 and	5 troops horse.
Sr. Willim. Stewart,	1000 and	1 do.
Sr. Robt. Stewart,	1000 and	1 do.
Sr. J. M.	1000 and	1 do.
Sr. Willm. Cole,	500	
Sr. Ralp Gore,	500	

And these were obtained at the Ld. Visct.'s and Sr. J. Montgomery's instances and recommendations (wherein Sr. Jas. appears mindful of his 2 fathers-in-law and friends) as is evident by the Secretary's letter to him, dated 26th of said month, and sent with the commissioners, by Mr. Galbraith afores[d], the original commission, 2do. f[m] (the Lds. Justices of Ireland) Sr. Wm. Parsons and Sr. Jno. Burlace, signed by

R

them and the Lds. Moore and Dillon, and many others of the Privy Council, sealed with the Council seal, and directed to the Ld. Visct. of Ardes, the Ld. Visct. Claneboy, the Ld. Visct. Chichester, Capt. Ar. Chichester, Sr. Edwd. Trevor, Sr. James Vaughan, Sr. Ar. Teryngham, Knt. and Sr. James Montgomery, Knt. (and every of them) for suppressing the Irish rebells. By which three foregoing papers you may observe, that the King's Secr[ty] and the Lds. Justices and Council afores[d] were no good heraulds, or at least, minded not the rules of that science (as to marshaling the persons' names) in the direction of that general commission; 3mo, the Lds. Justices and Council's letter, directed (only) to their very loving friend, Sr. J. M. Kn[t]. signed by them and Ormond Ossory, with the rest of the Privy Counsellors, sealed with the Council seal, and dated the 28th Feb[y]. 1641, (wherein the Visc[t]. Montg[y]. is mentioned to be also written to) for taking out sub[n] f[m] the country, etc. proout the same; 4[ly], the resolves of the House of Commons in England, dated 2d Aug[st], 1642, to give 3 mos. pay to the 10 troops joined with the Scotish army; 5[thly], the order of the Com[n] of Parliam[t] for one month's pay to the British forces, dated the 16th of Sep[t]. 1642; 6[th ly], authentick copy of the L$_{ds}$ and Commons' order, to pay Sr. Jas. Montg^y. Coll. Hill, and Coll. Mervin's regm$_t$. a certain share of the £14,141, 8s. 4d. out of the adventurer's money for Ireland, dated die Veneris, 5tb Octbr, 1642, and, no doubt, there was the like of the Ld. of Ardes' regm^t, and I find no more publick papers: 7th, Sr. Dan Coningham, of London, K^t. and Bart. his signed and sealed declaration, dated the 14th Augst. 1643, expressing, that pursuant to Sr. J. M.'s letter of att^y to receive for the Ld. of Ardes and himself their several shares of the £14,141, 8s. 4d. of credit was only a trust; 8th, a letter f$_m$ a Committee of the Lds. and Commons to Sr. J. M. (himself alone) expressing, and taking notice of, and thanking him for his special services ag^t the Irish, &c. dated 27th of 7ber, 1645. There may be many other authentick original papers (as the aforementioned are) extant to be seen.

I shall now write of some of them, w$_h$ relate to the general procedures of the British officers (reserving the residue to a proper place:) and 1st, an authentick copy of the council of war's conclusions at Antrim, begun the 14th of May, 1645, wherein it was 1st agreed by the respective Cols. undernamed, that a president should be chosen by lot (so it is phrased) this present council of war, and the same to be without prejudice to any of the Col[s]. rights of eldership, and the lot fell unto the L[d]. Visc[t]. of the Ardes, to be President of the s[d] Council, and so to continue unto the next general council; the names of the s[d] council were as followeth, viz.

 Hugh Lord Viscount Montgomery, President.
 James Lord Viscount Claneboy.
 Sir James Montgomery, Kn[t].
 Sir Robert Stewart, Kn[t].
 Audley Mervin, Esq.

 The Lieutenant-Colonels were

Sir Joseph Cunningham, under Sir William Stewart.
Hu. Coghran, under Sir James Montgomery.
Robert Saunderson, under Sir Robert Stewart.
Jo. Clotwortby, under Sir Jas. Clotworthy.

 The Majors were

Finlay Fevhardson, in the L[d]. Montgomery's regt. of foot.
Geo. Rauden, in Col. Hill's regiment of horse.
Geo. Keith, under S[r]. Jas. Montgomery.
James Galbraith, under S[r]. Robt. Stewart.
Theophilus Jones, under the L[d]. Conway.

 The Captains, Lieutenants, and Ensigns' names, and the subaltern officers of troops and company[s] there present, I omit as too many to be here inserted. In this paper are the council's resolves, with the articles of war and other matters therein concluded, w[h] are not to the purpose of this narrative, but are worth perusal; with it are wrapt up two loose papers (signed by the chief officers) the draught[ts] of S[r] James Montg[y] concerning the same councill; 9th, the other authentic papers, w[h] I have relating (more particularly) to S[r] Jas. Montg[y's] transactions as a Col. I reserve them for their proper place, and resume my discourse of our s[d] third Visct. I confess my ignorance of all his Lo[p's] particular proceedings before the s[d] council of war, and till the next summer, in which he headed the British party, in conjunction with a party of the Scotish army, both commanded in chief by Major Gen[l]. Munroe (thereunto authorised by the K. and Parliament) so commonly called, at the fight near Benburb river, (a place where in Q. Eliz. reign, Shane O'Neil had defeated the English prime forces) whereon our field was rashly fought in June, 1646, and his Lo[p] commander of the horse (warmly charging) being coldly seconded, was there taken prisoner, and by the enemy retained closely such, in a castle called Cloghwooter (afores[d]) whose situation was in a very small island (scarce bigger than its foundation) within a lough in the county of Cavan, then in the possession of Owen Roe M'Art M'Ever O'Neil; his army which gained that day at Benburb afores[d], and not thence released till about two years after that misfortune, during all which doleful days his uncle (the afores[d] solicit-

R 2

ous solicitor for his family, Sr Jas. Montgomery) was using all his endeavours in Ireland, and to the Committee of L^{ds}. and Comm$_{ns}$. (who had respectfully wrote to him as afores$_d$) in England, till he procured his Lo$^{p's}$ liberty from that solitary melancholy restraint, whence he could see nothing but woods and water and the stones which immured him (like an anachorite.) His only comfortable prospect was the heavens, in whose God (his ever-living father). he chiefly trusted for his delivery, w^h came to pass by means of his s^d uncle's solicitation, and obtaining a licence of Parliam^t to exchange the Earl of Westmeath snd Lieut.-Genl. (I think his sirname was) O'Reily, for his Lo^p and the s^d Theophilus Jones.

In this confinement, his Lo$_p$ ply'd his study of books, whereby he improv'd his knowledge in the military art, ags^t, the flesh, the world, and the devil, w^h he renounced according to his baptismal vow, that he might the better fight manfully under Christ's banner, both for religion and the King, laws, and country. So that his Lo$_p$ came out of Cloghwooter castle as to recommencem^t to take or reassume his degrees for command and glory. In the interim of his imprisonment, his Lo$_{p's}$ reg^t. and troop were ordered by the care of the s$_d$ Sir J. M. with the same kindness he had for his own, he being eldest Col. in those parts, and having his L_{p's} authority to command it. At length, this withering durance (for it impaired his health, tho' he wanted not wholesome vivers) being removed, had a safe conduct, and was rec^d in our frontiers by many Br^h. officers and some troops, and convoy'd through the county of Armagh to Lisnegarvagh (*i. e.* the Gamester's Fort,) where his s^d uncle, with a great train of Gents. met his L^{op} (my small self being one) and attended him through Belfast to Carrickfergus, where he made his first visit to the s^d Major-Genl. and to his Lady Mother. All the great guns and muskets in each garrison (where he came) wellcoming his L^{op} in their loudest thunderings. After these joyfull welcomes thus proclaim'd by Bellona's voice and the noise of drums and so of trumpets, and huzzas of officers and soldiers; I find nothing of this our 3d Visc^{t's} actions (for want of his papers) till his appearance at the council of war held in Lisnegarvagh (the town aföres^d) on the 14th and 15th days of March, 1647, stilo anglico, under the presiedency of Con^l. Geo. Monck. The names of the constituents were as follows, lire licet:

Colo. Geo. Monck, President, the R^t Honble the Lord of Ardes, Sr Jas. Montgomery, Cc^l. L^t.-Colo. O'Conally, Colo. Edwd. Conway,

L$_t$.-Colo. Keith, L$_t$-Colo. Frayle, L$_t$.-Colo. Conway, Major Geo. Rauden, Major James Clotworthy, Capt. Geo. Montgomery, Capt. Edwd. Brugh, Capt. Clemens, Capt. Jos. Hamilton, Capt. Hans Hamilton, and Capt. Augustin.—I will not recount all the passages at this meeting, but only a few, which (I think) are worth knowledge and memory.

Imprimis, it was resolved upon the question, that the Capts. and Field Officers should be involved (I use their own words) in one vote; that the Field Officers and Captains shall take place according to the antiquity of their Colo.'s commissions, not their own ; and it was (on debate) ordered by the President pursuant to the last said resolve, that Lieut. Colo. Coghran, under Sr J. M. should have the precedy in the courts of war of Lt.-Colo. Conally, under S^r. Jas. Clotworthy. There were (then) ordered forts to be made at certain passes, and men out of every reg^t. (not above 80 out of any one) to be posted in them, and to be relieved monthly by fresh detachments, and the quota of money is set down what pay every officer and common soldier, serjeant, corporal, and drums shou'd have; some debates, touching titles to command and pay, and to precedency, were likewise determined ; so the reader hath a brief acc_t. martial and (tho' he be one of the army) he may perhaps learn something there out.

I am now again at a loss for his Lo_p.s actions (for the want of his papers afores^d. many being burned in his house after his death) during the interval between the s^d court till the 12th of Decr. 1648, that I find Colo. Monck, Command-in-Chief of the Brits^h. forces in Ulster (so he stiles himself) in his declaration directed to and requiring all comm^ns and officers in the army in their several quarters, and likewise praying all pastors and ministers in their churches and parishes, &c. to publish the same, and a particular letter from him to Sr J. M^y. of the same date, to oppose the landing of S_r. Geo. Munro's men, who were coming over hither, after Duke Jas. Hamilton's defeat at Preston, in Lancashire, mensi Aug. the 18th, that same year, 1648. The last of Colo. Monck's doings (w^h I left at) were the declaration and the letter, both dated 12th day of 7^ber, 1648, as afores^d, whereby he threw off his vizard and appeared barefaced for a commonwealth against the K.

I am next to mention his letter to Sr Jas. M_y. and no doubt there was another to our Visc^t. for I have the copy of their joint answers, Monck acquainting him (the s^d 12th day afores^d) he had surprised the garrison of Carrickfergus, and that Belfast was delivered to him, and that he was resolved to go to Colerain, and therefore he had orders to the Ld Canbrassil and L^d. of Ardes, to send 200 men a-piece out of their regts. &c. with a fortnight's provisions, to be there as speedily as may be, to w^h letters of orders, I find our Visc^t. and the s^d Sr J. Mont^y. did give a joint answer as afores^d, of the date 17th same month, wherein they desire to know of Colo. Monck his intentions and reasons of surprising Carrickfergus, and of going against Colerain, and of making Major-Genl. Munro prisoner, say^g those two towns and Belfast were given by the K. and Parliament as cautionary towns, that the Scotish army shou'd receive their arrears of pay, and that the M^r.-G^l. was made commander (by them) in chief over the Br^h. forces in Ulster; to which Colo. Monck replys civily the 19th of the same month f^m Carrickfergus, where he kept the s^d M.G^l in sure (but favourable) restraint; his Lo^p's Lady mother, with his sister and brother, James Montgy, coming to Newtown (as soon as they might conveniently) and thence to her jointure-house of Mount Alexander; Colo. Monck, in his s^d reply, having accepted of his Lo^p's and Sr J. M. excuse for not urging their comm^ds upon that unwilling required party (indeed their whole regm^ts.

and the L^d. Clanbrassill's were extremely averse and highly stomached at such a march against their countrymen in Colerain) and praying their favourable constructions of the surprise he had made as afores^d, and promising kind usage to their relations and friends, and to give themselves satisfactory reasons of his doings. He forthwith marched to Colerain, and by getting the same (as he said he hoped without bloodsheding) he did complete his business in hand with a total breaking the Scotish army.

CHAPTER XVI.

In these cloudy times, our s^d Visct. appeared in his lustre, by going with a great train of attendance and the convoy of his troops to Mellifont (S^r. J^s. M. his uncle, making a figure suitable to himself,) and there his Lo^p wedded the Honble Mary, eldest sister of Henry, Ld Visc^t. Moor, Sr J. M assisting to have her Lap's marriage portion of £3000 secured by bonds of the staple, w^h her brother (the Ld Moor) gave for the same; and there was need of the best secuity, for his Lo^p's estate was entailed, and himself but tenant for life. This was done in the month of Decr. 1648. Then his Lo^p returned with his Lady and her sister and two of her younger brothers, &c.; the reception at Newtown was great as military appearance and good cheer could make it, and their entertainment suitable. For divers days, the Ladies had the pleasure to see several Gent^m. on horseback, with lances at their thighs, running at full career at glove and ring, for the scarf, ring, and gloves w^h her Ladyship had set forth (on the 1st day of that solemnity) as prizes for the 1, 2, and 3 best runners (a sight never beheld by any of the Ladies or any of the attendants before that time.) These exercises continued for two other days, matches for mastery being made among the Gent[n] runners themselves, and the wagers were mostly bestowed on a supper and good wine; other days there were horse races made to entertain her Ladyship's brothers, who were always guests at the consumption of the winnings. Among these cavaliers, Capt. Geo. Montgomery (his Lo[p's] uncle) bore away more prizes than all the rest, and to shew his good horsemanship (for he had in his travels learned to manage them) he broke his lance against the garden wall at high speed, and wheeled his horse upon his hinder feet, and rode back curveting and troting to the great admiration of fearfull Ladies and all the other beholders. I was then at Newtown school, and was a diligent spectator.

His Lo[p]. in a little while after these pastimes, gave visit to his uncle, Sr Jas. M. (whose third lady was before then dead) at Rosem[t]. and there his Lo[p]. with his own hands, begirt me with a silver-hilted sword. It was my constant fellow-traveller till (to my great grief) it was stolen from me, when our ship was broke at Amélandt, as I was going to Holland; and now our Visct. and the Earle of Clanbrassill, Sr J. M. Sr Geo. Moor, and the rest of the Scottish nation, being apprehensive (especially the officers under their command were) of being served by Monck in the same manner as he had done to the Scottish army, and that the King's party in Ulster would be shortly wholly ruined; therefore his Lo^p. a principal actor and Sr J. M. (as one chief contriver) and the persons afores^d. made up a friendship with the Presbitarian Ministers, who stirred up the commonality against the sectarians (for so they called their late dear brethren), and by their advice *the solemn league and covenant* was renewed, and by universal desire of all sorts, his Lo^p was chosen Genl. of all the forces in Ulster, and his Majesty Chas. the 2d, was proclaimed King, in Newtown, where I saw the claret flow (in abundance) from the spouts of the market cross, and catched in hats and bowls by who cou'd or wou'd, the noise of six trumpets sounding levitts, drums beating, the soldiers discharging three vollies apiece, as the brass guns also at his Lo^p's house did, at the healths drank to three royal brothers; and at night bonefires in the street and illuminations of candles in the windows, and good fellows in the houses with the soldiers (to whom a largess was given) encreasing their mirth and joy by good liquor.

    Now our L^d. Visc^t. (Genl. of Ulster) making

a numerous party, and declaring for the King, rendezvouzed an army and expelled Monck, who retired to Dundalk with his adherents, and they made friendship with Owen Roe O'Neil afores^d; Sr Chas. Coote (President of Connaught) being with a strong garrison at that time in Londonderry, holding the same, and Connaught for the Parlement; as these affairs took up many months, and the K. was then at Breda, treating with Com^rs from Scotland, and being advertised of his Lo^p's actions for him, and praying his authority to proceed therein, his Majesty sent him his com^n to be Genl of all the forces in Ulster, who owned his right to the crown, with divers powers therein, &c. This was brought by Sr Lewis Dives (whom I saw in Newtown house), and it was kept secret a great while, and became suspected more and more because of Sr Lewis (who was a known cavalier) had been with his L^p. but was not fully known till the seige hereafter spoken of.

But I must return to some remarkable passages after the s^d surprise of Carrickfergus. Colo. Monk returning from Colerain, which was surrendered to him the same Septr. 1648; he sent Major-Genl. Robert Munro prisoner to the Parliament, w^h committed him to the tower of London. Colo. Monk thus done, call'd a general council of war of all the Br^h Colo^s. L^t.-Colo^s. and Majors, to meet at Lisnegarvy, his head quarters, in Oct^br. 1648, to satisfy them of his doings, and to consult with them of the future safety and proceedings; but, in truth, with design of sending over (as appeared afterwards) more officers prisoners the same way. Our Visc^t. (by advice of his uncle, S. J. M.) and also the Earl of Clanbrassill (by like advice of his friends) stay'd at home upon their guard against the like surprise, and wrote their several excuses, sending some field officers (well cautioned and instructed) to represent, &c. for their respective regm^ts. Sr J. M. went out also to find out what intrigues he could learn, telling his Ld. and nephew, he feared much of his being snap'd, and undoubtedly believed his Lo^p the chiefest person aimed at, to be ensnared by his appearance (shou'd he be at that courtmartial), and it was better himself shou'd venture his liberty and life than his Lo^p. and the King's cause shou'd suffer by any circumvention ags^t his Lo^p's person; and as it was guessed so it happened, for the court being sat, and the two lords' letters of excuses read, Sr J. M. speaking to the same purpose, was, by order of Colo. Monk, made prisoner, but he giving Colo. Conway and others bondsmen for his appearance before the Committee of Parliam^t sitting in Darby-house in London, he had leave to return home to settle his own and nephew Savage, of Portaferry's affairs, and to prepare for his journey. About the same time, Sr Robert Stewart (who kept the fort of Culmore, w^h commanded the passage by water to Derry) was trepanned into a visit and christning of his friend's child in the town of Derry, and Colo. Audley Mervin also was insiduously taken, and both of them sent by sea prisoners to England. So the mask fell off Monk's face, and our Visc^t. with the Earl of Clanbrazil, were upon their guard still, and the Laggan forces, headed by Sr Alex^r. Stewart, Bart. (who sided with the Covenanters) was also upon his guard, having a strong party out of Sr Robt. Stewart's and Colo. Mervin's reg^{ts}. joining him, for it now plainly appeared that Colo. Monk wou'd not test at his breaking the Scotch reg^{ts}. who were born in Scotland, but (if he cou'd) he w^d also discard all the Br^h officers and soldiers of Scotish race, tho' born and bred in Ireland; which, therefore, made them cleave together the more (especially having renewed the covenant) both there and here.

There had long ago been great animosities betw^n the families of Ardes and Claneboys, by reason of the lawsuits which the first had against the latter; and the occasions of them (tho' partly removed before A°. 1639, was not fully taken away as yet; but a cessation began A°. 1641, when Danl. O'Neil gave the s^d disturbance ags^t them both, and then those animosities were laid in a deep sleep, by the Irish rebellion and the deaths of our 2d Visc^t. and of the first Lord Claneboys, for *inter arma silent leges*.

The hardships, also, w^h our third Visc^t. and the first Earle of Clanbrassill were now like to undergo from Monk, and which they actually and jointly suffered from the usurpers, who aimed at the total destruction of both their families, had totally mortified and burryed those differences between those interwoven neighbours, and had made them good friends as they were fellow-sufferers in one cause; so that the last two named Lords often met on divers affairs, both publicly and privately, eat and drank together, without jealousy or grudging to one another.

It happened in the time when consultation and strict union was most needful ags^t Monk, that the Earl of Clanbrazil stayed with our Visct. all night in Newtown-house; the Earle had taken medicine eno^h against fleabitings, but (as the story goes) was abused or rather affront^d. by a spirit (they call them 'BROONEY's in Scotland), and there was one of them in the appearance of an hairy man which hanted Dunskey castle a little before our first Visc^t. bot. it and Portpatrick lands from Sr Robt. Adair, Kn^t.); which spirit was not seen in any shape, or to make a noise, or play tricks, during any of our Lords' times. But it pleased his devilship (that night very artificially) to tear off the Earle of Clanbrazill's Holland shirt from his body, without disturbing his rest; only left on his Lo^p. the wristbands of his sleeves and the collar of the shirt's neck, as they were tyed with ribband when he went to bed. The Earle awaking, found himself robbed of his shirt, and lay as close as an hare in her form, till Mr. Hans (afterwards Sr Hans Hamilton) thinking his Lo^p had lain and slept long enough to digest his *histernum crapulum*, knocked at the door, and his Lo^p calling him, he went in, and his Lo_p showing him his condition, prayed one of his shirts to relieve him in that extremity, bidding him shut the door after him, and to discharge servants to come at him 'til after his return; and having put on the shirt w^h he was to bring him, his Lo^p s^d, " Cozen Hans, I w^d rather £100 than my brothers Mont^rs' of Ardes shou'd hear of this adventure, and therefore conceal it;" w^h was done till his Lop was three miles off. But the further mishap was, that Mr. Hamilton had no shirt clean but an Holland half shirt, that being then in fashion to be worn above the night shirts, wh did not reach his Lop's navel; but haveing got on his breeches and doublit, with Mr. Hamilton's help (for his Lop was excessively fatt) his servants were let in and dressed him; and his Lop having called for the chamber-pot, (now called in taverns a looking-glass, for reasons I know) his Lop found his shirt admirably wrapt up and stuffed therein; but his servants were enjoyned silence, and his Lop came to the parlour, where his brother, the Ld. of Ardes (as he called him) attended his Lop. They took a morning draught and dined; after which, his Lop went to Carnaseure, near Comer, the habitation of one of his Capt's. and cousin's, called, also, Hans Hamilton, and telling him his misadventure, had a long shirt, which he put on, and so went to his Countess at Killileagh. All I shall remark on this event is, that I presume to think that his Lop would not for the hundred pounds he spoke of have stayed another night (tho' he was heartily entreated), for he understood not *broony's* manner of fighting, tho' himself had learned in France to fence with a *câ câ et le pour pont bas:* as (himself did often say) he was taught and did in his travels.

I have inserted this story because but very lately told me by Mrs. Savage, in Newtown, whose first husband was the s^d Capt. Hans Hamilton, and because it is the first and last time I ever heard of a browney in any Montgomery's house, tho' in Sr Ninian Adair's time and his son's, one of them hanted his house of Dunsky. Therefore I proceed in my narrative.

You have heard of Sr Jas. Mont^y. his going to the Committee of Daby-house; he met with Colo. Mervin there, both of them being sent before any publ^k breach or rupture of friendship was made by our Brittish reg^ts. towards Colo. Monk. They appearing (as bound to do) found friends, who got them leave to return home; and you may be sure they did not procrastnate their departure, lest advice from Monk of the fermentation arising from his late actions, and the likelihood of rupture between the Presbeterians and him, should occasion their restraint; and therefore they rode post haste to Scotland, and seeing things therein genrl^y tending to an agreement for the calling home our King, they came (with all expedition they could make) to Newtown (where I saw them both), and they found affairs were soon ready to proclaim the King, wh was done as afores^d.

What our Visct.'s particular conduct was afterwards I cannot tell, for want of the perusal of his papers, and lacking some older than myself to assist me in the relation thereof; for I was then a boy at school, and was glad when I saw my father and Colo. Mervin returned with life, limbs and liberty safe. Yet I remember to see great clutter of mustering and exercising of armed men at Newtown; and my father, S^r Ja^s. Montg^y. going often to our Visct. and many officers also resorting thither, and the King and Colo. Monk was in every man's mouth almost every minute.

The sum of my knowledge of affairs about this time is, that our Visct. rendezvouzed his forces, marched to Lisburn, that Monk retired to Dundalk; that then his Lo^p had Carrickfergus surrend^d to him, and then his Lo^p marched to Colerain, w^h was deserted of Monk, and so went to Londonderry to visit Sr Chas. Coote in his garrison, where his Lo^p joyned Sr Alex. Stewart with his Lagan forces (so *they* were called who quartered in those northwest parts of Ulster), and Colo. Mervin came with his reg^mt. and then they encamped before the town and straitned it. Sr Chas. rose strong in it; he had good men and store of provisions and ammunition, for Monck and he had put up stores therein ags{t} a siege, and expected supplies from England, and had got Culmore to their hands by some artifice, when Sr Robert Stewart was trained into Derry as aforesd. Nevertheless, our Visc{t}. and Genl. was hopefull to reduce that important place to his Majesties obedience. The fault was not in his Lo{p}. but in those Laggan men, who no sooner knew of his Lo{p} having accepted a commission from the King, without their Kirk Pastor's leave, and that he w{d} no longer admit their Ministers into his councils, nor walk by their advice (that is in English would not act pursuant to their commands only) than the whole gang or crew of them deserted the siege and his Lo{p}; they all at once disbanding themselves with one text of scripture, viz. "To your tents, O Israel," which was certainly a precipitate course, to leave their country open to the impressions of Owen Roe O'Neil's army, w{h} was now confederates with Monk and Coote. But they did not think of that, nor of the duty w{h} they owed to their King, that had no fear of Coote, because thereby they put a necessity on his Lo{p} to raise the siege, and their Ministers helped it forward by preaching from him most of his men and officers (as they did more effectually at their return.) So that his L^{op} was obliged to march home with thin companys. So the covenant (as they called made on that desertion said) turned tayle on the King and his cause. The Presbiterians would admit of no cavaliers to assist them, and that proved the loss of the King's cause and their ruin now in this kingdom, as it did the next year in Scotland; from whence our Dominie preachers here were influenced to take measures for the Ministers and adherents intended to capitulate wth the King for their party and covenant here, as the com^{nrs} at Breda were doing, and to doo the Lord's work by themselves, so to get all the preferm^{ts} and profit in their own hands; tho' they could not pretend to merit by acting ag^t the usurpers or by loyalty to the late King.

But his Lo^p returned home in order, and fortified passes and garrisons, and was in safety till next winter; for in June, 1649, Michael Jones having routed Ormond at Remeins, [Rathmines, probably—ED.] near Dublin, and O. C. landing, had taken Drogheda, and the K.'s forces (like the wained moon in the middle of her last quarter) diminished to the last degree in Ireland, Ormond (deserted by many of the Irish) retiring to his defensive strengths, with his Protestant party, w^h he kept in a body

(as the rest of the Irish did to Limerick and other garrisons.)

Our third Visc[t]. with his few loyal followers and adherents, and the Earle of Clanbrasil, with his men (all that were preaching proof); their Lo[p's] kept their forces together, and being personally present (as they were afterwards with Ormond) and by ther example encouraging their soldiers, were routed at Lisnestrain (as it was s[d] by S[r] Geo. Munro's mismanagement near Lisnegarvey afores[d],) by S[r] Cha[s]. Coote and a party of O. C. army; Clanbrasil shifting with some flying horse, and his castle of Killyleagh standing out, he resorted to Ormond. The L[d] of Ardes had been too active and too much hated and feared and was wiser than to trust his person into Coote's hands (who he had complimented by an unwelcome visit at Derry.) Therefore, his Lo[p] collected his scattered horse and foot (much again, before last fight, being dismissed by the pulpeteer's preachments) the soldiers bidding, *Au diable* to the back-sliding covenant and its rebellious adherents, who disowned the K.'[s] commission and authority, and with this party (most of them officers and gents.) contented to partake of all sorts of fortune with so brave a leader as the L[d] Montg[y]. who made his way through many difficulties to join with his father's friend

T

and the K.'s chief serv[t]. Ormond, then a Marquis.

His Lo[p] thus leaving his Lady and house at Newtown, and his Lady Mother, his sister and brother at M[t]. Alexander, protection for them, their households and goods were obtained, but by whose procurem[t]. I know not; yet I confess the English are civil enemies, and I may think Colo. Monk (who had highly wronged his Lo[p's] family) took now an oportunity of verifying his promise of good treatment, mentioned in his reply to his Lo[p] and to S[r] J. M. dated the 19th Sept[r]. afores[d]) concerning his Lo[p's] relations. But S[r] J. M. might expect no protection, being so considerable an enemy, as he was (both for head and hand) feared by the Parl[t]. party, and his opposites being highly incensed ags[t] his loyalty, (this appeared by the Rump made after his death excepting him from life and estate) that he now must needs truss up his best goods, and send them and me to Greenock; himself soon flying after them, where he absconded, as shall be s[d] when I discourse of him in particular.

Our third Visc[t]. stayd with the Marquis and was included among the Protes[ts] (as the Earl of Clanbrasil also was) with whom O. C. made capitulations for their coming home and peaceably living there without deserting the realm or acting agst the Parliamt. and for being admd to their estates upon composition money to be pd by them as the Parlt. should think fit; wh done, O. C. went to Engd. in winter, 1649, leaving Ireton to attend the blockade of Limerick, to wh the Irish had retired for their last refuge, to obtain conditions of peace. The Marquis of Ormond went to wait on the K. (Chs the 2d.)

And now our Visct. came to visit his Lady and his daughter Jean, not three months old, and his mother, sister and brother aforesd. his Lop being afterwards brot under more severe bonds than his neighbour Ld and other Protestants, viz. to leave his family, friends, relations and tenants, by a certain time, and to travel to London by way of Dublin, and not through any part of Scotland, and to appear before a Committee of Parl. (to witt of the Rump) wh banished him into Holland. This was a trap or snare for his life and forfeiture of his estate; besides, his enemies considered that his being abroad cou'd do the harm but of a single man of his parts and interest at a distance; but if his Lop staid at home, he could do a general mischief to them (the usurpers) as formerly to Monck and Coote. So by removing him they prevented this, and watched him for the other danger.

And on his L^op they had laid a strict charge on several penalties of hard usage to his Lady and to his other relations afores^d; tho' he shou'd not go into the Spanish Netherlands or Scotland, nor come back to England or Ireland, without the Council of State's license, nor be any way correspondent with *Chas. Stuart.*

CHAPTER XVII.

ALL these rigid injunctions hindered not his Lo^p to see privately the court at the Hague. His Lo^p was then an unwilling traveller, to his great cost, in that dear country. His expense was that w^h his enemies always partly aimed at, and against his will; but he diverted melancholy the best way he cou'd, by seeing the Dutch neat towns, and going *incognito ;* among which, his Lo^p. in winter, 1651, visited Lyden, Carsacs Mount, and an Atomy Chamber, &c. and its university; it being the most inviting citie for many rarities (where I was at my studies among many Gents. of divers nations); and there his Lo^p came to see me to the great joy of my heart, (my father being then in Scotland very private), and I waited on him to Delft and to the Hague, and to see the Prince of Orange's houses at Reswick and Hunsterdyke, where (in a parish church) we saw a copper pan and a brass one, in w^h a Countess of Holland's birth were baptized, the males and the females separately, but at one time; the infants (in all) were 365. There were also hung (up by those pans) verses pasted on boards, declaring how this world's wonderment came on that Countess, viz. that she refused to give alms to a poor distressed woman, who went about begging charity for her little ones at home and for three sucklings on her back, which she fostered on her own breasts. The Countess conjecturing the beggar to be a common whore and the children to be bastards to three men, and telling her that was the reason she rejected her. The poor woman answered, God knows I am the honest wife of an indigent man, who is at home using industry to preserve our numerous family from starving. He sent me forth thinking a sight like this of mine was the best way to move compassion and to get relief, but seeing your Ladyship is so hardhearted to me and my babys, and so misbelieving of my having these children honestly and at one birth, may God convince your Lady^p. by giving you as many as there be days in the year; and so it happened, as is gen^{ly} there believed and reported.

In this province of Holland, this winter, 1651, we had the satisfaction to see many of the King's officers, who escaped from Worcester fight, it being *solamin* (a sorry one) *miseries socios habuisse doloris*. But all the entertainment w^h travel gave his Lo^p was full of pain and throes (like a woman's travell in child-bearing) for he cou'd have no comfort (or but very little) till he was delivered from that captivity in that Babilon of religions and nations. His earthly treasure was in Ireland, and his heart was there also ; and when the hopes of his Majesty's success in England ever dashed in that kingdom, (as in the other two) out of his grief for those disasters, an hope arose (for his good God always supported his mind) that his enemies being now out of fears of royalists, he should be permitted to return home, where he might wait for better times and opportunities to serve his Majesty.

It was very lucky I had the happiness to see his Lo[p]. because bound to my studies; and but this once I accompanied him to any village or town. When we were at Hunsterdyke, and gen[ly] alwheres (but publick certain rated ordinarys, where his Lo[p]. could hardly be unknown) he kept himself so as to pass for a Gent[m]. and we strove to do so ; in this dorp, Ensign Simeon Erskin was then his Lo[p's] only serv[t]. Lt. Col. Geo. Stewart (S[r]. Robert afores[d's] son), Capt. Hugh Montgomery and myself, had that afternoon walked from the Hague with his Lo[p]. as if we had been fellows. We went to a tavern in Hunsterdyke afores , and we had all got an apetite for victuals; so after two or three stoops of Rhenish (without distinction of hats or any extraordinary deference one to another), Simon and I were dispatched for meat; we had a cold veal py, but did not price it. This gave but small suspicion there was any Lord in company, yet for all the restraint that was on us all, that we should not drop one word or action w^h might discover that there was a Nobleman amongst us; yet this huisbrow and her maid watched like cats, peeped and perceived it. I did (and so did the rest) wonder at it, yet the matter was not so difficult to know, for notwithstanding the settled melancholy w^h was in his Lo$^{p's}$ heart, yet the rays of his noble soul often broke the prison and sprang out at his eyes, features, and presence, which were always (and when unafflicted) seen in his Lo$^{p's}$ generous countenance; and so we lost our labour of conversing in mascarade. In short, the landlady brought in all to maal bill (without paper), ag^t w^h we objected; for it was five times the price of the wine (w^h we drank liberally and wherein we agreed.) Then the covetous, imperious, wretched woman put into the scale (to make the bill relevant) imperious, the py, then the bread, butter, chees, small beer, spitting in the room, the smoking, her pictures and attendance, and chiefly she urged there was a great Lord there; bidding us in plain Dutch words be content and pay willingly, for if the Prince of Orange was there she would not abate one doit.

His Lo^p's exile continued long after this time, winter, 1651, that the King's armys and friends in all his three kingdoms were defoiled and broken. Then his Lo^p. (the spring time following, or thereabouts) caused solicit O. C. (who had made the capitulation afores^d) to allow his return home, which was granted by the Rump (so was the fagg end of the long parliament called), but with all he must appear before the Council at Whitehall, where (as an innocent) I was petitioning for my birthright, at least to be admitted (no other Protestant) to a composition. I was in Westminster from June, 1652, to May, 1653; and when his Lo^p came thither, he made the required appearance afores^d. No sooner had his Lo^p received his pasport for Dublin, to appear there in like manner, but he hasted gladly away, for he might be put to keep Major-Genl. Robt. Munro company (whom we divers times formerly visited in the tower.) Then being so dismissed, his Lo^p bro^t me with him to Dublin, and we loytered not by the way. His Lo^p having arrived at Dublin, he presented his letters to the council and after some short stay, he came home and now obtained a breathing time for some few months) to enjoy himself with his Lady and children, and his mother, sister, and brother, to their mutual great comfort, and the rejoicings of the whole country; where I was before him, Dublin not suiting with my light purse.

Now when I contemplate on his Lop's past and future sufferings, I am sometimes drawn to think of the worldly implicities w[h] (invariable times) attended persons of great spirit (such as his Lop) when as their neighbours (like his) of mean capacity in mind are suffered to rest at home unsuspected. This seems to be hard measure, but it is a fate imposed on the noble souls for their outward glory, to go ℣ *ardua ad alta,* and to make them strive for true happiness, and so the said way is the high road to Heaven also.

But now again his Lop was commanded up to Dublin (for his compositions business requr[d] his attend[cc]) therefore his Lop took with him his Lady and children, and settled them at Milifont (his brother-in-law the L[d] Visc[t] Moore's stately capacious house) where hospitality was kindly given to them and requitted by allowance out of the interest payable for the forbearance of ceding the staple bonds given for security of paying the marriage (portion) money afores^d. But it seems the deluge of troubles was not abated, for tho' his Lo^p was let out of confinement and was abroad and might fly whither he pleased, yet he found no station of ease to the soles of his feet at Milifont. There he must not be, nor haunt nor harbour long ; for he might plot with his brother Moore, and by their respective intelligence (w^h came to them f^m their several friends) they might hold multiplied correspondence, and contrive disturbances ag^t the state. This made the governers at Dublin call his Lo^p up hither, both to take away the comfort of that society and his conveniency of living cheaper and more retired than elsewhere. Likewise, at Newtown (among the disaffected) his Lo must not be suffered to stay, with his friends and tenants and former officers dwelling in neighbourhood. That place was too far from their jealous eye and from a ready close lodgings in Dublin Castle. The s^d Newtown was too near Scotland, w^h (about this time) was uneasy to those prevalent usurpers, by reason of Glencairn's, Sr Arthur Forbeses and s^d Sr Geo. Monro's, &c. parties, which stood up for the King a great while in the unpacefied lands.

When his Lo^p had stayed at Dublin a while under their malevolent aspects (especially Forbitt's evil eye) who told his Lo^p he hoped to see his head off, allowance was given to his Lo^p (for recovering his health, much impaired at Dublin), that he might retire to the L^d of Howth's (on his warranty of his being forthcoming when called for. This was his Lo^p's next best retreat, he had a full freedom and the delightful and endearing company of (always) his most beloved Lady and sweet children, and of the ladys of the house, they being his kindred by blood; tho' by this remove he must make his purse lighter, w^h was troublesome for weight, since Sr Luis Dives saw him, it being exhausted by the publick service, by his removals, banishm^ts, and many confinements, as shall be further s^d hereafter.

I do believe the usurpers had it for a necessary maxim to impoverise the Royal Party pinching them by considerable crooked serpentine ways last spoken of, and by their composition money and untolerable taxes on their lands (whereof their rents must answer near to the half, having no consideration of creditors, but that they might take the other half moiety, and so starve the family, and also by tying them to all attendancies as aforesd. This hardship (used to such as his Lo^p) must oblige them to borrow money, w^h cou'd not be had but on land and personal collateral security, and if any of Oliver's men (who had the baggs) lent

What the other party needed, those huksters (who, from robbers, were now become usurpers) for sure w^d put them to expensive suits at law, as I found in my own case ; for Colo. Barrowston (at one and the same time) sued myself and both my bail kinsmen severally ; or else if any of those pinched Cavaliers (so K. C^h. the first's party were called, as the parliaments were nicknamed Roundheads) had money to spare, they wanted not good will to lend it to their distressed comrades and fellow-sufferers for loyalty : then the disbursing that or any other ways did weaken them all ; but these intruding rulers delighted most to see the King's friends worry one another at law, and perhaps they put our 3d Visc^t. to the greater hardships that his necessity might force him to sue his brother Moore aforsd. ; for they encouraged privately animositys among the loyalists, and publicly let loose upon them all their creditors like fierce mastives, whom the wars had for some years chained up. Our Visct. had no reason obliging him to gratify the desires of the Government any way, much less troubling his brother Moore for his Lady's portion money to make their common enemies sport, and he was so far from suing for it that he borrowed from Dr. Colvill £1000, to pay his own composition; and that portion money

U

was not called for till long after his Lo^{p's} death (by the ex^{rs.}) for payment of his debts, which then (by misfortunes) grew up yearly and plentifully like hemlock and thistles in the furrows of his son (a minor) his estate.

This unactive manner of living at Millifont and Howth, and the temptation of a bottle of wine (which in the city was often offered and accepted f^m the loyalists to remove heaviness of heart, to forget poverty and to remember misery no more) made his Lo^p corpulent and unhealthy; yet this infirmity of his body was not regarded by Corbet and his gang, but his Lo^p was enjoyned to present himself at their council door twice a week, and dance attendance there till word was sent out that he sh^d come in or might retire himself; which dancing (without musick) being troublesome and costly, and his Lady falling sickly at Howth, necessitated his Lo^p to remove her with his family to dwell in Dublin, where (her Lad^{p's} distemper encreasing upon her) she died, and was buried as the times w^d allow; and his Lo^p expressed his grief and her worth in an excellent elogy of his own composure, which I have still by me.

After his Lo^p had continued some small time in Dublin, and settled his children in Orthodox schools, or had them sent to his mother, &c. After this great misfortune, whither Corbett's malicious maggot bit him, or the council for private reasons thought fit, (perhaps some of the former motives urging it) his Lo^p was sent prisoner to Kilkenny, where he fell sick in body (his grief in mind contributing great help to forw^d and encrease this disease) and there continued some months, and in long run his Lo^p petitioned and had leave to come to Leixlip, and to stay at Madam White's (his Lady's aunt's house) seven miles to Dublin; and his Lo^p a little recovering, he was commanded to Dublin (where he being now a single person) was more than formerly watched by spies on his words and actions. Thus they had placed him (without promotion) in slippery places, that he might slide and fall into the pitts they had digged (and in the snares he had laid) wontly for him. Thus his Ld^p continued in Dublin (as it were on the brink of perdition) soliciting liberty to attend his affairs in the country, and to provide payment of his composition money. At last, upon bail he was suffered to go home, and so he did; and by the way (as always his custom coming and going was) he visited Millifont and came to Newtown, where, watering his empty couch with his sorrowfull tears for some nights, he was persweaded to reside with his mother at

Mt Alexander; whose desolate case (as to a conjugal bedfellow) was all one with her son's, his Lo^p, they spoke comfort to one another: the news of her husband's health and hopes of his enlargement, and our Ld's children being boarded with a careful friend within three days journey, and his sister and brother M. to attend him with their best caresses, and the visits of friends, and sometimes business, these were all the visible alloys of melancholy w^h the s^d mother and son had, yet their good God (as he gave those) added the comforts of his spirit, and gave them grace to trust in his delivery and salvation, w^h gift was always sufficient for them.

About this time, her Lad$^{p's}$ husband, the afores^d Major-Genl. was released from the tower of London, and had a pass to return by Dublin, (w^h citie he never had seen till now, he had landed there) for so he was enjoined to do. His s^d Lo^p, after some months stay, was called up again, with w^h he was well pleased, being informed that the former Governors were laid aside, and Heny. Cromwell was to be Ld Deputy; his father, Oliver, (as Protector) having regal power, his Lo now hoped for more fav^r than f$_m$ the Rump Republicans, Anabaptists, Independents, or such like locusts, w^h the bottomless basis of anarchy had vomited upon us. It was likely that O. C. to ingratiate himself with the gentry, and that they might not countenance the s^d locusts (who now were a common enemy to them both) would mitigate the compositions, or give long gales for payment (because his exchequer was full, and he had all the undisposed forfeited Irish and Bishop's lands un possesssion), or it was thought probable, at least, he w^d hold and make good his capitulations afores^d; and we found this change much to our ease and advantage, as we loyalists hoped it w^d be; for when Henry Cromwell came Ld Deputy into this realm (for the title of kingdom was rejected by former Governors) of Ireland, he had (as I was told) and do believe it, (for I was much then in Dublin about my purchased debenture) secret instructions to manage the reign, and spur tenderly toward the royalists, and to conciliate (as much as he cou'd) friendship or acquiescence from them towards Oliver's government and to his successor (whom he might nominate by virtue of the instrument of Government, w^h he swore to observe when he was instated Protector), and this made H. C. civil also to all the fanatick factions, for they were fermenting and designing against his father, both Lambert and Fleetwood secretly contriving parties in the armies for themselves, each of them thinking to fill Oliver's chair when he died. H. C. also cajoled the Presbiterian Ministers; for quietness he invited them to send up Commissioners from their Presbyterys, and they had several conferences with the Independants and Anabaptists, and all the doctrinal points or principles of religion wherein they agreed were printed; but to no purpose, for these parties cou'd not be twisted together more than a rope can be made of sand. However, the chief of each sect were closetted apart by H. C. and had favours put upon them. Dr. Owens was the great leader of the Independants, and was chief Chaplain to the castle. I do not remember any Presbiterian congregation then in the city. Now H. C. his Excellency (for in what I am now to say he deserved (as he was called) that title) was very respective and gracious to the Marchioness of Ormond, and to our Vis^t. (and to myself); for his favour allowed me to try those loose unsatisfied debentures, and to have them satisfied on my hands in Castlereagh barony, notwithstanding Colo. Barrow (a ringleader of the Anabaptists) had *costodium* thereof, for w^h I paid that Colo.'s son £150. This favour was some months before O. C. died. H. C. (as I was saying) was more favourable to the s^d Lady and Lord, and to the L$_d$ Moore, and some few more of the jovial compounders (so Noll's people termed us) than to any of the Papists' nobility or to the rest of the Protestants, and generally gave them good gales for payment of their composition money, and was mild to them all. Nay, moreover, he owned a favour to our Bishops, and allowed them pensions out of the rents of their bishopricks, w[h] so pleased Maxwell, the diocesan of Kilmore and Ardagh, that he addressed his Excellency with a printed copy of about ten hexameters and as many pentameters, wherein he stiled him, *Deliciæ humani gœneris* (as Vespasian was called) and to complete the verse, he added and gave him the title of *Mitissime prorex*, thereby calling him a Deputy King. Our Visc[t]. came now (unsent for) to Dublin to salute his Excellency, and was received favourably as afores[d], but was taken with sickness, which did cast him into a deep palsy that seized all one side of him; and being lodged next house to Dr. Ffenell, after many weeks his L[op] recovered, and was permitted to go and live in Newtown, as most agreeable to his constitution, where often he enjoyed the company of the Countess of Striveling, his grandmother, and of his mother, sister, brother, and honest kind Major-Gen[l]. Monro, fitter than the other four to converse with his melancholy; myself also, and his other relations and friends visited him often.

CHAPTER XVIII.

WITHIN a few months after this, viz. Augst. 1658, O. C. finding by his sickness (w[h] was concealed carefully) that he must go off the stage of the three kingdoms, (because he had played all the mad pranks he had to act thereon) he therefore made his testament, wherein he declared his eldest son, Richard, to succeed him as Protector of the Commonwealth of England, Scotland, and Ireland, and he was proclaimed accordingly. I saw it done in Dublin with great concourse of the people (but not by armed men, save those of Henry Cromwell's guard, who attended him) who made great huzzas and throwing up of hats; the fanaticks did not expect their white devil wou'd die so soon, and were surprised with amazement at the proclam. wherein all joined but themselves. But how soon they found a soft part in Richard's head and little courage in his heart! Fleetwood, his brother-in-law, and Lambert, &c. agreeing (like Herod and Pilate), got themselves and their partisans chosen members in that Parliament w[h] Richard had called, and also they held a grand council of officers of the army at Wallingfordhouse (within a pit and strides length of Whitehall) under this new mean-spirited Protector's nose, and in view of his long gallery, and they sent Richard frequent messages (mixed with their saint-like canting) and civil hypothetical menaces, w^h with promises to take care of him and of his debts for his father's too sumptuous funeral and of his families welfare, obliged his newly erected highness to demitt and render up his place and the instrument (that fiddle (as it was called) on w^h his father, Oliver, play'd any time he pleased) to his Parliament, w^h he did (cap in hand) confessing his inability, &c. And so the chief authority of the three nations (as they called the kingdoms) rolled into so many forms (in a very short time) as one would think impossible—that I I will not disturb this narrative (w^h is special) with the history of those general revolutions, which may be briefly read in Hobb's Behemoth, a book in octavo. Richard, for this womanish condescending, got the name of Queen Dick; and for the confusions which followed on this dimission of his sceptre, he was called Tumbledown Dick.

Among the turns of state (wherein Lambert and Fleetwood cou'd not agree w^h should be uppermost) it happened the Rump to strike into the Comm^{ns} House of Parliament. H.

C. had fair offers to stand for himself, and might have prospered (as Monck did) and played the game w^h Orrory and Coote won, but he was schooled by Dr. Owen and his Lady's tears, that he gave way to Commissioners sent by the Rump, and went to England. Our Visc^t. was at home, Sr Geo. Booth was up in Lancashire, Colo. Cromwell (afterwards Earle of Arglass) and Colo. Trevor were secretly consulting with our Visc^t. what to do to advance the King's cause. The Anabaptists bore the greatest sway in the Council at Dublin, and they ordered Colonel Cooper, Governor of Ulster (then in Carrickf_s) to send up our Visc^t. prisoner. His Lo^p had some sickness and recovered health in Dublin, where I was when the council was surprised and seized, in w^h his Lo^p was covertly active, for tho' he staid in his lodgings, he sent myself and his servants in messinges, and allowed his horses and mine to a friend, called Geo. Wilton, who mounted himself and others on them, joining Theo^s. Jones, who was in the action of that surprise, in scouring the streets hindering the Anabaptists to get to a body. I will not here relate that Sr Theo^s. Jones (my kinsman and great friend in usurping times) and the persons who surprised the Council Chamber and Castle (both at one time) made a rendezvous on Oxmondtown green; declared to restore the secluded members of the Long Parliament to sitt with those now in the Com^{rs} House at Westminster, and nor how they made S$_r$ Hardress Waller their Major-General, for the Ld Burhill and Coote were not yet appearing in Dublin; nor will I write what they declared for more than afores^d, nor how K^t Waller relinquished his promise to help to restore the s$_d$ secluded members; nor how he was (by siege) obliged to surender up the Castle of Dublin, wherein he had nested himself for the Rump, nor of any other occurrences consequent thereupon, because it is not my business: and I stayed no longer in the city to see them, but went home and surprised by artifice (without siege) my house of Rosemount and castle of Quinlinbay (als. dict. Collinsbay) in one day, and keeping possession of them.— Tho' Colo. George (in his circuit to cajole the Presbet^n Ministers) came to view the pretended forcible entry, but he did not disturb me. This was done by me on the 12th Feby. 1659, four months (bate fifteen days) before the K. came to Whitehall, and was wonderfully and happily restored by God to his people on the 29th May (his birth-day) 1660, without bloodshed. And now, having mentioned myself, I must not forget our 3d Visct.

whom I left in Dublin, where he stayed but a few days; wherein he understood from Theo[s]. Jones (who was released with him from the Irish as afores[d]) what was designed for the King's restoration; and now his was free from attend-tendances, therefore he hasted home, and by the way went in at Millifont, and concerted with his brother Moore their councils for the King, not doubting that the confusion and stirs wou'd all end for his Majesty's and his kingdom's welfare; they wishing that the several parties of Oliver's army might overturn and governments till the King (whose right it was) should come and rule us. And now every party minded their own knitting, to work the best for themselves respectively. Then our Visct. came to Newtown, and sent messages to C[h] Comwell, Colo. Trevor afores[d] (afterw[ds] he was L[d] Dungannon) and communed also with the Earle of Clanbrassil's friends (for himself was dead) whom he thought true loyalists, and with his own friends and followers, whom he knew best of all and trusted most. Whilst these matters were under consultation, Cap[t] Campbell going with instructions from Coote to Gen[l] Monk to Scotland, and Colo. Clifford, Gov[r] of Edinborough Castle, coming from his Excell[cy] Gen[l] Monk and to Broghill and Coote, now in Dublin. The s[d] Capt.

and Colo. as they came and went communicated their business privately to our Visc^t. at Newtown, and his L^{op} gave them (at each meeting) steadable advice, incouragement and furtherance, and imparted to them what he was doing, for they were both enjoyned to apply themselves to his L^{op}, whose interest and abilitys (fit for the present purpose) Monk and Coote well knew by experience; and Theo^s. Jones found private means (as his L^{op} and he had agreed at parting) to send his L^{op} intelligence and advice how to demean himself, and by what steps to proceed, as Sr Art^r Forbes (afterwards Earle of Granard) had in Dublin informed his L^{op} on what message he went from Coote to the K. I am sure I write not by guess or bare hearsays, for I was admitted to the wine that the Capt. (who came fm Dublin first to us) and the Colo. had in Newtown, publickly with his L^{op}, tho' I was not private at their opening their instructions afores^d; but when they were gone, his L^{op} imparted the secrets to me, having the honour then to be one of his cabinet council and confidents, as formerly I had been his solicitor both in Whitehall and Dublin (in his absence from those places), and as having embarked my life as well as my late purchase, and surprised houses and lands in the cause of his Majesty's restoration; and therefore my relation touching his Lop shall now again begin fm that the happy epocha. Having accounted our former passages from many dismal hours, because they were most remarkable and best inhering in memory, rendered the narrative the more certain; but before I enter on that delightful theme, the reader may please to peruse a reflection I had on Colo. Cooper, his taking and sending his Lop prisoner as afores^d. It was in Decr. 1659, and the last of his hardships fm the usurpers. When I ruminated on the many bad usages w^h my dearest Ld Montgomery had, and the noble serenity of spirit wherewith he endured them, I did not doubt, but confidently immagine, that his good God (in whom he trusted always) supported him with assured hopes of particular deliverys and supplies in all his streights, and with a full persuasion of his Maj^{tys} restoration, for which his Lop waited with omnt Christian patience, and often advised him to take his carriage for an example. Yet all the experiences his enemys had of his Lop^s candour and veracity, cou'd not make them secure of his quiet living according to the promises they too often extorted from him by force, and therefore, knowing their doings to be unlawfull, (both in spirit and military courts) they dreaded he wou'd break those exacted engagements. In this contemplation, I was at first and on the sud'den a little amazed, to think that men cou'd be so stupid and blinded, that they cou'd not confess that they perceived his Lop's honour (wh he always reserved unsullyed and entire to all men) obliged him more than all the bonds that tyed him; and yet, to such sordid, covetous men (as the Rump officers and O. C.'s generals were) me thinks it had been argument and pawn enough to trust his Lop's single parole without suretys, because that (on the least forfeiture of his word) they cou'd levie his rents and his houses goods; his dear mother (who nursed him) his sisters, his brother, his children, and (more than all these) they had (for some years) his entirely beloved, loving Lady in their autched claws, they being like harpys regarding nothing secret; for nevertheless of their fast holds, they were still jealous and affraid (without cause given on his Lop's part) their guilty consciences telling them that retaliative justice was due to themselves. This does solve the riddle, and dissipates my wonder, because, (after all the promises proved often) gross ignorance did not, but only fear and malice prompted and actuated them to perpetrate the barbarity wh his Lop suffered, (alas too many) whereof they had not the grace (tho' they all pretended to walk by the spirit of God) as to relent; nor had they human nature enough as to be ashamed or blush for their enormitys. This anatomys (on which I have lectured) please me not; their scent is unsavary, and therefore I return to my proper duty of relating his Lo$^{p's}$ better fortunes. Our third Visc^t. went cheerfully to see his Majesty and to kiss his hand at Whitehall, where he also joyfully met with the Duke of Ormond (the friend to his father and himself) who was then steward to the King's household, and saw many other friends, but ere he inwent his Lo^p made his betamt relative to his former settlement, the will bears date in May, 1660. There was no enmity (now) or strangeness between Monk (D. of Albemarle) and our Visc^t. The K. had forgiven all persons but the regicides, whom the Lord Earle (to vindicate the kingdom's honour) wou'd not forgive, but capitally punished them as paracides, according to the law. And then the affairs of Ireland falling soon under consideration, there issued a commission for putting in execution his Majesty's gracious declaration at Breda, and our Visc^t. was named among the chiefs of the commissioners. I saw him and them sit in court at the inns of law in Dublin, where were determined many claims of adventurers soldiers (who shared in the benefit thereof) and many innocent Papists and also Protestants retored to their estates. At the insuing the first com[n] for justices of peace, I was named one for the county of Downe, and his Lo[p] was Custos Rotulorum Pacis, and he (unrequested) made ne his deputy in that office. His Lo[p] was also Privy Council[r] and his name (as other Privy Councillors are) was inserted in all the commissions of the peace, and so his warrants cou'd run through every county of Ireland. Then also our third Visc[t]. had his patent of honour for being Earle, dated 1661, and might have had the precedency of date before his brother Moore; it was offered to his Lo[p] to be, but he declined that compliment (that might raise envy) which brotherly concession was ill requitted, when the trial about S[t]. Wolstan's came to be heard. His Lo[p] assumed the title of M[t]. Alexander, in honour of his descent by his mother, from the family of Alexanders, Earles of Strivling, in Scotland, and his Lo[p] (in the patent) had this epithet gave him, viz. *Qui nec Regem nec Religionem reliquit.* Whereas, in those troublesome turning times many men deserted both, nor wanted he temptations to shake the foundation of loyalty (which were laid at Oxford as afores[d]) but neither promises nor threats, nor the sufferings (wh you have partly heard of) nor the frequent danger of death (hoped for and therefore intended by Corbet) cou'd divert him fm deserving the s^d short character, or a better one. Before or about this time, our s^d Earle was made Master of the Ordinance and Military Stores in all Ireland, w^h is (in campaigns) the 3$_d$. post of honour in the army, and he had foot, &c. allowed to attend the train of artillery, with waggons, &c. besides a troop of horse to himself. After this, our s^d Earle married a very good lady, the widow of Sr Willm Parsons, B^{rt}. named Cath^r Jones (daughter of Arthur Ld Visc^t Ranelaugh); by her he had one son (who died in his early infancy) and the Ladies Cath^r and Eliza, whose pictures (drawn when children) now are in Mt Alexander house, and show their comliness. They both married after the death of her Lad^p. who survived his Lo^p. and died his widow A^o. D. 1675. The Lady Cath^r married (with her brother's consent) Sr Fra^s Hamilton, Bar$_t$. and had a daughter, w^h died an infant, and her La^p departed this life soon after it; in her sickness, recomm^g to her husband's choice his cousin-german (A. Hamilton, a good and pretty one) to whom he was married before A^o. 1695. The Lady Eliz. (so called for her aunt of Rosemount's sake) married Mr. Hunt (a gen^t

of a good estate) and dying, left him no ssue. Both these young ladies were as well humoured and bred and dutiful to their husbands, and loving to their kindred, as an honest heart can wish.

About the time of our Earle's marriage a Parl^t sat in Dublin, wherein I was burgess for Newtown afores^d, and then was passed the act for settlement of adventurers soldiers and others in Ireland. This was done in pursuance of the gracious declaration afores^d, and another commission was granted, wherein I was adjudged as an innocent Protestant restorable to my father's estate; and I procured the Papists, under whom (as thro' my father's purchase f^m them) I claimed a right to part of Quintinbay lands, to be also declared innocent; and so I was confirmed in my paternal estate. In this Parliament, there was a recognition and address made to the K. and our Earle was one of the commissioners for the Lords House, and he went to Westminster, taking his Countess with him. And the commissioners having spedd their business, they returned to attend the Parliam^t, w^h (before they went) had made a recess by adjournment. The Earle had obtained a grant of the lands of St Wolstan afores^d, but by the favour of the Court of Claims and knavery of his Lo$^{p's}$ Papists' witnesses, and the cunning cheatry of a supposed friend, who tore the lease, where was Allin's name, out of the record that was made of rebels' actions. That nigrum theta (w^h w^d have cond^d his claim) cou'd not be found. So by virtue of £2000 bribe and Colo. Talbot (afterwards D. of Tireconnell) his close agency (for which he was well rewarded) the s^d Allin was declared innocent Papist, and our Earl defeated of the King's grant afores^d. Nevertheless, our Earl was well enough to pass, and had contrived his debts to be paid by gales out of his rents, w^h w^d have cleared him of them all in five years, for he was to have took out of his estate but £500 per annum to maintain his daughter and his two sons (by the first venter) at boarding-schools in Dublin, over w^h his Lady had a motherly, careful, kind eye and heart, tho' they were not lodged in the house with her; and his Lo^p's table, w^h was publick and free to gentl. was furnished by his Lady out of her jointure, and his pay supplied him in cloaths and coaches, (w^h were very splendid) and in attendants and spending money, and a round yearly sum to spare, besides accidental profits arising f^m his office, but these last his Lo^p applied to some poor friends' and servants' behoof; and in this manner his Lo^p lived in grandeur, highly esteemed and respected by all, and for his ripe judgment appearing when he spoke in the House of Lords or at the Council Board, where he was revered by understanding persons, and his conversation (for the obliging gentility thereof) much comended and coveted by both sexes. His Lo^p. (amidst these felicities and dearest earthly enjoyments he cou'd desire) had fallen into a discentery, w^h lay sore upon him, changing its complexion twice or thrice. It was very dangerous, his body being grown unwieldy and bulksome ; but, by God's blessing, (on Dr. Fennell's endeavours) he recovered and was but weakly well mended, for that flux had bro^t him low too suddenly, by evacuating a great abundance of humours and fatt, by which he was become formerly uneasy to himself. Yet his Lop (not fearing a relapse or other disease) was earnest to go into the country to finish his private business afores^d, but chiefly to serve the country and his King.

For upon a design of surprising the Duke of Ormond and the castle of Dublin, one Maj^r Blood (who was in the plott) went through the North of Ireland privately, and in like manner conferring divers Presbeterian Ministers to engage them and to learn what assistance they w^d lend to a cause on foot for God's glory (so he called the rebelliou he was hatching) and their profit, they being now ejected by the B^{rs} and not suffered to preach. Our Earl had some small notice of this, but no description of the man. The Duke had more perfect intelligence, and sent for his Lo^p giving him a character of Blood, and where and with whom he had been, and desired to have him apprehended; his Lo^p, therefore, sent Mr. Hugh Savage (one of the Gents. of his troop) called commonly old Rock (because it is supposed he is descended of the family of Rock Savage) and with him the Duke's warrants and his own order to take such and such out of his s^d troop, which then lay at Newtown, and to search for Blood, who escaped very narrowly. But this sad plott for surprizall afores^d, being fully discovered by seizing the body of Thomas Boyd (designed treasurer at war) Col. Warner, Col. Jephson, Col. Shapeot, a lawyer, and Lecky, a Scotish Minister, &c. his Lo^p thought it a fit time to be at Newtown, and to send for the Presbeterian Ministers (his quondam backsliding friends) when he sh^d please, and to receive the addresses of such as came (unbidden) to him voluntarily. His Lo meant to try all their pulses and to mind them of their duty as subjects. So his Lo^p, at the desire of the D. and by his own inclinations to see his friends and to his private business, took journey the sooner (for he might not be long f^m the Government, nor f his post and family) and came to Millifont, now a table visit, for his Lo^p, and the beginning of that lethargy w^h killed him. His Lo^p being come to Mount Alexander and Newtown, and having visited his sister and me at Rosemount, his drowsy distemper grew fast upon him, that in a fortnight he was much indisposed to write (with his own hand) the dispatches w^h he was obliged to send to the D.; his cl^k (Loftus) doing the ordinary affairs. Yet by his directions his Lo^p first of all laboured at the publick business with the Presbeterian Ministers, many of them (on discovery of this plott) had been taken (at one time) and sent to Carlingford (and other places) under confinement, because they were suspected, and would have kept possession of the churches and glebes f^m the re-established and legal preachers; and practised clandestine meetings, and resorted to the people, met by their appointment in bye places, on mountain-sides, and in dry turf-bogs; which was suspicious and dangerous to the peace in those times, when all the sects were plotting to unhinge the Government in church and state (as appeared by the intended surprize afores^d); yet his Lo^p had procured leases for many of them, upon bonds of peaceable living, and his Lo^p had pass'd his word for his mother's chaplain, Gordon, and for Mr And^w Stewart, a good, loyal man, and a moderate Minister (in covenanting times.) So they were not troubled, and therefore the obliged and the relaised came to pay their thanks unto his Lo^p (who was then, as heretofore, the most regarded Scottish man in Ireland.) Most of them answered most ingeniously what he asked them in private: others of them were dismissed upon bail, with this advice—sin no more, lest worse things befal you. His Lo^p got but few of his debts settled, or business (with tenants) done, tho' he had Ma^r-Genl. Monroe, myself, and other friends assistants, by reason of shoals of visitants, and the daily increase of his distemper, w^h was plethorick; his liver was large and strong, and sent more blood to the heart than it could vent fast enough (for his heart was wissened and shrivelled to less than it sh^d be (occasioned by defect of the pluræ) to preserve which f^m corruption, the lotion afores^d was used every morning and at bedtime, by injection at the s^d orifice with seringe.) ; and this surcharge of blood upon the heart caused the swimming and obfuscation in his brain (wh^h in itself had no fault the abundance thereof) and made him drowsy every 3^d and 4th hour. The first remedy was to let his veins often breath out part of that superfluous mass of rarefied blood; but Primrose, the Belfast apothecary, (who practised physick) understood not the matter, and was timorous to tamper in that case. Wherefore his Lo^p hasted back to Dublin, and (by the way) died in his bed at Dromore the 15th night of September, 1663: the next morning Dr. Gray (who had been sent for) averred, that if his Lo^p had often been bled in several veins, and his blood sweetened and thickened, it had not gushed out (as it did divers times) at his nose, nor so oppressed his brain making it giddy and his eyes to be bemisted. This D^r. disembowelled and embalmed him, and being well searclothed, corded and coffined, his corpse (now no man) was bro_t back in his coach to Newtown. *Quis talia fando temperet a lachrymis*, for the sight or news of the loss of so great and good a man might have brought tears even from Oliver's mirmidons. The 16th day (before it was light) I took horse for Dublin, and met Capt. Hu. Montgomery at Dundalk; he had gone fm Newtown on the 12th day early, because of his Lo^p's hopeless condition, and was bringing Dr Fitzwilliams, which being now needless, the Dr. returned when he thought fit. I rode on well mounted, and was with the Countess about 8 o'clock that night, and left her in tears, I sympathizing with her good La[p]. The 17th I left town as soon as I could sod the roads, and went to the D. at Kilkenny before night (and ere he had heard the sad news from any other;) his Grace was heartily sorry. I made supplication (and added reason to it) that the troop might be reserved for the young Earle as his support, and shewed a precedent, but it could not be done. His Grace desired to know wherein he could place respect upon myself. I thanked him, and said if he pleased he w[d] commend me to his Lo[p] Chancellor, that I might have the office of Custos Rotulorum Pacis in our county, now vacant by the Earle's death: for, as his deputy, I had taken pains to regulate it. The letter was signed by his Grace next morning, and I had it when I came to receive his comm[s]. I had not made this unprofitable request, but that it disgusts grandees to make offer of service in vain; as I was not prepared to take a better thing. However it was an honour put upon me, a private Gentn. to have patent for that office, which is always conferred on the primest Peer or discerningest Nobleman in the county; so that I believe that favr hath no precedent. I had not seen the children, wherefore I returned a great part of the way on the 18[;h], and came to Dublin the

19th day, and stayed with them three days, consulting the Ld Ranelagh and the sorrowful Countess; leaving the care of sending as his Lo^p sh^d think fit. I stayed a night at Millifont, and conferred with his Lo^p Visc^t Moore, who said he w^d advise with the Lords Ranelagh and Charlemont about the young Earle's affairs; and now his Lo^p, our Earle, and his brother being put in mourning, followed to Millifont, and thence to Mt Alexander with their conveniency.

CHAPTER XIX.

PREPARATIONS were making at Dublin in blacks, torches, and scutcheons, &c. to be sent into the country by the order of the Lords and Countess, in which Cap$_t$. Hu. Mon^{ry} (then clerk of the stores) and Capt. Hu. McGill, controller thereof (both of them so advanced by the late Earle's fav^{rs} and kindness) were at hand and busy (all their pains cou'd not be called officiousness) to advise and see the premises gott together and sent by the carriers, and I was near Newtown ready (and present at a call) to see things done as ꝑ advice by post from Dublin. The funeral geare and provisions for entertainment being laid and the day appointed, I drew the forms of the cannon (and of the more especial invitatory) letters to the funeral, w^h were transcribed and endorsed as the s^d two Captains directed, and the letter to the B^p was left to my care: therefore, I wrote and sent an express with it, w^h prayed that Right Rev^d Lo^p would be pleased to preach the sermon; but his Right Rev^d Lo^p excused himself, and sent D$_r$ Rust, whose discourse on that occasion was printed and distributed by the Countess her order (as I believe, the other expences for the premises were also at her cost.) Yet the kindred and gentry furnished themselves and servants in mournings without charge to the family. The Hon[l]. Col. Cromwell, Major-Gen[l]. Monroe, S[r] Arthur Chichester and S[r] John Skeffington, and many other gen[s] neighbours and officers out of Clanbrasil's and L[d] Conway's estates (whose names are lost, and not in the following lists) assisted at the obsequies, as also did the s[d] Col['s] own troop and the defunct's, which horsemen (at the enhuming of the corpse) did fire three volleys, and the time thereof being adjusted with the gunners in Dublin, the ordnance on the castle and custom-house quay gave three peals about the same instant. So his Lo[p] was layed in peace in his grave within the chancel of the church, to sleep and rest with his Rt. Honb[l] father and grandfather and grandmother afores[d], and some of his brothers and sisters, who died before the rebellion. The chief of the gentry (w[h] came to the burrial) dined with the Earl in the parlour, and the rest in the dining-room or with the steward and seneschal at their tables, and others in the common hall; which done, I gave the following order (or marshalling methods) for the procession unto the four captains (bearers of the

y 2

bannerells) hereafter named, desiring them to see it done accordingly, the same being consonant to he rules of heraldry, leaving the ranking of the inferior people to their own discretion. The corpse being taken down the stairs by the gate-house entry as daylight was gone, and the torches and flambeaux being lighted and the procession ready to march,—the names of the chief persons who stay with the Earl and his brother were called in the order they were to go, and they went to their several posts; and the Earle, attended by next of kin and family, repaired to the coffin and (a signal being given to move) they walked leisurely in due distance. In the first place, Col. Cromwell and his troop (whereof Maj^r. Saml. Stewart was Lieutenant); then the defunct's troops, their Lieutenant leading them, marched with their trumpets, banners and standards in mourning and folded, sound Chancel Wail. The rest went into the church. Then followed the procession walking from the gate-house into the street, which is on the south side of the School-house hill, and so onwards to the north side of the Market-cross, and turning about it, left on the left hand; and came down eastward through the street which leads into the west gate of the church, wherein the seats were ordered and kept to receive the mourners of all sorts before the common people were admitted. So that all the solemnity was observed and performed with great decency and order; more reverently by far than was expected. This great deference which the vulgar had for their late most loved landlord restrained their curiosity and rude behaviour, and listened to the prayers (w^h was a novelty to them) and to the learned pious sermon (such being also rare among them); yet with great silence and reverence they contained themselves whilst this was doing in the church, the same being thereby well illuminated.

The same procession, taken out of my fragments which escaped the fire in my house, was as followeth, viz.

[Following M.S. imperfect]

Imprimis,—Two conductors, with black stalves, Alex$_r$. Crawford and Hu. Montgomery.

2, Thirty-eight men in black gowns, by two and two, his Lo^p having lived full so many years.

3, The French page, bareheaded. 4.th, The grand standard advanc^d by Pat. Mont^y. of Creby, Esq.

5, Serv$_{ts}$ to Gent^s mourners and strangers, how many I know not. 6, Serv^{ts} to the defunct, Jo. Davison, Ed^w. Kelly, Jo. Edwards, Jo. Francis, Ja. Norwell, John Corry.

7, Stranger^s Mourner^s { Mr. Burly, Capt Alex^r Stewart, Mr. Bowyer, Mr. John Law, Mr. Thos Simms, with many more out of Clanbrasil's and Conway's estates, whose names are lost.

8, Newtown and Donaghadee men freeholders, whose names are lost.

9, Freeholders and Kindred { Capt. Chas. Campbell, Capt. Hu. Dundas, Capt. Dan. Kenedy, Mr. Fergus Kenedy, Capt. John Keeth, and Major Willm Buchanan.

10, Gentlemen Freeholders or Relations { Hugh Montgomery, of B. Skeogh, J. Montgomery, of Tallynegry, Mr. Oline, Thos. Nevin, of B. Copland, Jo. Cunningham, of Drumfad, Hu, Montgomery, of B. Henry, Mr. Hu. Campbell, Mr. Hu. Savage, of Carnesure, Lt Col. Cochran, Mr Lindsay, Wm Shaw, Provost.

11, The great banner, carried alone by Jo. Monty Gent^m. second son of the Honbl Geo. Mongy.

12, The steward, Capt James M'Gill, with his white rod in his right hand.

13, Strangers legal Minnisters { Mr. Wallace of Hollywood, Mr. Mace, of Porteferry, Mr. Robt. Echlin, of B. Culter, Mr. Goldring, Mr. Hudson.

14, The defunct's Minnisters { Mr. Dowdall, of Comer, Mr. Heald, of Donaghadee, and Mr. Mont^y, Curate of Greyabbey, Mr. Robt Pierce, to whom his L^oP pay ½ salary.

15, Mr. Robinson, the defunct's Chaplain, Curate of Newtowne alone.

16, Dr. Rust, Dean of Connor (who preached the sermon.)

17, The cushion and coronet on it, borne by Hu. Montgy. eldest son of the Hble Geo. Montgy aforesd.

18, Dudly Loftus, the defunct's clerk aforesd. and Hu Montgy his best Gentn. both bareheaded.

19, The coffin, covered with a deep velvet fringed pale, and above it was laid the defunct's naked sword and scabbard by it and his gauntlet, and on the sides were taffety scutcheons, and underneath

20, The corners and sides of the pall by { Andw Monro, Esq. Jo. Savage, of Ardkeen, Esq. 2 Sr Jo. Skffington, Barts. Sr Edw Chichester, Kt Sr Robt Monro, Gentn Major Garrett Moore, Capt. Hu. Shaw, Capt Hu. M'Gill, Capt. J. Lessly, Capt Hu. Montgomery.

21, 22, The banners on each side of the coffin by { The present Earle alone, as chiefest mourner, at the coffin head, his train supported by Robt Crawford, Gent bare-headed (he is now Governor of Sheerness, at the mouth of the Thames, and is called Col. Crafford)

And next to the Earle walked

23 The Honbl Jas. Montgomery, his uncle, and Henry Monty his brother, Willm Monty of Rosemount, Esq. his uncle, and Geo. Montgomery aforesd. his grand uncle.—24, Hugh Savage, of Portiferry, Esq. the defunct's cousin-german. They followed by two and two the servants of the persons undernamed; of the Earle's six, of his brother's two, of his uncle Garret now

afores^d one, of his uncle Ja^s one, of his grand uncle Geo. one, of his uncle W^m two, of cousin John Savage afores^d one, of the Major-Genl Monroe one, of all 16; those were on the outsides, and many followed us (who were nearest the Earle) in long black cloaks, w^h they hired in Belfast for that service—Nota, that in the order of funeral processions (by the rule of heraldry) those who march next to the coffin or hearse (before or after it) the nearer the better, and they who walk on the right hand, have the precedency. Here nota, they are to go in pairs, except in the cases where it is otherwise hereinbefore used. There be other preeminences, we had none at this time, either to puzzle my skill or memory, as Privy Counsellors, Judges, younger sons of Marquises, and other Nobles, &c. The first afores^d doth contain some few mistakes (as to places) not occasioned by my deviation, for I was obliged to attend the Earle and brother (in their behalf) partly to bear up discourse to the best of the company, however it must be confessed that the s^d list or acct of the procession is short and defective in names of our neighbours, friends and their tenants, and of the tenants of his Lo^p^s three man^rs. w^h are lost as afores^d. this being drawn out of paper of fragments. All needful (w^h I can now think of) to be added, is, that the defunct and the s^d Col. Vere Essex Cromwell were very intimate (as their fathers were mutually to each other always) and that he died Earl of Ardglass; and that he, the Knights and Esq^rs. and the best of the country, who were strangers, were entertained in Newtown-house the night before and on that of the funeral, and that the s^d Col^s troop and officers, with other gent^n strangers, in like manner were quartered two nights in the town at the young Earle's charge: and after all, the strangers, who lived not far off, and his relations dined next day; they parted his Lop, giving them thanks for their respects as they came to bid him farewell. This funeral was the   day of   1663. The elegy, w^h is inserted in my opera virilia, being too long to be herein placed, I have therefore only given the reader the epitaph which I made on his Lop, as followeth:

HERE lies the much-lamented, much-belov'd;
One greatly hoped of, and one much approved;
Kind to the good, he was to all men just;
Most careful in discharging of a trust;
Compassionate to the poor, devout towrd^s God;
A cheerful sufferer of the common rod,
Which scourged thousands—not proud when he was
    high,
Nor yet dejected in adversity;
Unalterably loyal to his King;
He truly noble was in every thing;
Yet dyed in his prime   this;
But do not pity him who blessed is.

It may now further be expected, that I should add some description of his Lop's person and parts. I protest I can fully give a character of this great good man; for tho' his earthly half be laid in the dust, his honour shall never be confined there nor in obscurity, whilst there is any desire in his posterity or relations to read or know what sort of person a Christian here is, or shou'd be. The eulogetical elegy aforesᵈ, which I made (as better poets also wrote) on his death (wʰ was little past the 38th year of his life) is the nearest resemblance of his Loᵖ wʰ I could draw, but if you carefully read his actₛ (wʰ rather may be called the history of his sufferings) hereinbefore partly mentioned, and but lately collected from my few written memoras and memory; and do weigh well with what fortitude, discretion, Christian patience, affyance on God, prudence and pity on men, and foresight on affairs, he made his way through the different passages of his life, since his return from his travels and wrote man; and in like manner shall trace him to his death, you may then dive deeper and find more oriental pearles to adorn his coronets, and so understand his noble mind better than my speculation can penetrate into it; and you will rather lose yourself in wonderment than be truly able to express the ideas you or I may have of his Loᵖ, what his improvₛ might have been (had not death too early stop't his career in his life's race) is a subject profound enough for a metaphisical divine to study; but because it is sayed *dolus versatur in generˢ.* therefore I take leave to recount a little of what his Loᵖ was in person, pedigree and parts, as my present thought and memory will assist my pen. His Loᵖ of stature was among the properest of middle-sized men, well shaped, of a rudy sanguine complexion, his hair had been reddish and curled, w^h denoted vigour of brain to give council, according to the proverbial advice, namely, " At a red man read thy reed ;" his eye grey and quick, and his countenance smiling and complacent, his arms and thighs sinewy and brawny ; his legs and feet very comely, as if they had been to adorn dancing, which he performed very well ; his gait (without affectation) stately ; and his   (among strangers and in publick) was neither French nor Spanish altogether, but an admirable mixture of gravity, with a (*Je ne scai quoi*) courteous humility. His Lo^p was noble, and his extraction, &c. ancient from both parents; and their families (whose genealogies you have read before in this narrative) were issuing from untainted fountains ; his own and his progenitors' blood (of each side) not being corrupted in any one instance (that I could learn by all my researches) of his loyalty to the crown. His and their matters were very honb^le and their beds were undefiled. The servants next about him endeavoured to estrange his Lo^p from me, that they might have his ear to themselves, the better to work their own ends ; but his Lo^p was past his own minority, and cou'd dis-

z

cern and would receive no bad impressions of me, who had served him gratis on my own expence, and was seeking nothing (for it) of him. His Lo^p had no hatred or love solely for country sake; English, Scotts and Irish were welcome to him, yet he liked and esteemed the English most (both his Ladys being such) and bore the greatest friendship to the most loyal, and (unaddressed to) often received those of them (in the first place) that most needed and deserved help, and when it was not in his own hand to give it, he then bestowed his recommend^s as it were a debt or wages he owed to this honest hireling serv^t, and moreover, his very enemys found his Christian forgiveness and generosity. His justice was exemplary, and his readiness to give it made men bold and cunning to overreach him. He did not suspect any old servant his father had, tho' there was too much cause for it; but his father, had he lived, might have prevented the cheats (as I have credibly heard) put on his Lo^p, by those who were agents to them both. The rebellion in Ireland kept them both from prying into their s^d servants clandestine and outward mischiefs; and the rebellion in Scotland (by sending an army into England) laid on the country as a support or contribution for their maintenance, and the acc^t for arms sent over to his Lord father's regm^t and his own, were the spurious pretences for those agents and supposed friends in Scotland to draw that long and dear taylor's bill, and the use upon use, and liquidate expences (as they call them) and the colloguing suits raised against them in Scotland for caution^g (so) the resconning, that the lands of Portpatrick and Braidstane (being valued by sham in friends) were accounted too little to pay the debt of his Lo^p's father and himself incurred on these scores, and therefore his Lo^p sold the premises to those agents and friends who were baile for the debt, that no man should in the least be loser at his hands; and gave his bond for what was unpaid thereof, w^h his son, the now Earle, hath paid; it coming heavy by reason of his father's death and the neglect of his tutors (in his minority) to see the interest money paid annually, w^h was also obstructed by the two joynters on his (this said pres^t Earle's) estate. His late Lo^p, from the civility he received in his travels in France (his ancestors in Scotland and the Montgom^{ys} of England deriving their original from a Count of that sirname in Normandy, yet standing there in that degree of nobility) had bred in him an inclination towards French servants, (they being very ready and towardly to please their m^r) he brought over one of them as his valet de chambre, to confirm his skill in that tongue, and in touching the lute; and this man was with his Lo^p all the while he was confined in Cloghwooter afores^d, but after his Lo^p's enlargment and marriage (when misunderstandings fell out between him and Monck) this ungreatful fellow betrayed his councils, and fled for it : and his Lo^p (after the King's restoration) bringing from London another ingenious Frenchman with him, was, by that knave and his French trumpeter, robbed of his clothes and money to a considerable value, yet he retained his page of that nation, and he is mentioned to be one in the funeral procession. A kindness and courtesy done to his Lo^p was an inviolable tie upon him of gratitude and of making suitable returns; his Lo^p was a constant friend to those he professed to love, but neither hasty nor lavish to declare his mind therein. His Lo^p was good to the servants of his household, who all did thrive under him, and he was industrious to get promotions for his Lady's relations. His Lo^p's devotion was pure and unmixed, being done for duty's sake, not to serve secular ends; and this appeared in the worst times of schisms and heresy; he vowing his religion and loyalty, and educating his sons by Dr Bayly and other episcopal teachers, and himself was intirely addicted to worship God by the Canon Prayer Book (in publick or in his family) when he could have it, and therefore was hated by the Scotts of all sorts, and so by them cross'd or kept under hatches. Whereas, had he complied (as great names did) he might have flourished in Long Parliam^t, Rump and Oliverian times, and had also been loaded with honour by helping the restoration, but his Lo^p was the heart of oak for honesty and fidelity in right principles, and would not bow to the idols of those days; so I may say he was *quercu non salice*. In fine, his Lo^p was well bred and well read in men and books, and had a judicious soul, which improved and cultivated all he learned, and was a complete Gen^t and Nobleman, for his virtues alone made him such. His frugality, in times of scarceness and bounty, when he had affluence, were managed with singular dexterity and address. Now, after all I have said of his Lo^p, I must not omit his facetious chearful comportm^t in society, w^h was natural and improved, much obliging and lov'd, nor leave out his courteous condecendencies, which were not so low as to disgrace his birth, station, or discretion. And his Lo^p lived in his exalted state without pride, and bore his humbled condition without dejection; for he never flattered or fawned on enemies (tho' often in their cruel hands), but argued strongly (with an even temper of spirit) the justice of his demands; and tho' they (many times) had broke the capitulations with him, yet his promises (w^h by hardships were wrung from him) were justly performed. I will now withdraw my pen, seeing I can do no better with it; having (as I think) used it enough to prove my averment that I w^d write affectionately and without flattery; as likewise having made appear what I have lately, concerning my own and the reader's speculations, in order to express our true and full ideas of his Lo^p's worth; for indeed it must be in this theme as is afore (upon the matter) said, viz. *Superat admiratio captum.*

INCIDENTAL REMEMBRANCES

OF THE

TWO ANCIENT FAMILIES

OF THE

SAVAGES,

IN THE LOWER HALF BARONY CALLED THE

Little Ards.

Collected out of my narratives of the lives of the three first Lord Viscounts Montgomerys, of the Great Ards, and of the Hon[ble]. Sir James Montgomery, of Rosemount, Knight, and out of relation of my own acts and sufferings. Written and attested this St. Taffy's day, Ano Domini 1700.

IN or about the said year 1623, the said Viscount married his daughter Jane to Pat. Savage, Esquire, whose predecessors, by charters from Queen Elizabeth, and formerly (as I am credibly informed) was stiled, and in their deeds of lands they named themselves Lords of the Little Ards, and principals of their own nation.

This family is reputed to be much above four hundred years standing in Ireland, and these Lords were men of great esteem, and had far larger estates in the county of Antrim than now they have in the Ards, so that the Earls of Antrim coveted alliance with them, and one of them married Sheely, a daughter of Portaferry, and the last Marquis thereof called those of this family cousins, and the Lord Deputy Chichester would have had the said Pat's immediate predecessor and brother, called Rowland, to marry his niece, but Russell, of Rathmullan (as is reported) made him drunk, and then wedded M[r]. Savage to his own daughter, by whom the said Rowland had one daughter, who was married to one O'Hara, a Gentleman in the county of Antrim.

This Patrick was reported to be the 17th son, and succeeded to the manor of Portaferry (by virtue of ancient deeds of feofm^t in taile) for want of heirs male by his brethern. He was the first Protestant of his family, thro' the said Viscount's care to instruct him, giving him also (as I am credibly informed) above six hundred pounds stl. as a marriage portion, which was a great sum in those days. He was captain of a troop A.D. 1641, in the regiment of horse un-under the command of his bro^r-in-law, the 2^d Viscount Montgomery ; and the said Jane dying in Anno 1647, himself also departed this life in or about the beginning of March, 1644, leaving orphants only two daughters, and Hugh, his 9th son (so he was, as the said Hugh himself told me) to the care of Sir James Montgomery, their mother's brother (who performed that part with fidelity and love) to their great advantage, compounding debts, and paying them out of the rents (which then were high) for he waved the benefit of the wardship he had of the said Hugh's estate and person, and bred them all at Rosemount (his own house) though widower, according to their qualities, till harvest, 1649, that O. C.'s army, triumphing over us all, obliged himself and son to go to Scotland, and leave them at Portaferry aforesaid.

The said Hugh being educated at Rosemount, Newtown, and Carrickfergus with me (as if we were two b{rs.}) his love and trust to me was such, that he boarded himself with me in Rosemount many years, wherein his affairs were set to rights, and he died unmarried at his sister Wilton's house in Gaalstown, in the county Westmeath, on the 10th of Feby. 1683, and was buried in the chancel of Kellucan Church, and his incumbered estate came (by virtue of the said and a cater of his own) feofmt. to his nearest kinsman, Patrick Savage, who deservedly now enjoys it, he having, by his prudent management, recovered it out of great incumbrances, especially to Mr. Maxwell, of £500 sterling, and to the said Hugh's sister, to whom he gave, by accord, £800 sterling, and brought the said estate to great improvements of rents and buildings.

This Hugh was a nimble, active man, and witty in his repartees, delighting in tennis, and such like stirring exercises, by which taking cold the sciatica seized him many years, and made him lame till his death: he was greatly beloved, particularly by our said Visct. Montgomery, and all the branches of his Lop's family. Coll. Vere Cromwell, last Earl of Ardglass, and all the gentry of Lecale, coveted his conversation, which he many times afforded to them; but all could not remove his melancholy, because his lameness and pain always much disheartened him, for he could not ride (for a long while) but on a side saddle, nor walk with ease but on a plain floor.

As to old Conn, his widow Eliss,ng Neile afores^d. she, in or about Anno 1628, married Henry Savage, of Archin, Esq. (the son of Shenickenboy, who, with his brother Elder fordarragh, were killed by the O'Neills, in the county of Antrim) This is another ancient family of that sirname in Ireland; his clan or sept were, by the Irish, called *Slut ne teneschal, i. e.* the offspring of the Seneschal, which (I am credibly told) was a title equivocal to a President, which (this family avoucheth) their first ancestor to have been over all Ulster; yet it would seem likely that this family hath risen from a 2^d brother of Savage, of Portaferry, called chief of the tribe or nation in Ireland as aforesaid, who, before Q. Eliz.'s reign, had some territories in the barony of Lecale, and also in the county of Antrim (as is credibly asserted) that family being always sore enemies to the O'Neills, and in those days this house of Archin had (it may be) the appointment of Seneschal, the office being then honb^{le}. though now despised, and they had the lands they now (and which their cadetts lately did) possess from the said

Lords of the Little Ards (as is supposed) tho' they now hold only of the Crown.

Which lands lie on the frontiers of that half barony, to be as safe out guards against the O'Neills, in the Great Ards and in Castlereagh barony, for the old castle of Archin (when built none can tell me) stands on an eminent hill, (fortified after the Danish manner of forts, and perhaps thence called Archin, (*i. e.* the head of the Ards) is almost environed by Loughcone and Ballygetgit; another castle in view of (and about a mile and an half from Archin) stands in the middle between it and Kirkistown, alias Eren Castle, later built and near the sea; the lands of both these two other castles were belonging, (by deeds from Archin family) and built by Rowland, a cadett of Archin. I say the owners of said three castles belonging to all of one blood, and by occupying by their tenants the full breadth of the said frontiers, could not but be (as thus posted, each castle within sight of the other two) a notable safe outguard to the Lords of the Litle Ards, whose lands (and the Bishops and the lands of Castlebuoy, long ago the possession of the Knights Hospitallers of St. John's of Jerusalem,) lie within them, and are surrounded by the sea, so that long running risks, the Savages were convinced that castles of stones were necessary to save castles of bones from being broken.

Moreover, that which makes the descent of Archin from Portaferry more probable is, that these Savages give the same coat armorial with the said Lords, without any distinction (that I can perceive by their seals) which they ought not to do if these likelihoods be real truths. And altho' Portaferry hath had the precedency (for a long time) yet Archin pays him no chief rent; Pat holds off the crown as aforesaid, by patent on the Com^n of Grace for remedy of defective titles, which is ratified by act of Parl^t. A^o. Car primi; but as to the right of precedency, or as to the antiquity of these two families, I cannot determine, neither will I assert any thing which may make discord among these good friends, or may savour of partiality in myself. The said Henry told me that the two first Viscounts Montgomery and Hamilton offered him five thousand pounds sterling, if he would sell his wife's (the said Ellis) jointure to them, which had been happy for him, because she died about a year after their marriage. And he next married Elizabeth Nevin, the Laird of Monkroddin's eldest daughter, niece to the first Viscountess Montg^y. and cousin-german to Lad$^{p's}$ daughter, M^{rs}. Savage, of Portaferry aforesaid.

Since which time, the said Savage families have been good friends and Protestants, only the said Henry did not put himself out of the Roman communion, but did read our Bibles; and on his death-bed, bid be assured that he would die in the faith of being saved by the merits and mediation of Jesus Christ only.

Only he not hindring any of his offspring to be Protestants, the said Sir James, his sister Jane being married to Patrick Savage aforesaid, he found his estate much in debt, and not one stone walled house in Portaferry, 'till that match, (as was credibly informed me) only some fishermen's cabins, and the old castle near it out of repair, nor any such mills as now are, and very little grain to employ one, that country being much wasted, 'till the Viscount's plantations, which was not suffered to spread into the Little Ards, 'till their own greater was furnished with inhabitants, and no trade by sea, nor no convenience for it, before the said year 1623.

Therefore the said first Viscount employed his 2d son, the said Sir James, to settle his brother and sister Savage's affairs, for themselves remained with the Viscount at Newton above 18 months, till a long but low house was built for them, and olitary garden was put in order, where they lived about two years.

In the meantime, the said Sir James was seting and leting the lands, and laying out tenements to best advantage, but the freeholders and followers, (who were mostly degenerate old English or meer Irish) were obstinate, and would not renew their deeds, nor alter their holdings from their old way. And besides these misbehaviours, they cosheered much upon Mr Savage, who bore with them, in those customs in which he was fostered; so that his debts encreased, and he was persuaded to go with his family to the Isle of Man, to live privately, but plentifully, yet much cheaper than at home, and so to be rid of Cosheerers, and to stay two years at least in Peeltown, 'till Sir James should improve his estates in rents, and build for him an house befiting his quality, and should bring his freeholders to submit to him. During this recess Sir James put the most stubborn and refractory to the law, to make them examples, for there were flaws in their deeds, and their titles were defective, sealing leases of ejectment against them, whereby they were overcome, and submitted, some paying fines, and encreasing rents, to be paid in money, besides the usual duties and services; and obliging them to the English way of living, habit, and building : others of them he brought to stoop to his lure, partly by threats to take the severity of the law against them, partly by conferences and gentle speeches, shewing also kindness to those he found willing to support their landlords. But the most effectual course he took, was to get wastes filled with British planters, on the lands, and builders of stone houses in the town, (whose examples taught the natives husbandry and industry) and to cause build mills on the loughs, tying the tenants to grind and pay the 16 grain as toll, or thertage (commonly called moultre) and other helps for reparations, which atchievements soon brought plenty at home, and traffic from abroad, and merchandize ware to the town. And afterwards he brought matters to fuller settlement and prosperity, by encouragement of which monied men had from his passing two patents to remedy Mr Savage's defective titles, and thereby ascertaining his royalties and customary profits, both at sea and land; but this last effect came not fully to pass 'till *Caroli primi*, that the last of these patents was passed.

Sir James (during Mr Savage's stay in the Island) repaired the old castle, by roofing and flooring it, and by striking out longer lights, with freestone window-cases: and also building (and joining to it) a fair slated stone house, as may be seen, with the Savage's and Montgomery's arms above the door thereof. It is now of late years much bettered (by this Mr Savage) in the contrivance within, which had not been so necessary as now, had not the old castle been almost ruined by an officer's family, which quartered therein the first three years after the Irish Rebellion. The aforesaid buildings being made, Sir James sent for Mr Savage, (who had run in debt among the merry Manxmen) but now he came home, and lived splendidly like himself, much better for the helps of additional portions given by the first Visc^t Montgomery, to discharge debts compounded for in his absence. There are some other instances (partly spoken of before) of Sir J. M. kindness to the children of the said Patrick Savage, viz. their education at Rosemount and elsewhere aforesaid, his preserving safe, and leaving to his nephew, the said Hugh (the only surviving son of the said Patrick) all his parchments and papers, and by using the benefit of the Wardship, (which he waved as aforesaid) and by his codicil annexed to his will made anno 1648 (when Monck oblidged him to render himself in London) declaring he did not intend to affect that estate as Ex^r to Lt Barry, but thereby to awe his nephew to do brotherly duty to his sisters, and to have respective regard and kindness for the family of Rosemount; which intimation made me freely give up to the said Hugh, all his father's bonds for the debt due to the said Barry; and for the same ends I have endeavourd and shewn my love and respects to the present Mr Savage, and his late father of Ballyvarley.

In all the fermentation raised by the Covenant teachers, against the peaceable Irish Papists in the Lower Ards, yet Sir James Montgomery still protected them, and procured the Lord Conway's order, dated De^cr. 1642, that only bonds should be taken of Henry Savage, of Archin, Esq. for the delivery of the arms in his house at any time when called for, and the rest of the Papists to be disarmed, which privilege Sir James got confirmed and enlarged on another occasion, and there was need and reason for granting that safeguard, because of the unruly Scottish mob and common soldiers, who would make the pretence of searchiag for arms and ammunition, an opportunity to quarrel and plunder; this Gentlemn. was loyal and moderate in his Romish religion, and read the Holy Scriptures, and in his death bed, (whereon he lay long,) assured me that he trusted for salvation only to the merits and mediation of Jesus Christ. He kept no images in his house, nor used beads at his prayers, (that ever I could see or hear of,) and he said if he had any such images in picture, he would meditate on, but not worship them. He used to say that invocation of saints was needless, (although it were supposed they heard us or knew our wants,) because he was sure his Saviour was God all sufficient, and our intercessor as man and priest.

He was (by marriage,) next cousin to our 2d Visc^t. and to Sir James Montg^y. and that was related also to some of his reg^t. officers, to whom he was kind and hospitable to the rest; yet all this did not release the fear he had of the vulgar people and the inferior officers, wherefore the 3d Visc^t. and Sir James, at the league in Armagh, signed an order, dated the 22d August, 1644, directed to Quarter-master John Hamill, prohibiting all persons whatsoever to give any disturbance to the person of Henry Savage aforesaid, or to his wife, children, servants, tenants, houses, or goods, and requiring restitution to be made if any thing hath been seized or taken from him or them, as all persons concerned should answer for disobeying this their order, requiring and ordering the officers and soldiers to give assistance for recovery of any thing so taken, and to protect him and his aforesaid from such injuries; for granting which order Sir James was complained of and made to answer (and other trivial dust was raised against him,) before Sir Robert Meredith, Sir Robert King, and Sir John Clotworthy, commr[s]. of Parliament, for these parts of Ireland, Anno. 1646. Thus worth is attended with envy and obloquy—such malice had the Covenanters against them both.

At Rosemount I found my cousin, Hugh Savage, of Portaferry, in May, 1644, and his two sisters. The women were taught vocal and instrumental music by Thomas Naule, adduced to that end, and they had a schoolm[rs]. to other purposes, and we had for our teacher, Mr. Alexander Boid, (and Master in the liberal Arts, who had travelled into France, as tutor to Mr. Eclin of Ardquin's sons); we had divers sons of Henry Savage aforesaid, our cousin, at school with us, and we the males were removed to the great school of Newtown, Mr. Boid having the oversight of my cousins, the Savages, and me.

Soon after Benburd fight, June, Anno. 1646, my cousin, Hugh, and his sister and myself, were removed to Carrickfergus; they to be under their aunt the 2d Viscountess Montg[y's]. care; for she lived there with her 2d husband, Maj^r. Genl. Robt. Monro, and we were put to shoool under Mr. George Leslie, (the B^p. of Down's brother,) having the said Mr. Boid, with my said cousin, Hugh and me, as our tutor.

At my first coming to London from Holland, I met with my said cousin Savage of Portaferry, and was steadable to him, his servant Plunket being sent home for supply of monies.

I conclude the description of this territory, with brief remargats of the Savages therein, viz.

The lower half barony was planted by a colony and recruits of the English, not long after de Courcey pierced unto their parts of Ulster and sacked Downpatrick. The chief name and commander of that colony, with the assistance of the Russells, Fitzsimmons, Audleys, Jordans, and Welshes, &c. in Lecale, and of the Whites and others in the county Antrim, (many of which families depended on, and were as the Smyths *alias* M'Gowans,) fosterers and followers of the Savages. They have hitherto kept their ground in the Ards, against all the incursions of the O'Neills and divers clans their vassals, although the York and Lancastrian broils drew many of their people to take the part they best wished to, which was the York side.

The chief of those Savages, in grants from themselves, were stiled (in Q. Elizabeth's time,) Lords of the Little Ards, and *principales suæ nationis;* I have seen a letter from the Lord Dept[y]. Chichester, to Savage of Portaferry, directed thus, viz.

His castle is that of Portaferry aforesaid, the largest old pile of them all, and a fair slated house, built A°. 1635, by the care of Sir J. M[y]. the reputed and so called then being Pat. who married a daughter of the first Visc[t]. Montgomery of the Great Ards, and the Earl of Antrim, in the said Q'[s]. time, married Sheely, a daughter of one of those Lords. Other ancient family of the Savages, is that of Archin Castle, it is of good account and hath another, as they called Sketrick, the oldest, (as is said) of them all, and 13 islands in Lough Coen, both are very tenable for war, (if fortified and repaired) of whose family a cadet called Rowland, (an officer of the Queen's army against the Irish.) He, since K. James's entry into England, built the two castles of Ballygalgit and Kirkiston, *alias* Erew, being high square piles, as are usual in Ireland, and gave the same (with lands adjoining) to two of his sons. This family of Arkeen have matched their sons creditably, (as I am informed;) this I know, that Henry aforesaid, grandfather to Hugh Savage, Esq. purchaser, (as it were,) and inheritor of Arkeen, and Richard his brother, were married to the two sisters, nieces to said 1st Visc[tss]. Montgomery, and daughters to Nevin of Monkroddin, near Irvine in Scotland, wedlocks, in old times, being made more for creditable and strengthening alliances than for money. About all these castles are divers Irish Papists, but inconsiderable, being mixed with British Protestants in this territory. The Savages of the Ards, have always been a stout and warlike people, loyal to the crown of England, who, however they might have had some few civil broils or contests among themselves, on acount of the Tannestry custom, when they were out of fear of the O'Neills, and so became, as many noble English families in Leinster, Munster, and Connaught, too much addicted to the Irish customs, feuds, and exactions, yet of a long time past and now they are as much civilized as the British, (perhaps the more since having married with these nations,) and they do live decently and conformably to the church re-established by law, and enjoy good houses, orchards, and enclosed fields, which they improve and hold all the possession they had at the entry of K. Ja[s] aforesaid, except Kirkistown and the lands adjoining before men[d], which nevertheless of the late said purchase made thereof, doth pay chief rentto the Savages of Archeen, and do suit and service to the Courts Leet and Baron in said Manor thereof, they having taken out letters patent, pursuant to the Comm[rs]. of Grace, for defective titles granted in the reign of the Royal Martyr of glorious memory.

Another remark, I made on occasion of vindicating my liberty in the way of writing my sirname, and I bring in these Savages among others—for an instance I write thus :

The late Mr. Savage, his ancestor, *imo*, July A[o]. 1573, by his Latin charter to Denis Smith, wrote himself *Patricius filius et heras Rowland defuncte suæ, nationis principalis & signes ;* his subscription to that deed, Patrick Savage and the same Patrick, the 17th of the said month and year, in a bond made to Phelimy Smith, the 15th of the said Q. Eliz. subscribes Pat. Savage, and his successor the late Patrick, and his said son Hugh wrote their sirnames, Savadge. Item Henry of Archeen, in a deed dated 15th Jacobi, (whereof I saw the counterpart,) made to Rowland of Ballygalgot, his sirname is spelled Savadge, also in another deed, from the said Henry himself, writes Savadge, item 6th Junii, A°. 1641, Edmund Duff of Derri, and Margaret his wife; he was grand uncle to the present Mr. Savage of Portaferry, subscribes their names Savadge, but both Portaferry and Archeen do now write Savage.

The Frenchmen of that name write Saavage (this word sounding after their pronunciation, as if we should write it Sovage,) which they acknowledge to be an adjective noun, or word to signify a wild creature. Now, may I not think that the Eng^d and Irel^d people of this sirname brought themselves from the French, and also from the ancient English way which last) was to write Salvage, that likewise imports wild or untamed, to shelter themselves under the similitude of the French word afores^d, lest if at all understood by the vulgar, or that they brought in the letter D to make the sirname vary from both the other ways of spelling it, to shun the imputation of wildness, imposed on them by the said French and ancient English way of writing it. However it be, I may say that there needs no tergiversation on that account, because many brave men think it no disgrace to be of the sirname of Wildman, for perhaps it was given so at first, when sirnames came to be in frequent use and vogue, from the representation of such alike untamed uncloathed man depicted in their shield of arms, and thus the Deburgos, Fitzursulas, and in many others obtained their sirnames, which yet adhere to their offspring.

This I am sure of, that our Savadges, their Lyons Rampant are as wild and untamed like, (being in that positure, and armed and langued Gules) and are seldomer if ever reclaimable from their ferity, as the wildest man that ever ran frantic and naked out of doors to the woods and mountains.

FINIS.

S^{r.}

ACCORDING to my promise, I send to you all the foregoing Remembrancers (worth your notice) which are any where scattered in my writings, that they may obtain a room in your *escritoiri*, to be a vindication that I have writ nothing for my posterity's perusal which may disgust your family, if I should be aspersed so to have done. The paper on every leaf is attested by the first letters of my name and sirname, as I usually subscribe them in letters: miss eve and the whole ten pages is transcribed from my original, and now com-

pared with me by Mr Rob Walker, school-
master in your town.
And is presented by,
S
Your affect^e Friend and Servt
WILL. MONTGOMERY.
For Patrick Savadge of
Portaferry, Esqre
(A true copy from the Original.)

ALTARE VOTIVUM.
An humble Doxology to the holy and undivided Trinity
in Unity, the only one God over all things (ever way)
most blessed, for ever and ever—amen.

Adore the Father of all things,
As Lord of Lords and King of Kings,
For he who sits upon the throne
Hath absolute dominion,
And rules the world with wisdom's love,
By fiats of Almighty pow'r;
Ascribe all glory to the Son,
By him was our redemption done;
His mercy, love, and truth recite,
Which boundless are, and infinite,
Th' eternal word and lamb who was
Slain for our sins and happiness.
The spirit's comforts, O! declare,
By Him, we pure and holy are—
He guides to the right and shields from wrongs,
Extol him with most grateful songs,
For He proceeds from both, and's one,
God, with the Father and the Son.

MASCHIL.

Strive with this God and persons three,
To live (then) everlastingly,
And to this ancient of days,
Sing chearful Halelujahs.
My soul, O! take thy chief delight,
Of this, to think, to speak, and write—
Thou art his gift and shall return again,
Judged (as thou dost) to endless joy and pain.

THE AUTHOR'S SLENDER OFFERING TO HIS JEHOVAH.

I praise and thank thee, Lord, who doth supply
My wants, when I don't think thy help so nigh;
Ten thousand times and more, my hopes have found,
Thy pity, and thy goodness, without bounds,
Let me not thee provoke, to anger, Lord,
Who so much mercy such sweet hopes afford;
All mine are thine, myself, too, is thy lone,
I now resign, O! save and take thine own,
By many titles due and bound to thee,
Thy poor, sincere servant, Montgomery.
        Amen and amen.

To fill up blanks, I have here inserted (as a corollary *(Hybernice a Duragh)* to the foregoing pages) this sudden meditation, excogitated at Donaghadee on Sunday morning, the 20th Jan. 1699—1700, and then rough drawn before sermon, being transcribed after evening service the same day, touching the innate desire of perpetuity naturally rooted in all mankind, which, to me, is one strong argument to prove the immortality of our souls.

Thou thinking man who would'st for ever live,
Dost from two fountain heads thyself derive,
And in one stream, glides through this worldly life,
With much self-fondness and too little strife;
Thou art of form and brittle matter made,
(Which thoughts and accidents do still invade)
Thy different parts are wonderfully join'd,
But by what thongs, none tell us how combin'd—
Nor how thy earthy substance grows and's fed,
(By food digested) prop'd up, nourished—
Nor why thy form doth all the powers contain
Of thy whole matter, for therein remain
Two distinct knowledges and wills in one,
(Which hath a three lived) composition.
 The mind aspires to live with God on high,
 Body would stay on earth and never die,
 (Which is a foolish, selfish, vanity.)
O, cornes of flesh, go to your dust again,
And dy and rise the most refined grain;
Return, O, everlasting spirit, to thy sire,
He can (with pleasures) fill thy strong and large desires,
Or else can thee torment (as mortals are) by fires—
After this life he'll fully thee restore
To be one person as thou wast before;
That he should take his way and time, 'tis fit
Thou know'st, then humbly wait and look for it;
For, if thou lov'st him, and obey his word,
He will thee blessed happiness afford,
And make thy corps (like Christ's flesh) glorious be,
T' enjoy (and be with him) eternally.
Rosemount, September 1701.

HONBLE SIR,

To end (as I begun) with an address, it is not so much to inform your knowledge, which is universal, and hath digested far more than I have read and writ, but to refresh your memory, for which I crave to use St. Peter's apology, made to the scattered Jews, in his 2d epis. iii. chap. ver. 1, and, in the same epis. i. chap. verses 12, 13, 14, 15.) *parva silicet componere, magnes.*

Dear Sir! Man dies not a whit the sooner, that he prepares a grave vault, a coffin, a winding sheet, shroud, with other necessarys and decencies (according to his own mind) for his funeral; thereby leaving as little ground as he can for another to boast of, in performing that last duty to his body.

Yet the sooner that the impotent, infirm or aged person, doth make these provisions, the wiseleir it is done. In health let us look for sickness and death, because he will have the less to think of when God's visitation comes, which may be unforeseen and quickly dispatching.

Furthermore, by his frequent meditations and actions relating to his dissolution and departure, he will *(obere mortem)* meet them and their terrors the more courageously, and with chearfuller resignations of himself unto God, esteeming and expecting that change to be, but as a door to an happy eternity of a better life.

Now, Sir! after this act of faith as to his soul's concerns, he may lawfully and commendably, as he ought, to take some care, but not too solicitously, of his fame, because a good name is preferred to great riches—Prov. 22, i. and it must not be slighted or neglected.

The Emp^r. Cha^r. the 5th, caused make an an obit for himself, and personally joined in the funeral solemnity, and prayed most devoutly for the rest of his soul, which set all the congregation a weeping and mourning. He also had prepared his tomb *(Humili Tam jacet in vina)* and caused it be inscribed with these words, viz.: *Quis est inlus, Carolus Quintus.* And this was well enough for so eminent and well-known a personage as he was, but private men are as good Christians as he, and ought to have some of their virtues mentioned (as a diagram) on their grave stone, for the honour, emulation, and imitation of their posterity.

Caius Caesar on his lection of Alex^r. the Great of Macedon's monumental epithets, was inflamed with ambitious desires and resolutions to act heroically.

D^r. S^r. I ask leave to beg, that this following brief (and, indeed, too short coming an) epitaph, (unless one more elegant and full be provided) may be engraven on your tombstone, for I know of none, or but few at the cost and pains to do the like, (because out of sight is out of mind often) I must acknowledge it will lisp out, but only a small parcel of your worth, yet may be accepted rather than want altogether.

This one, of my shallow contrivance, will (at least ways) shew my aim and respects to your character, which will be attested also by many (I say) very many more, than
   Dear Sir,
    Your very affectionate
     Friend and servant,
      WILL. MONTGOMERY.

In semper, Honoratum, nec non, pro retore et Generositate Dotum, Corporis Atque Animi, bene admodum Reputatum et Approbatum virum, nempe Honorabilem Franciscum Annesley, de Clough prope Dundrummi Arcem, in Comitate, Douni, Qui ex hac luce migravit, in Cœlis, Anno Æræ Christianæ MDCCI. vitæ suæ LXXII. ΕΠΙΤΑΦΙΟΥ.

Qui fide dignus, erat vir Laude et Amore Piorum
Ille nec Invidium, nec capit obloquium.
Or thus, for and instead of the last above line you may take this hexameter to make the whole epitaph heroic.
Non odium meruit multominus obloquium ve.
   { Teste me Gul. Montgomery de
     Rosemount Arm.
       W. M.

A DESCRIPTION
OF THE BARONY CALLED THE
ARDS,
DEDICATED UNTO
Patrick Savage, of Portneferry, Esq.
BY
WILLIAM MONTGOMERY, ESQ.
Anno Domi Christi 1701.

THE barony of Ards is thick and well peopled, being about seventeen miles long and three broade, except between Gray Abbey and Ballywalter, where it is narrowest. It is separated (on the south end thereof) from ye barony of Lecahill by a great and swift flux and reflux of the sea (thence called Stronfoord River) a muskett shott over. In w^h, neare ye Ards side, under an hill (by the Irish) called Bankmore, there is a whirlpool or eddy of the returning or incoming tides, called (by the Scotts) the Rowting Well (from the sound it makes sometimes in calme weather), near to which, if small boats come, they will be sucked in and swallowed up, except about full sea, when the water is smelt and even; a great vessel, with top sailes and a good gale, doth hardly pass through it, without being laid about, yet we have not heard of one boat or person lost by it, for sailers and fishermen shun that place.

From thence, in a mile, stands the Thursday mercat town of Portneferry, where store of great barques belonging to it doo anchor, and at half ebb ly dry; hence, and from the daily passage to ye other land, perhapps the town was so called. Here was a wooden kay, which one of the proprietors pulled up, selling the timber for building of Drogheda bridge (is reported), because Kildare's family had got the custom-house fixed at his town of Strongfoord.

About half a quarter of a league up ye river, great shipps may saile to a cape (or lands end) at the entry of Logh Coan, which, from an hill that extends its taile in the s^d river, is called Ballyhendry point, giving under shelter thereof a spacious place to ride in at anchor, safe from ye north and east wind's fury.

Some minors offered to ye late M^r. Savadge to find good coales in ye bank above this place, but want of money and encouragement hath hindered the tryall thereof.

There is another such harbouring place (just opposite thereunto) on Lecahill side of the river, called (from a castle above it) Audley's Roade, and a little shallow bay contiguous to it; in the bottom whereof is a pleasant seat, good buildings and plantations, called Castleward.

On the same side stands Strongfoord town, where is the residence of a collector for excise; under which town there is a creek or small bay for barks to anchor in (five faddom deep almost) at lowest ebb. This poole is fenced with a large rock, called Swan's Island, and is out of the current of the s^d river.

The moon at due south causeth high water at ye bar of the said river, which is not safe to be attempted by strangers but at half flood, which comes from the northward, and in calm weather the outgoing strong current against ye inblowing wind makes rough seas.

The barrony is divided in lower and upper (otherwise called the Little and Great) Ards, the former hath ye parishes of Ballyhalbert and Ballywalter adjected to it in all assess^{nts}. of public taxes, to make it bear equally with ye other parts of the barrony.

The said Little Ards, next Lecahill, sends (every winter) great store of good wheate, beare, oats and barley to Dublin and elswhere; and all the eastern coast thereof (from whence Scotland and the Isle of Man are seen, and is but four hours sailing distant) abounds with fishes, as herrings, in harvest, also codd, ling, mackerel, barins, lythes, blockans, lobsters, crabbs, gray lords (which are near as big as codds) whiteing, haddocks, plaice and large dogg fish, &c. and hath good cattle, especially sheep w^h (feeding often on ye sea oare) keep whollsome and fatt all ye winter and spring time; within the said land are many fresh loughs, in which are store of pike and eeles, ducks, teel, widgeon and swans.

It is supposed that the ducks and widgeons have brought into these loughs and turff pitts of the spawn of these pikes on their feathers, because in many places no stream runs into or from those waters, to bring that fish therin.

The hills, wherof some be craggy and full of furzes and heath, and the corn and pasture fields, afford partridge, quails, curlew, and plover, of both sorts, and abundance of hares, and some store of rabbits, and no want of foxes.

This whole territory doth much want fewell, for with great pains they make it of bogg mudd, clapped together and formed with hands, and turned often to dry in the sun; but the gentry supply their parlours and lodging rather with coals from England or Scotland.

THE LOWER ARDS.

This lower half barony was planted by a colony and recruits of the English not long after De Ceurcy pierced into those parts of Ulster and sacked Down Patrick.

The chief name and commander of that colony was SAVAGE who with the assistances of y[e] Russels, Ffitzsymonds, Audleys, Jordans and Welshes, &c. in Lecahill, and of the Whyts and others in the county of Antrim, many of which familys depended on and were (as y[e] Smiths and M[c]Gowans) fosterers or followers of the Savages; they have hitherto kept their ground in the little Ards ag[t]. all y[e] incursions of the Oneils and divers clanns their vassalls: altho' the York and Lancastrian broils drew many of their people to take y[e] part the wished best to, which was the Yorke side.

The chief of these Savadges in grants from themselves were stiled in Queen Eliz: time, Lords of the little Ards, and *Principalis suæ Nationis.* "I have a letter from the L[d] Deputy Chichester stileing on of them L[d] in the direction on thereof to him. This family had great quantitys of lands in y[e] county of Antrim of which their were defeated by one of their sonns-in-law called   who joyned

c c

with y⁰ McDonnells family, and resigned to hold of them. There is Castlesavage now y⁰ Custom house in Carrickfergus, and M^r· Savage of Anacloy now hath freehold tenem^ts, in that town."

This Lord's Castle is that of Portnoferry, the largest old pile of them all, and he hath a fair slated house built A° 1635, by ye care of Sr James Montgomery added thereunto, for the reputed Lord (and so call them) being Patrick, who marryed a daughter of ye first Ld Visc^t Montgomery of the great Ards. And ye Earle of Antrim, in ye s^d Queen's raigne, marryed Sheely Savage, a daughter of one of those chiefs in Portnoferry, perhaps to fortyfy his title to ye said lands resigned by McQuillan affores^d and to have allyance.

An other ancient family of the Savages is that of Ardkin castle: It is of good account, and hath also another castle called Scatrick (ye oldest pile of this family as is said) and thirteen islands in Louth Coan; both castles are tenable if fortified and repaired. Of this family one Cadet named Rouland, an officer in the s^d Queens wars ag^t, the Irish, hath (since King James entry into England,) built ye two castles of B. gallgot and Kirkestone (being high square piles) and gave the shore with lands adjoining unto two of his sons.

This family of Ardkin hath matched their sons creditably, (as I have heard), and this I know that Henry (grandfather to H. Savage now inhabiting Ardken) and his brother Richard were married to two sisters, neices to y[e] first Vic[tss.] Montgomery, and daughters to Tho[s] Nevin, Laird of Monkroddin, neare Irwin, in Scotland, an ancient worshipfull family; matches for wedlock (in those former times) being made more for creditable and strengthening allyances than for money.

About these castles, are divers Irish Papist households (but inconsiderable), being mingled with Brittish Protestants.

Neare Portneferry (northwestward) is y[e] old Abbey of Ardquin, with seven towns y[e] Bps. lands, seased to John Echlin, Esq. whose great grandfather, (of the same s[r] name) was Bishop of Down and Connor at y[e] beginning of y[e] Brittish plantation under King James afores[d]. These lands are said to have been given to y[e] Church by Savage of Portneferry, in an expiatory devotion or penetentiary benevolence, when all Ireland was popish.

The said John Echlin, Esq. hath also seven or eight townlands in freehold belonging to a great ruined pile called Castleboy, one of the seats of the prior of S[t] Johns of Jerusalem, which hath a mannor court also, but by which of y[e]

Savadge's donation, I know not: but it is environed by Ardkin lands. There are some inferior households of ye Echlins which are well to pass, and thrive under their chief (as I may call) the s^d John, whose younger brother is one of the Barrons in ye Exchequer.

There is likewise on the eastern shore (one league from ye s^d Barr) Cottins bay, als. Quintin bay Castle w^h commands ye bay, that is capable to receive a bark of forty tunns burthen. Sr James Montgomery of Rosemount purchased the same, and lands adjoining therunto, from Dualtagh Smith, a depender on ye Savadges of Portneferry, in whose mannor it is: and ye s^d Sr James roofed and floored ye castle, and made freestone window cases, &c. therin: and built ye baron, and flankers, and kitchen walls contiguous; all w^h, Wm Montgomery, Esqr, and his son James (joyning in ye sale) sold unto Mr George Ross, who lives at Carney, part of the premises.

Neare it is a ruined pile called Newcastle, formerly belonging unto
another dependant of Portneferry, which, wth diverse town lands adjoining, now doth belong to James Hamilton of Bangor, Esqr.

Thence on ye same coast (three miles northward) stands Kirkestown castle afores^d, which, wth B, gallgott and Quintin Bay, are the only ones in repair in this half barrony whose garden walls are washed with a pleasant fresh lough near the sea, and opposit to ye rock. James McGill of Ballymonestragh, Esqr improved this place very much, by building garden walls, and houses, and repairing in and about. He purchased ye same, and some lands adjoyning, from ye grandson of ye s^d Rouland: and hath also built a wind miln there, wh^h is seen farr off at sea, and serves in day-time in good steade as a land-mark for saylors to avoyd the north and south rocks, wh^h are noted in all mapps for the misfortunes that ships, especially forreigners, have had on them, in stormy and dark weather: so that it were to be wished that a light house were erected and maintained there.

Next lyes a small island called Green Isle, and beyond it a lesser patch of rocky land called Burialh; wh^h are the most easterly parts of Ireland. The island being a place where vessels often ly at anchor, expecting the desired wind to runn their begun cours. This is the furthest north extent of this lower half barrony, wh^h hath in it the small parishes hereafter named, viz. Bally Phillip, B^r Trustan, Woughter, Slanes, Castleboy, Ardquin, and Ardkin, all which are now served at Porteferry, w^h only hath a large church in good repaire, the rest are unroofed.

I conclude the description of the s^d territory, with brief remarks on the SAVAGES afores^d, vizt, that they have always been a stout and warlike people, loyal to ye crown of England. Who, however they might have had some few civill broils amongst themselves, on account of ye Tannestry custom, when they were out of fear of ye O'Neils, and so become, as many noble English families in Leinster, Mounster, and Connaught, too much addicted to ye Irish customs, fewds, and exactions; yet of a long time past, and now, they are as much civilized as the Brittish (perhaps for having marryed with those nations), and doo live decently and conformably to ye church re-established by law, and do enjoy good houses, orchards, and enclosed fields, wch they improve, and hold all the possession they had at ye entry of King James as aforesaid, except Kirkestown, also Erow and the lands adjoyning (before mentioned) w^h nevertheless of ye s^d purchase made thereof, doth pay chief rent to ye castle of Ardkin, and doth suite to ye courts leet and barron of ye mannor thereof. The said Henry haveing taken out letters patents (as Patrick of Porteferry also did) pursuant to ye com^n of grace, for remedy of defective titles, granted by King Charles ye martire of glorious memory. And so here I stop my further observations, having wrott els'where other matters to ye advantage of ye s^d two familys not proper in this place.

Then next to ye lower half barrony, mearing on ye north, is ye GREAT ARDS, wherein are first the parishes of B. Halbert and Bally Walter: in this lays a smal village of the same name, a slate quarry, a creek for smal two sail boates, and a place very fit for a great harbour, if a kay (as was spoken of in y^e last Earle of Clanbrazill's time) were built there. They now belong to Sr Robert Hamilton's son, Mr Hans.

In these parishes are handsom slated houses lately built by John Bailie, Hugh Montgomery, Esqr and Mr Hugh Hamill, Gen^t$_s$, raised by them from y^e ground on their respective fee farms, all within prospect of the firth between Scotland and Ireland; and Mr Hugh Maxwell is now rearing a new edifice on his fee farm lands in B. Halbert parish.

THE UPPER ARDS.

Contiguous, and a little more northerly on y^e west side of this half barrony, is Gray Abby parish, half wherof by letters pattents from

King Charles ye First, belonged to S^r. James Montgomery, K^nt. and descended from him to his son W^m. who conveyed the same unto his son James, in which was a double roofed house (now burned) and a baron and fower flankers, with bakeing, and brewing houses, stables, and other needful office houses; they are built after the forraigne and English manner; with outer and inner courts walled about, and surrounded w^h pleasant gardens, orchards, meadows and pasture inclosures under view of, ye said house called Rosemount, from w^h ye mannor taketh name. "The same was finished by ye s^d Sr James A^o. Dom^i. 1634, only some small convenient additions of building and orchards are made by ye s^d William, and improved lately by his s^d son James.

King James afores^d granted a port to be at Grey Abby islands, with pilotage, anchorage, keelage and other advantages and priviledges to the same, and licenced exportation of all native commodities thereout, (except Irish yarn) but there is no trade there at this time. The market day of Greyabby village is on Friday, but as little regarded as the port.

Neare and in view of Rosemount house, are ye walls of a large abby of curious work (ruinated in Tireowen's rebellion); it is called in inquisitions and patents Abathium de fuga

Dei; in Irish, Monestrelea, in English, Gray (or Hoare) Abby, from the order of fryars who enjoyed it; and had, in ancient times, belonging thereunto, all its own parish, both in Spiritualibus et temporalibus conferred by De Courcy at ye inshanes of his wife, the King of the Isle of Man's daughter, as Cambden reports (if I remember aright) in the annales of that island. To this abby belonged also diverss lands and tithes in ye county of Antrim, viz. out of Ballymena.

And also, tithes in the Lower Ards and Lecahill, w^h I can name; and also, (as tradition reports) in ye Isle of Man (likely by ye s^d De Courcy's wives gift) and in the High Lands of Scotland; near this abby is a spring of most excellent water, over which y^e s^d W^m built a little cover, and there are many other good ones in y^e fields thereabouts.

Campion reports, page 69, that the s^d Abby, Innis and Comer were built Annis D$^{mi.}$ 1198 and 1199; but, in all my researches, I could not find figures, or any stones, either of y^e abbey or in y^e castles afores^d, to denote the year when they were erected, and who views y^e walls and ruines of this monastry, will allow many years to the building of it.

The church thereof was in part roofed and slated and re-edifyed, and a yeard thereunto walled about, and a competent stipend given for that by ye s^d first Lord Montgomery; and, in Anno D^{ni} 1685 it was new roofed again by ye heirs of Wm Montgomery, and by contributions of gent. concerned therein.

About a mile thence is a small ruined abby, with some lands adjoining (called Blackabby) from fryars of that coloured habit, belonging to the Lord Primate in right of his See of Ardmagh, hitherto leased to and still in possession of ye Lords Montgomerys; the rest of this parish (called Temple Cron lands) being a thousand acres at 18 foot and 9 inches to ye perch, belongs to Hugh Colvill, Esqr as purchased by his late father, Sr Robt Colvill, Kn^t.

Then is ye parish of Donaghadee (in Irish called Down da ghee, that is, ye buriall mount of ye too worthys); this is ye large mannor of Montgomery, wholly belonging to ye Earle of Mount Alexander.

In ye town (of ye same name with ye parish) is ye said Earle's slated house and walled garden, and office houses adjoining to it. Also, there is a fair slated church (in shape of St George his cross) having four roofes meeting in ye midle and a square bell tower at ye north end of it. Also, here is a great kay for barks (a great work indeed) 'w^h with ye church, was built by ye s^d Lord Montgomery, and here is an handsom mercat town w^h is ye usuall port for transportation of horses and cattle to England, and for trading elsewhere. It is ye nearest to Portpatrick, in Scotland, and is a Collector's custom house port.

This town hath bred and now hath many good navigators by means of allowances, w^h ye s^d present Earle gave unto Mr Robert Watson, who teacheth that art very well; and is a good writing master and arithmetician, and skilled in keeping merch^ts books.

About a mile and an half from ye town southwards, is Patrick Montgomery, Esq. His house of Creboy, now conveyed to his eldest son, Capt. John, slated and seen a far off at sea, having orchards, and inclosiures, and his lands about it, and within a mile and half thence are quarries, the slate of which are used at Belfast, Carrickfergus, and elsewhere. Neare this place are ye ruins of a small church, called Temple Patrick, where it is said S^t. Patrick first landed in Ireland; there is his well also, and other traditions among ye Irish concerning it.

About a mile westward from ye house of Creboy, (which the Irish so called it from ye soil, which is yellow clay,) there is ye house and lands of Gransheo, orchards and grounds well inclosed, lately belonging to Major Hugh Montgomery, whose grandfather was descended of the family of Braidstaine, and was cousin-german to the first Lord Montgomery, who was 6th Laird of that place and family; the said house end lands of Gransheo, now belongs to W[m]. Montgomery of Maghera, in y[e] county of Derry, as his fee farm, being son-and-heir to the said Major Hugh, who also possessed y[e] said Maghera in lease from y[e] B. P.

Then about two miles from Donagadee, is James   Esq[r]. his great house of Portavo, and large office houses—all of stone, brick, and lime, slated; gardens walled in, and fenced orchards and pastures—all his own erection, since K. Ch. y[e] 2[nds] the happy restoration, all wh[h] and his estate in lands, he conveyed by feofment to his coson Geo. Ross, called Gaaston, himself wanting heirs of his own body.

In view of Portavo are y[e] Copeland Isles, part of his estate, being convenient places for a deer-park, warrons, and other chaces, now well inhabited.

About a mile more northerly is Graham's Port, (a kay and harbour for small barques,)

These three last mentioned places are ı
gor parish, wh^h belonged to ye s^d Earle of Clanbrasil, but now unto James Hamilton, Esq.

And from thence neare two miles distant, the next considerable is a town corporate (a mercat one) of the same name with the parish. It hath a provost, twelve burgesses, and freemen. It sends two men chosen by ye burgesses and provost to sitt in Parliam^t. It hath denomination from an acient monastry, (whereof some walls yet stand,) believed to be the mother (at least ye eldest daughter,) of Banchor in Wales.

Here is a large church and a bell tower, which were part of ye monkish buildings, but raised out of its rubbish, much re-edified and wholely roofed and slated, by James, first Visc^t. Claneboye, who also built a great stable and other houses, and planted orchards and fenced grounds near unto the same, and is a noble seat capable of improvement, w^h ye s^d Esq. hath begunn.

In the middle of this town is a large lofted slated house, w^h. may serve a master who loatheth Latin to live in, and students for a schoole.

At ye end of ye town is a small bay for barques, and on it a large slated house double lofted, intended at first for a custom-house, both built by ye said Lord Claneboye, from hence is an usual passage to Carrickfergus.

Now having traced all the north-east coast of ye whole barrony, lett us note—that all along from hence to the barr of Strongford river, the inhabitants do manure and dung the the land wi^h sea oar, (by them called tangle,) w^h. being spread on it and plowed down, makes winter grain and summer barley grow in abundance, cleane without weeds, cocle or tares. The roads are pleasant and smooth in depth of winter. In this whole barr. there are no great graziers, as in other parts of Ireland, but every man grazeth and ploweth with his own farm.

Now returning from Gray Abby, (which is near ye center and on ye west side of this barrony,) wee come next to view the PARISH OF NEWTOWN, w^h. is a large mannor. The town of the same name is called mostly Ballyno; it is five miles of good smooth way distant from Gray Abby, three from Comer, three from Bangor, and six from Belfast. It on Saturday hath a weekly good mercat, &c. is incorporated, sends men to Parliament, &c. as Bangor doth.

Herein is a faire, neate, circular, octogonal building, (all hewn freestone) carved, painted, and guilded it was in diverse parts therof, with a smal doore and stairs within it, ascending to a batlement, which is brest high from y^e vault, and from y^e pavement of y^e s^d vault issue severall spouts carved wth antique heads, w^h at y^e coronation and nativity days of our kings, have dissembogued wine to y_e glad and merry multitude. In y^e middle of this fabric, upon y^e vault afores^d, stands a pillar of hewn stones of eight squares, about twenty foot high, with a lyon seyant on the topp. This whole piece of work is called y^e mercat cross: whence are made publiq (with y^e town solemnitys) all proclamations that come from our chief governor, and their own town business which needs an outcry.

The body of this building (which is seen of four streets) hath ye King's arms fronting to ye great street, with this subscription, ' These arms which rebells beat down and defaced, are by this loyall burrow now replaced.' And the town arms on another square therof thus blazoned, Azure a crescent wth both horns upwards proper, from ye nombrill wherof ariseth a dexter arm and hand, armed, holding a flower de luce, reaching to ye cheif of ye feild, or: with this motto, viz. *Tous-jours croisant;* it being Sr James Montgomery's contrivance, also other shields armoriall belonging to y^e s^d first Visc^t Montg. and his matches and alleys, wth the badges of these kingdoms, on y^e rest of y^e squares aforesaid.

William Montgomery of Rosemount, Esqr being this town's burgess in Parliam^t, A$_o$ D^m 1662, bestowed the king's arms painted in oyle and guilded, and a large seale to serve this town hall and corporation.

In this town, which hath good springs and pump wells, with a brook or bourn runing at each end of y^e great street, there is a great school, wth good encouragement of an annual stipend for a master of arts, to teach Latin, Greek, and Logicks, continued by ye s^d Sr Robert Collvill, who was purchaser and proprietor of ye said town, and of all ye lands in this parish, who, by help of a contrabution from his tenants, hath built a stately mercat house, fitt for ye sessions of ye county.

Here is also a fair long church, part wherof were ye walls of a priory, but new walls were erected, and a new church (w^h hath a square tower five storys high, and a great bell in it, joyned without any partition, but large freestone pillars and arches; all w^h now roofed, sclated, and made by ye s^d first Lord Montgomery, (in his life-time and by his order and legacys after his death) and Sr Robert Colvil hath made a beautifull large chappell at ye eastmost end of the s^d church, w^h formerly was not used for divine service; but there ly the bones of the three first Lords Montgomerys, the two first Ladys, and many of their familys. The s^d Sr Robt hath built a large burial place, wherin himself and his third lady are layd above ground.

Contiguous to ye s^d old church walls (where stood ye Lord's house, accidentally burned, A^o D^{mi} 1664) the s^d Sr Robert hath (from ye foundation) built up one double roofed house, stables, coach houses, and all other necessary or convenient edifices, for brewing, bakeing, washing, hunting, hawking, pleasure-rooms, and pigeon-houses, &c. with inner, outer, and back courts: and a spacious well planted olitory, fruit and pleasant flower gardens, w^h have a fish pond, spring wells, (thence conveyed in conduit pipes to y^e kitchen court) long broad sanded without as well as within, and a bowling green; all therof walled about, and set about with trees, and adorned w$_{th}$ diverse curious hewn stone gates, and balls uniformally placed in a regular comely manner.

And hath also built a great and neat dairy house, lofted in y^e fields near unto y^e premises.

The whole considered, there are few such or so much work to be seen, about any one dwelling in Ireland, nor any so great done by a gent^n, at his own expence, tho' the sluces, draines, and inclosures adjoyning be not reckoned into the account, w^h was an annuall mighty benefit to the artists, laborers, and to the town itself.

Near Newtoun is a piece of ground called Kiltonga, in which hath been ye cell of some devout person, but few remains therof are now to be seen: yet at ye old ruines of it were found (a few years agoo) some medalls and crucifixes: this lyes on ye north syde.

But towards the south of ye town stands many ruined walls of ye church and ancient abby called MOVILLA, which had large lands, besides revenues scatered at a distance from it; now it is inclosed with an old wall, w^h serves for a cemetary to ye whole parish and town. None but persons of ye best sort being buried in ye new built church, parcell of ye priory afores^d.

The s^d houses gardens and church stand on a level on ye head of Lough Coan, (which is salt water) and is thirteen miles long and five broad at some places. This lough washeth all the west and south sides of this barony from Newtown downwards, and hath in it many Islands, whereof some are accessible at low water, for it ebbs about two miles downward from Newtown, leaving a large rideable strand, and this Lough hath also in it oysters, which are dredged in deep water, and some gathered from rocks on which they grow and from off ye sand banks within ye sea, which are thrown thereon after great south and west winds, and are good as well in summer as in winter. There be in this Lough also store of mullets, plaice, sand eels, strand cockles, and in harvest time (some years) herrings are taken and everywhere on ye western coasts of ye said barony are abundance of wild foul of all sorts, viz:— Barnacles, wild geese, sea pys, cormorants, sea larks, red-shanks, and some swans, besides those other before named in ye lower half barrony.

And, within ye land from Bangor to Kirkestown afores^d is a long red bogg, which gives passages by land, from ye s^d Lough to ye main sea, but at five or six narrow places. All this bog over it affords the green harrowgoose, land barnacles, grouce, snyps and (in ye season.) woodcocks (w^h haunt mostly among orchards) also hares and foxes for game.

The corn and grass fields have—plevers, quailes and larks: the trees and hedges yield many thrushes, blackbirds, feltifaris, about one bigness, linnets, goldfinches, and other melodious and small birds in plenty as elsewhere.—This part of ye barr, is called the ye great Ards as afores^d, hath good grain of all sorts, and abundance of fewell, cutt by the spade and dryed in ye sun, in the said long bogg out of which are digged up (many times long and great fir and black oak trees without branches, w^h are good and fresh timber; the oak serves for great beams for floors, and so doth the fir, wh^h also afford good deales.

Lastly as part and appurtenance of the mannor of Newtown afor^d is ye high hill called Scrabo, formerly intended for a deerpark, and therein is a quarry of the best freestone that may be seen anywhere, if either ye durableness or smoothness and variety of green vaines therein when pollished be considered. The shades whereof are well known in Dublin, and taken thither and elsewhere in abundance.

Also within ye libertys of ye s^d Newtown is a large salt marish full of medicinall herbs: the grass is wholesom for diseased horses and cattle, for w^h ye Netherland Dutch (before they had well learn'd and practised navigation to ye East and West Indies) offered above two thousand pound sterl^g fine, and fifty pounds, sters per annum rent, to have it for sixty one years in lease, from ye s^d first Ld Montgomery, but his Lo^p, being bound to a British plantation, and (if that had been dispensed with) fearing the trade of ye Brittish might be absorped in ye Dutch industry, and the towns of Newtown, Comer, (now vulgarly called Cumber) and Bangor, (which are at furthest but three miles from ye s^d marish) would have been hindered and discouraged in their building, therefore that proposal was not accepted.

I conclude with a few remarks more, viz. that from ye s^d long bogg issue many rills and streams, w^h make small brooks (some of them almost dry in ye summer) that run to ye sea on each side of ye upper half barrony, and on them each townland almost had a little miln for grinding oats, dryed in potts or singed and leazed in ye straw, w^h was ye old Irish custom, the mealle whereof called greddane, was very cours. The milns are called Danish or ladle milnes, the axeltree stood upright and ye small stones or querns (such as are turned with hands) on ye top thereof; the water wheel was fixed at ye lower end of ye axeltree, and did run horizontally among ye water : a small force driving it. I have seen of them in ye Isle of Man, where the Danes domineered as well as here in Ireland, and left their customs behind them.

Some waters or brooks being inclosed in walls of loose stones on ye strands of Lough Coan, (in little bays) made weirs or fish yeards, which wells did suffer ye tides to come insensibly thro' them for four hours flood, w^h for ye last two hours of the tide, flowed over the said walls: then did the sea run strong and the fishes followed ye stream, and finding food brought down thither, by ye fresh water brookes and that ye bay was calm, the fish remained therein, untill y^e ebb left y^e wall to appear and then shrunk thro it, insensibly as it came, so that the fishes not getting back (thro' the wall,) were taken easily; but since fish dayes were neglected, these yeards decayed.

WORTHY HONORED S^R.

The foregoing is pages coppyed by M$_r$. Robt. Watson from my own draft of them; You may please to acept as a token of my love and respects to you. I promised to send to you this description; it is attested at y^e bottom of every page by the two capital letters of of my name and surname, as I usually subscribe them. This account of y^e barrony was more gen^{lly} written (long agoo) at ye desire of my kinsmen (W^m. Molineux and G. Usher, Esqs.) who were collecting materialls to make an atlas or description of Ireland; you will see ye printed quires which are concerning ye same sent herewith to you, w^h I received from them by ye post.

This part of my labours may (if you please) find a plaice among yor papers w^h you lay up for entertainment of strangers, to save yor pains of writeing yor knowledge in ye premises; but before you expose it, I pray correct or scrape out what are my mistakes therin, and add what you think fit to ye description now written, and thereby oblige to further service,
 Sir,
  Your very humble serv^t.
  And affectionate friend,
   WILL. MONTGOMERY.

For Patrick Sauage,
 of Portneferry, Esq.
    these

3d *April* 1701.
 Sir,
 To fill up ye blanks that was where I now write, I send the following fancy that took me in ye late King James of our troubles, to express my notions of brass, which was too currant among us.

Brass moveth men to board, to church, to field,
Wee all (someway) to its temptations yield.
The trumpets sound to arms, and death doth call,
The bell to prayers and meate invites us all ;
But stamped brass gaines more than both these doo:
It courts not, yet we daily doo it wooe,
As means to make us happy, merry live ;
Yet (on a sudden) guns our death doth give.
How diff'ren shapes, one substance hath and ends ;
Some on ye body, some the soul attends ;
Some both destroys, some booh would scape alive:
Thus ! forms (which beings have) make all things strive
W. M..

A CATALOGUE
Of several writings of W^m. Montgomery, Esq.
MISCELLANIA OPERA,
Juvenlia virilia et senilia mentis atque manus,
or
Recreations in vers and prosaick collections, partly Poetical, Historicall, Morall and Oeconomicall.

Among all wch there are some pieces the fruits of pious and serious meditations and reflections on divers subjects. By reading whereof, it will be seen how men's genii alter (especially my own) in every of those stations of life, and that as yeares and experience encrease so that writeings are meliorated; and yet that youths' notions (on some ocasions) have been clearer, higher flown and better expressed, than when they became men or grown old.

But still (upon yearth) it is found that age hath ye judgment and methode, which ye other two generally want. It is observable again, that in these three periods men doo say, write or act things much beyond their greatest talents (natural or acquired), even more than their utmost study and paines could at other whiles affoord; tho' they be put to straine their endeavors to shew an excellency wch is not aimed at by ye author;(of ye following pages) W. M. yet he is of opinion, that viz.

"Aut prodesse solent aut delectare poetæ."

The catalogue afores^d beginning at the Opera Juvenilia.

ΠPOΛΕΓΩΜΕΝΟΙ or introduction page.........	2
Printed Disputations de Habitibus	14
Printed Philosophical Question	26
Verses on ye Prosperity of ye Usurper, etc.........	36
A Melancholy Meditation, in prose.................	38
A ntation on Ambition, with ye blazon of our Coats Armorial..	46
A Narrative to ye reader	48
Verses on James D. of York.....................	49
Verses on Poverty	50
A Paraphrasis of ye Grave, in vers........	52
The 52d Psalm paraphrased, and its tune............	55
Psalm 79 paraphrased to ye s^d tune	57
Psalm 58 paraphrased to ye s^d tune...................	58
Psalm 74 paraphrased, in lyrick vers, it is tune is page 76 of ye Virilia	60
Verses on Friendship and Kindred, unfinished, and a Criterion, in prose thereon	63

E E

Fuller's H. Warr compendized, beginns................ 66
Verses on ye effects of Brass, according to its fower
   cheif shapes and usages 113
A description of Arithmetick .... ibid.
Verses on ye dissolution of ye Rump Parliam^t......
Preface to ye satyr on ye English Rebell............ 129
The satyr itself beginns..................................... 125
The Hector's complaint or dirige 132
Meditations on a Scull..................................... 135
The instalment to a club among poets............... 136
A petition, in vers... 138
Verses under ye pourtraiets of Socrates............. 140
                           of Plato....................... 141
                           of Aristotle .... ibid
                           of Pythagoras 142
                           of Diogenes .... ibid.
To ye reader of other encomiums is lost 143
Verses under Cardinal Wolsey's pourtraiet 144
Verses under ye s^d first Cromwell's pourtraiet...... ibid.
Elegy on Thomas Venables, Esq...................... 145
Divers foren am^{ds} interpreted............................ 149
Tailor's several stitches 151
On the attempts of faln mankind...................... 152
Translations of Latin and French verses............ 154
Apology for Lucretia, ye Roman....................... 169
Her picture and epitaph................................... 173
Verses in praise of Geo. Sandys........................ 174
Verses on Adam and Evah's picture................. 175
Verses on Cleopatra's picture............................ 176
The picture itself .... ibid.
A short conclusion to ye foregoing juvenile works... ibid.
The D. of Gordon's

SOME MEMOIRS OF CAPT. GEORGE MONTGOMERY.

The Honble. Geo. Montgomery, (so called for our B^p. Geo.) was born in Newtown and bred at school there, but he not inclining to be a bookish man, (as his paidagogue said,) was sent to travel to learn (in Holland,) how to beare and uss armes; I never saw him carry a rapier, but a keen-edged broad sword, (called sweet lipps) fittest for hors service, in which he delighted: he loved S^r. James more than the Visc^t. his eldest brother, and upon his father's death bed contrived to gett to himself his sword (wch his Lo^p had borne when he was an officer abroad,) and afterwards bestowed it to S^r. James, who carefully kept it and left it to his son W^m. who gave it to his son when he wrode in the 2^d Earle's troop, without altering the old fashion hilt or handle: it was so trenchant and well metled a blade, that the edge did neither break out nor turn, tho' struck ag^t. a bar of iron—the old people in S^r. Hughe's days used no other; for these swords could cutt through a sleeve of maile, and break ye arm bone.

You have heard of his marriage with the ancient Laird of Garthland's daughter, with whom (after two years stay there, and his eldest son Hugh, being born,) he came and lived on his estate, neare Lisnegarvy, and prepared timber, &c. to build his house at Dunbratly, (by which name himself and his mannor court were stiled,) but ye rebellion afores^d. made him and his family retire to Newtowne, and there he gott a com^n. to be capt. of a troop (in his 3^d brother's regiment of hors,) wch. he loved more than latin books, for he liked not any but *propria quæ maribus.*

He was the last issue of Dame Elizabeth Shaw aforesaid, and on that acco^{nt}. (as is usuall with mothers towards such,) he was in his youthhood indulged by her in his pleasures, (as she had seen him provided for in lands;) he delighted in hunting, hawking, and fowling, in which his aged fathers, masters of those games, were willing and ever ready to please him at his beck, and this Jacob's venison, (whereof there was plenty before the contry became populus,) was ever dressed by his mother to relish with her old husband his father.

But these exercises could not make him the man wch his father desired; and his mother's milk must be removed by travell as afores^d. and a master of arts waited on him to instill (by discourss,) into him, the knowledge of what he had learned, and of what he should see, hear, or read abroad.

There was no court then at Holyrood house, yet Glasgow college and towne, Strivling castle, towne and bridge, and Edinburg with the King's palace above named, and ye Parliament house and other places, besides the castle and maiden's tower, (which is the glory of Edinburgh, and was the seat of ye Pictish King's family, and ye nunnery of ye Royal Virgins,) now all worthy to be seen and observed, besides the visits he was to make to ye Earle of Eglinton, and the Earle of Striveling's daughters and sons, and the kindred of both sides whence he was decended, were also dew, and so he was sent to Braidstane and thence to make ye s^d visits and views.

Which being performed he took sea at Leith and sailed for Holland, (then ye school for warr,) where he was welcomed for his ghelt, and to ye Scotish officers of his kindred and of his father's old acquaintance, where he stayed a campaign and a winter, and gained knowledge fitt to make him an officer, serving that summer as a voluntary cadee.

His person was portly, his discours manly, and his heart stout. He could drink, smoake, and can woimgh sproken, like a Dutchman;

but more soberly and courtvously than most of them.

His discourse was neither of philosophy, divinity, nor phissik, but good round (home spun) rational sence, and both in body and inclination he was fitt for a wife, and indeed he was a desireable man of ye women, haveing natural allurements enow to gain their good will.

He was, (at his mother's entreaty) called home, and required to take a view of ye court at Whitehall, and to see friends there, as well as to kiss ye king's hand, and to return thro' Scotl^d by Edinbrugh and Braidstane, repeating his said visits, and to make two or three dayes stay at Garthland, because now he was become a man of good carriage.

His mother had enjoyned him this last visit, that he might appear as a wooer, for here was the fair lady designed for his wife, viz. Grizel, eldest daughter of Sr John Mc Dowell (ats Mc Dougall) laird of that ancient place last before spoken of.

This our George liked ye match, wch he heard was intended for him, and being a fresh, young, and well complexioned spark, and a traveller, made his adresses, wch were civilly receaved; on this encouragement he returned to Newtown to his mother's joy, that he had come home safe, and was liked of his mistress as she told him, but said she was not to declare her love, but according to her parents pleasure, wherof he had no doubt ; and had spoke to them, who wrote therof to our Vis^{ct} and Visc^{tess} that they liked of their sonn whom they for their daughter above named ; our George plyd his sollicitations to his mother to speed ye affaire by making preparations for his return to make a wife of his m^{rs}, being over eares and head in love.

He was called by ye agnomen (Scotice too name) of Kinnshoker (Anglice the hauke head) from his eagerness (perhapps after his game,) and it may be also from his readynes to stoope at female quarrys, because he was easily lured that way.

This gentl. (by ye 3^d Viscont, and by his brother, and by ye contry) was called Uncle George; by Sr James and Mr Savadge was termed brother George, and by their descendants named uncle George without other addition : and the 3^d lord's brother was called Sq^r James, and y^e 4th lord's brother was, and is called Squire Henry and no more, and now are properly called Squire Montgomery (*sans eul* as is spoken of Le Mounsieur, y^e Frenchking's next brother) and no more without designm^t of y^e X^{tian} name, but onely the l$^{d's}$ eldest son, *vivant son pere.*

This hono^{ble} gentl. was but a tenent for life, and held his land under y^e 2^d Visc^t, and his posterity, as his chief landlords in fee, at a smal rent, and an acknowledgm^t to be paid by every male heire in possession (after his father's death) if he be arrived at 21 years of age, or when he comes to bee so old, and this is named a releif in law.

The case being so, and this gentleman (who lived a widdower from A^o 1646 till 1669 that he dyed) being, since his lady's death, none of ye best managers of an estate, and his eldest sonn Hugh (comonly called Ballylessan) being grown up, and an honest discreet man, he ye s^d George was perswaded to betake himself to a certain yearly rent-charge during his life, and his s^d son Hugh bound to pay it.

His affaires being thus setled by consent of his feo fees, his said eldest son Hugh managed ye states, and was obliged, for paym^t of a portion to his brother John and sister Jean; and marryed the daughter of Coll. Hercules Hanks (who had not any other childe or grandchilde) and yett ye s^d Hugh had no portion by her, tho' her father had been a moneyed and landed man, and none could tell (that I could learn) how his estate of both sorts vanished away, tho' he lived very obscurely.

This Hugh hath, by his s^d wife, one son named Hercules (after ye s^d Coll) who is now A° 1698, a comely well humoured gentl. unmarryed.

The said Hugh marryed ye Lord Blayney's widdow, by whom he hath a considerable estate in fee farm and bish^ps. leases renewed in his own name and cypher, a pretty lusty young gentl. named Hugh, who is marriagable, both for discretion and yeares.

This very good lady and her husband, the s^d Hugh, are of age and can speake for themselves, and tho' they doo not, I hope their respective sonns will doo it, both orally and in black and white, as I have done for my parents, so that I need not to be their histriographer, only I have this to add, that this Hugh (the father of these two young gentl.) had a com^n. for Coll. from y^e Prince of Orange (our good King W^m.) and raised a regiment of foot, w^ch, with y^e rest of y^e North Western and Lagan forces, now broken by Majo_r Genl Hamilton, at or near Clady foord; as for any thing els I shall forbeare to mention the same, yet I heartily wish wellfare to him and to all his concerns, as I hope he doth to mee and mine, wee two (and his sister) being the onely persons alive of y_e first Visc^ts. grand children, hee and I being born before his Lop^s. death; and so I take leave of him and return to his father Capt. Geo. Montgomery, who, being retired to Newtown as afores^d. had occasions to try his courage and skill, and to vent his anger and revenge ag^t. the Irish rebells, who had wasted his lands, so that he went gladly to make them pay him rent, and behaved himself to approbation with his troop, continuing in service till O'C.'s army defeated ye K's forces in Ulster.

The s^d Grizzell, his loving and entirely beloved wife, dying A^o. 1646, left him another son named John (for her own father's sake); this son resembled his father much, and he haveing served as a gentleman in our 2d Earle's troop, he raised a foot company and went a Cap^tn. in ye Earle of Roscommon's regiment into France, where he died of sickness, unmarryed.

She left also to him a daughter named Jean, (after ye 2d Viscountess) who is now, A^o. 1699 ye widdow of W^m. Shaw, (formerly called of Newtown and afterwards of B. Stockart) Esq. unto whom she hath at this present living Hercules, Elenor, Ann and Sara; this last is maryed and hath a daughter to M^r. Hugh Montgomery, whom I call ye gentle mariner, both from his extraction and occupation.

The s^d Capt. Geo. (to whom I now turn again) after divers years being boarded at Rosemount (to his heart's content) dyed in his son Shaw's house at B. Stockart, A^o. 1674, and was burryed in the chancel of Newtown by his father, brother and nephew, the first three Lords Montgomerys of ye great Ards.

He was a good horsman (having practised at riding houses abroad) and expert he was at running topp speed with a lance at his thigh, to take up glove or ring as afores^d, and at making hors matches and discerning horses, and was a man gott honor in our warrs, and had ye true principles of honesty, affection and civility in him.

Belfast: Printed at the News-Letter Office.

COLUMBIA UNIVERSITY LIBRARY

This book is due on the date indicated below, or at the expiration of a definite period after the date of borrowing, as provided by the rules of the Library.

DATE DUE

GAYLORD　　　　　　　　　　　PRINTED IN U.S.A.

929.2 M761

ImTheStory.com

Personalized Classic Books in many genre's

Unique gift for kids, partners, friends, colleagues

Customize:

- Character Names
- Upload your own front/back cover images (optional)
- Inscribe a personal message/dedication on the inside page (optional)

Customize many titles Including
- Alice in Wonderland
- Romeo and Juliet
- The Wizard of Oz
- A Christmas Carol
- Dracula
- Dr. Jekyll & Mr. Hyde
- And more...

Emily's Adventures in Wonderland

Ryan & Julia